MUSTANG 5.0 LITER PERFORMANCE HANDBOOK

Peter C. Sessler

Motorbooks International
Publishers & Wholesalers

First published in 1992 by Motorbooks International
Publishers & Wholesalers, PO Box 2, 729 Prospect Avenue,
Osceola, WI 54020 USA

Library of Congress Cataloging-in-Publication Data
Sessler, Peter C.
  Mustang 5.0 liter performance handbook / Peter C.
Sessler.
    p.   cm.—(Motorbooks performance handbook
series)
  Includes index.
  ISBN 0-87938-580-4
  1. Mustang automobile—Performance—Amateurs'
manuals.   2. Mustang automobile—Maintenance and
repair—Amateurs' manuals.   I. Title. II. Series.
TL215.M8S482   1992
629.28′722—dc20   92-8714

On the front cover: A 1988 Mustang 5.0 liter convertible
basks in the Florida sun. *Mike and Denise Mueller*

On the back cover: A turbocharged Mustang launches
off the line *Texas Turbo Engineering*; the most
modern small-block to date, the fuel-injected 5.0 liter
HO engine rated at 225hp *Ford Motor Co.*; a 5.0 liter
Mustang fitted with several Saleen accessories *Saleen
Performance Parts Inc.*; an SAAC Mk 1, which is heavily
modified over stock but remains street legal.

Printed and bound in the United States of America

Contents

Acknowledgments

I would like to thank all those who have helped me by generously contributing their time, information, and assistance. Special thanks to Bob Atwood, Kenny Brown, Steve Collison, George Klass, Jerry Walsh, Quality Engine Distributors, and of course, Special Vehicle Operations of Ford Motor Company.

All photos are courtesy of the author, except where indicated.

Introduction

Third-generation Mustangs have been with us for a long time. For a car that hasn't changed its basic configuration since 1979, the Mustang has shown its staying power. It outsells its chief rivals, General Motors Corporation's F-bodies, the Camaro and Firebird, and for many reasons remains America's most popular performance car.

From its very beginning in April of 1964, the Mustang has had a youthful image. For Detroit in 1964, a youthful image meant a car that was stylish, smaller than what mom and dad drove, one that performed better than most (or at least *felt* that way) and, of course, it had to be affordable. The original Mustang did all these things. The youthful image also meant performance, and although it took Ford Motor Company a year to introduce the GT Equipment option, you could have optioned out a performance Mustang from June 1964 on by ordering the 271hp (horsepower) 289 High Performance, or Hi-Po, engine. With the GT option, the Mustang also had a performance image, though it could not compete with the hot street cars of the day—such as Pontiac's GTO—in terms of all-out acceleration. Later on, it was a different story.

The Mustang grew in size with the 1967 model, yet it managed to retain much of the original's flavor. Larger engines kept the Mustang competitive on the street, and until 1971, you could have ordered a Mustang with a big-block V-8. These big engines were popular with the street racers, yet by far, most Mustangs were equipped with either a two- or four-barrel carbureted version of Ford's small-block V-8, the 289, which grew to 302ci (cubic inches) by mid-1968. With the exception of the 271hp version of the 289 and the Boss 302 of 1969-70, the 289 and 302 were low-performance engines. Still, the small-block proved to be responsive to the usual hot-rodding modifications because of its inherent good design.

Through 1968, the top-performance Mustang was the GT (excluding the Shelby Mustangs), particularly those powered by the aging 390ci big-block. However, most of the Mustang's reputation as a street racer was due to the 428 Cobra Jet engine, a late-1968 introduction. The 428CJ continued to be available through the 1970 model year.

Although the Mustang was extensively facelifted in 1969, its basics were little changed from the 1967 model. Choice of engine grew to ten options, yet it was still the small-block 302 that provided the motivating power for most Mustangs. New engines for 1969 included the 351ci Windsor, the massive Boss 429, and the high-winding Boss 302.

The last of the first-generation Mustangs were those produced from 1971-73. A larger car, the Mustang still retained some of its sportiness, but by 1971, the pony car market was in decline. In fact, 1971 was the last year for the true high-performance Mustang engines such as the 429 Cobra Jet, which replaced the 428, and the Boss 351. During the 1972-73 period, the largest engine available was the 351 Cobra Jet.

Receiving a drastic redesign, the 1974 Mustang II tried to emulate the feel and proportions of the 1965-66 model in the context of the post-Arab oil embargo era. The Mustang II continued on until the 1978 model year. There wasn't much available for those interested in high performance, as the "big" engine was a two-barrel 302.

The current third-generation Mustangs debuted in 1979. The basic body shell and suspension design has remained the same, although it has been constantly refined through the years. The start of the current performance era with the Mustang GT did not begin until 1982, when the GT model designation was resurrected after a twelve-year hiatus.

Throughout the Mustang's long history, with the exception of one year, 1974, only one basic engine has been common to all—the small-block V-8. It took Ford a long time to come up with a small, compact V-8 engine to compete with Chevrolet's very successful small-block which debuted in 1955. Ford's version came out in 1962, measuring only 221ci. Later that year it was enlarged to 260ci and in 1963 to the well-known 289ci. The 289 was by far Ford's most popular street engine in the 1960s. The big-blocks may have made more power, but the sheer number of 289s made them available to the typical enthusiast. The 289 also formed the basis for Ford's road-racing activities, and the small-block was also the recipient of extensive factory experimentation and a wealth of factory performance parts.

The 289's stroke was increased to 3.00in in 1968, resulting in 302ci. With the exception of the 1969-70 Boss 302 engine, the 302 was a low-performance engine. In the 1970s, low-horsepower versions of the 302 were as much as the enthusiast was going to get from Ford as original equipment, but the aftermarket industry was there to remedy that situation.

When the third-generation Mustang was introduced in 1979, the 302 was the top engine option, but Ford made a serious (and largely unsuccessful) attempt to replace the 302 as top-performance engine by turbocharging the Mustang's standard 2.3 liter four-cylinder engine. During 1980-81, a 255ci version of the small-block was all that was available in V-8 form.

The horsepower wars started again in earnest in 1982, however, when General Motors introduced the redesigned third-generation Camaro and Firebird, which were available with injected 305ci Chevy small-blocks. The 1982 Mustang GT powered by a two-barrel version of the 302 put out 157hp. Four-barrel carburetion followed in 1983, and fuel injection in 1986.

Ford once again made an attempt to persuade the performance buyer to go for four-cylinder power. A more reliable, revamped turbocharged 2.3 liter four-cylinder powered the Turbo GT Mustangs of 1983-84 while during 1984-86, Ford tried to build a Mustang that was on the same level as Europe's best performance sedans. The SVO, named after Ford's performance arm Special Vehicle Operations, was powered by a more powerful version of the Turbo GT's four-cylinder, but again, to no avail. The Mustang was too heavy for the four-cylinder, its platform too unsophisticated, while the 302ci V-8 proved to be far more attractive to the typical Mustang buyer—and was cheaper, too. Poor sales finally did the SVO in after the 1986 model year.

Since its inception, the Mustang has always provided the enthusiast with a solid foundation on which to build. Beneath the skin, the third-generation differs from the first two in two areas. The current Mustang uses a MacPherson strut front suspension and a coil spring rear—these don't present much of a problem for suspension modifications. The second area involves fuel injection and electronics. When you come down to it, modifying the 302ci engine for more power is a fairly standard procedure. Most of the combinations were worked out years ago. The big difference today is that all of Ford's engines are computer controlled and in order to meet the ever tighter emission requirements, fuel injection has replaced carburetors. Thus the hot rodder has been forced to re-educate himself.

Mustang 5.0 Liter Performance Handbook explores all the current avenues that are available for those wishing to extract more performance from their third-generation Mustangs—from engine swaps to supercharging to even better handling and braking. Some effort has been made to keep everything on a realistic level. After all, for many owners, their Mustang is their only means of transportation and they may have to cope with the realities of a limited budget. Still, those who have to have the latest modifications no matter what the cost, such as a set of $6,000 four-valve cylinder heads, aren't forgotten here.

There is one final point that should be explored. In late 1990, a new set of Clean Air Amendments was approved. The Environmental Protection Agency (EPA) sent a policy letter to automotive parts manufacturers, distributors, retailers, and installers stating that the EPA believes the new regulations prohibit "any person from manufacturing, selling, offering for sale, or installing any part or component intended for use with, or as a part of any motor vehicle, where a principal effect of the part or component is to bypass, defeat, or render inoperative any emission control device or element of design and where the person knows or should know the part or component is being put to such use. A civil penalty of up to $2500.00 may be imposed for each violation of this defeat device prohibition."

Except for California, which had already prohibited the car owner from tampering with emissions equipment, there wasn't previously such a federal mandate. No longer can the "Not for sale or use in California on pollution controlled motor vehicles" disclaimer be used in the rest of the forty-nine states.

Unfortunately, the law is ambiguous on what constitutes a "defeat device." If the law is strictly interpreted it would mean that you can't make *any* modifications to a street car and if you wanted to turn your Mustang into a racer, well, you couldn't do that either. Until clear guidelines are issued, you shouldn't tamper or disable any of your engine's emission devices. This means don't disconnect the EGR (Exhaust Gas Recirculation) system or take the catalytic converters off. But it *doesn't* mean you can't replace the stock catalytic converters with aftermarket units that flow a lot better. You don't have to be a genius to know that future guidelines will prohibit any disabling of emission control systems.

Still, things aren't as bad as they sound. There are many parts that, although they can affect the engine's emissions output, won't disable the stock emission control systems, such as a more radical camshaft, headers, intake manifolds, superchargers, or freer flowing cylinder heads. In the past, when such parts were sold in California, the California Air Resources Board (CARB) certified them acceptable for sale as long as they passed tests showing that they did not increase emissions. It seems likely that the EPA will go along with such procedures, too.

More and more performance parts are being certified—for example, the Paxton supercharger has been certified as acceptable. The reality is, with technology being what it is today, you can build a high-horsepower engine and still meet current emission standards. The outcome of all this will be clean-running performance engines, and when you think of it, there is no reason why it shouldn't be that way.

Chapter 1

Mustang Performance History

When you look at the Mustang, you'll find that its history is steeped in performance. There were always performance Mustang models. Sometimes they didn't perform well, such as in the mid-1970s and early 1980s, but that was the case for most American-manufactured cars at the time. Still, even when high performance wasn't much of a priority at Ford, you'll find that the Mustang never lost its performance image.

Besides the Mustang's obvious sporty styling and flair, it is the engines that made it the performer it was and is today. Practically every engine that Ford built has at one time or another powered Mustangs. In this chapter, we'll take a look at the great Mustang engines as well as their packaging.

1965-66

Ford Motor Co. didn't need to produce a performance-oriented Mustang when the car first came out in April of 1964—the Mustang was a phenomenal seller as it was. In fact, most enthusiasts consider the GT Mustang to be the first performance Mustang, and that didn't go into production until a year later. Still, in keeping with its policy that the Mustang be a car for all people, Ford added one additional engine to the Mustang's option list in June of 1964 and that was the famous 271hp 289ci V-8. Mustangs so equipped became known as K cars, as the letter K indicated this engine in the Mustang's Vehicle Identification Number, or VIN.

The 271hp Mustangs were good-performing cars, but their performance in no way equaled that of the supercars of the day, such as Pontiac's GTO. Mustangs weren't that kind of car anyway, and only 7,273 were built with the 271hp engine in 1965. A significant move toward a stronger performance image came in April 1965, when the GT Equipment Group option was made available on all three Mustang bodystyles. This option combined the Mustang's best suspension and drivetrain pieces, such as heavy-duty suspension, quick-ratio steering, and disc brakes, along with GT emblems, stripes, a couple of grille-mounted fog-lamps, and a slightly revised interior. This gave the

The Mustang at its purest—a 1965 convertible powered by the 289ci small-block. Most first-generation Mustangs were powered by either the 289 or 302ci V-8.

It was the 1965 Shelby GT350 that made high-performance enthusiasts take notice. Properly modified, the Mustang could keep up with most muscle cars of the day and easily outhandled them. This is a 1965 GT350R (competition) version which still sees action on the Vintage race circuit.

You could even rent a Shelby Mustang from Hertz in 1966. These were identical to the regular street Shelbys, but most were painted black with gold stripes.

Mustang a performance image to go along with the 271hp 289ci V-8 which could be ordered with the GT package. The standard engine was the 225hp four-barrel 289ci V-8. When you look at enthusiast magazines today you'll see a preponderance of GT models featured, but the reality was that only 15,079 cars in 1965 and 25,517 in 1966 got the GT option. That isn't very many when you consider that more than 1,200,000 Mustangs were sold in the 1965-66 model year.

1967-68

Bigger is better, or so that's how the thinking of the day went, and the Mustang, after its first major restyle became longer, wider, and heavier in 1967. The small-block engine was still the main motivating force for the Mustang, but because the engine compartment was larger, Ford's big FE-series 390ci V-8 rated at 320hp was shoehorned in. There were several reasons for this move. First and most important is that 1967 was the year GM brought out the Chevrolet Camaro and the Pontiac Firebird—both cars designed to compete head on against the Mustang. Both of these cars were engineered to accept big-inch V-8s from the very start—396ci with the Camaro and 400ci V-8 on the Firebird. And although not many Mustang GTs were built in the first two years of production, it's quite likely that the GT's image brought many plain-Jane Mustang customers into the showroom. And so in 1967, if a customer was considering both a Mustang and a Camaro, it wouldn't

In 1967, the Mustang was restyled for a more aggressive, broad-shouldered look. The engine was enlarged to accommodate the 390ci big-block.

The Mustang finally entered the muscle car race in 1968 when Ford installed the 428CJ powerhouse. Its forte was quarter-mile acceleration. This is one of the fifty pre- *production 428CJs originally sold by Tasca Ford, East Providence, Rhode Island.*

have looked good for the Mustang not to offer a big-inch engine option—even if the customer wasn't interested in one. The Mustang would have been perceived as being a lesser car, especially to the all-important youth market. So if GM went ahead and installed big engines, so did Ford.

Ford had to go with the big, heavy 390 V-8 because there was nothing else available. A medium-size V-8, in the form of a 351, was still years away. As a high-performance car, the 390 Mustangs weren't a match for the big-block Camaros and Firebirds. The 390 was a lazy, slow-revving passenger-car engine. A 390 GT Mustang just didn't elicit the same response that an SS396 Camaro or a Ram Air 400 Firebird did. These cars were solid 14sec quarter-mile performers while the 390 was lucky to get out of the fifteens.

When it comes to performance measured in terms of acceleration, which was how most saw it back then, the 1967 Mustang was better, but only in relation to earlier Mustangs. To some enthusiasts, Mustangs with the 271hp 289ci V-8 were preferable because they provided more balanced performance in better handling and cornering.

Also in 1967, Chevrolet made available for the Camaro what was then an obscure option package. It was known as the Z-28 Special Performance Package. If the Camaro was going to participate in Sports Car Club of America's (SCCA) Trans-Am series, then at least 500 street Camaros had to be built, equipped in a similar fashion. The Z-28 was high performance in all respects—it could handle, brake, and accelerate and was equipped with only a small-block Chevy V-8 displacing 302ci.

Although the Mustang was outselling all the other competing pony cars in 1968, when it came to performance, it was still in the boonies. The 390 V-8 remained the big-engine option, even though for a short time Ford made available an FE-series 427ci V-8. It put out a healthy 390hp, but it was not available with a four-speed manual transmission and it was a very expensive option. Meanwhile, GM's pony cars were getting a reputation for performance, especially the Super Sport Camaros and the Z-28s which had suddenly caught on.

Late in the model year, in April of 1968, the 428 Cobra Jet engine was introduced in hope that this engine would give the Mustang a much stronger performance and image. The 428CJ was again based on the Ford FE-series engine family and outwardly, it did not differ from the 390. The additional cubic inches, coupled with cylinder heads that breathed better and a larger Holley carburetor transformed the Mustang into a hot street car. The 428CJ was a deceptively smooth, quiet engine but it produced an enormous amount of torque. The Cobra Jet-powered Mustangs effectively silenced those who complained that the Mustang couldn't put out, but it would take another year before Ford could come up with a car that could take the Z-28 Camaro on its own terms.

Up to this time, the Mustang had been reasonably successful in racing, particularly road racing. Mustang had won the 1967 Trans-Am series and prior to this, Mustangs were successful in SCCA B-Production class. The Trans-Am series, which began in 1966, caught the public's eye by 1968 because the series provided some really great racing, big-name drivers, and most of the factories were represented on the track. In 1968, the series became a classic Ford versus Chevrolet confrontation, with the Penske Camaro convincingly defeating the Ford teams. Here was a company that had won Le Mans and Indianapolis and even with its immense resources, couldn't beat a Chevrolet back-door operation. The Mustang teams fared better in 1969, but lost the series once again to

Chevrolet. Finally in 1970, the Mustang was the Trans-Am series winner.

Of course, the Cobra Jet-powered Mustangs proved to be very successful in drag racing for years to come.

1969-70

It seems that 1969 was the culmination of Ford Motor Co.'s efforts to transform the Mustang from an image performance car to a performance car in fact. Although the Mustang platform for that year was unchanged, the car received another facelift transforming the fastback (SportsRoof) body into a sleeker car. The GT option group was still available (its last year) but it was rather tame when compared to the new performance model, the Mach 1. The Mach 1 was available only as a SportsRoof. It came with reflective side stripes, a rear deck stripe, a blacked-out hood, a simulated hood scoop, body-colored rear-view mirrors, a special deluxe interior, special chrome steel wheels, and a new 250hp 351W (for Windsor) V-8 engine as standard equipment. Optional engines were a 290hp version of the 351W, the old 390, and the 428CJ. There was also a special version of the

A 1969 Boss 302 Mustang powered by the ultimate development of the 302 small-block, also called the Boss 302. The Boss 302 was a production Mustang built in the guise of the early Shelby Mustangs—it could handle and brake as well as accelerate.

10

428CJ available, dubbed the 428 Super Cobra Jet. The SCJ didn't produce any more power, but it came with stronger internal components. Also new on the 428CJ Mustangs was the Shaker hood scoop. The Mach 1 was a good-looking Mustang and the public showed its acceptance by purchasing 72,458 of them.

While the Mach 1 may have been enough for the typical performance enthusiast, Ford also brought out a Mustang variant to compete against Chevrolet's Z-28: the Boss 302. The Boss 302 may not have had the brute acceleration of the 428CJ powered Mach 1, but it was almost as quick and it could outhandle it. Sharing the same SportsRoof body, the Boss 302 also had a blacked-out hood along with a blacked-out rear deck and taillight panel, unique side stripe treatment, body-colored rearview mirrors, and special 15in Magnum 500 wheels with Goodyear F60x15 tires—the cutting edge in 1969. Accessories that are taken for granted today originated on the Boss 302. This includes the rear wing spoiler and the rear window slats. It also came with a standard front spoiler. Unlike the Mach 1 which gave the buyer the bare essentials, the Boss 302 included disc brakes, heavy-duty suspension, and a four-speed manual as standard.

The heart of the Boss 302, just as it was with the Z-28, was the 302ci version of the small-block. Unlike

For those favoring traditional street performance, there was the popular Mach 1 Mustang which could be optioned out with the 428CJ engine.

previous small-blocks, the Boss 302 had completely new cylinder heads which featured large, canted valves. The engine was a high-winding screamer. More details on the 302 are included in the next chapter.

If the Mach 1 and Boss 302 weren't enough, there was also the Boss 429 for those who wanted the ultimate. While there were two reasons for building

The ultimate Mustang was the Boss 429, powered by an aluminum head hemi 429. It was produced in low numbers in 1969-70. This 1969 model lacks the stripes and graphics typical of the Boss 302 and Mach 1.

the Boss 302—to compete against Camaro Z-28s on the street and to homologate the car in SCCA's Trans-Am series—there was only one reason for the Boss 429, and that was to qualify the massive 429 engine for National Association for Stock Car Automobile Racing (NASCAR) competition. The Boss 429 was based on the SportsRoof body and was understated compared to the Mach 1 and Boss 302. No blacked-out paint treatment or fancy side stripes, the Boss 429 came with two small fender decals and a small front

One of the rare Boss 302 Mustangs that was raced in the late 1960s. From a visual standpoint, it closely resembles the street Boss 302.

The 1970 Boss 302 race Mustangs are valuable collector items, but that doesn't stop their owners from racing them once again on the Vintage circuit.

spoiler. It did, though, have a rather large hood scoop. Because of the engine's large size, the Boss 429 had to be specially modified for the engine to fit. The front shock towers were relocated and at the same time the suspension was lowered. The Boss 429 was also the first Mustang to come with a rear antisway bar.

There were no surprises in 1970, just a minor restyling. Both Boss Mustangs were available as was the Mach 1. There was yet another engine to join the line-up—the 351C (for Cleveland). Whereas the 351W was an outgrowth of the small-block, the 351C was a totally new engine which had cylinder heads similar to those found on the Boss 302.

1971-73

The Mustang got a new body in 1971 while a new big-block V-8, the 429CJ, replaced the aging 428CJ. The Boss 351, a new 351C, also replaced the Boss 302. For all intents and purposes, 1971 was the last year for performance 1960s' style. The Mach 1 continued to be the performance image Mustang with the new 429 as the top engine option, while the Boss 351 Mustang replaced the Boss 302.

The model year 1972-73 saw the elimination of the 429ci V-8 and the Boss 351. High performance was

Even fewer 1970 Boss 429s were built, only 499. Its distinguishing feature was the black-painted hood scoop.

in image only and limited to graphics and the 351CJ which pumped out 266hp. There was a brief, last-gasp attempt at a high-performance engine in 1972—the 351 High Output (HO) rated at 275hp. This engine was similar to the Boss 351 engine, but production ceased after about 1,000 or so were installed in all three Mustang bodystyles.

The year 1971 proved to be the last year for big-block-powered Mustangs. This particular car, with only open   *headers and slicks, has recorded low-12-second quarter-mile times.*

While the production Mustangs could be ordered with the 390 V-8 in 1967, Shelby went a step further and stuffed the dual-quad 428 Police Interceptor V-8 in the GT500 for easy mid-13-second quarter-mile times in a truly distinctive package.

Shelby Mustangs were produced until 1970. This is a rare 1969 GT500 convertible. Note the integral roll bar.

1965-70 Shelby Mustangs

No consideration of high-performance Mustangs can be made without mentioning the Shelby Mustangs, the GT350 and the GT500. Built in small quantities, their effect was considerably more than their numbers imply. Until late 1968, they were the only true high-performance Mustangs that could hold their own against other high-performance cars of that era.

The 1965-67 Shelby Mustangs are considered by some to be the only true Shelbys because Carroll Shelby still controlled to a large degree what these cars were all about. The original Shelby was a highly modified Mustang that got state-of-the-art engine, driveline, and suspension modifications in a visually exciting package. Based on the fastback Mustang

Hottest street configuration of the 289ci small-block was in a 1965-66 Shelby Mustang. It was rated at 306hp. It came with tubular exhaust headers, high-rise aluminum intake manifold, Holley four-barrel carburetor, and a mechanical-lifter camshaft.

Of course, if you wanted to impress your friends and neighbors, you could install one of the aftermarket Cobra kits sold through Ford dealers and Shelby. This 289 has two four-barrel carburetors.

The Mustang II was a disappointment in terms of performance. It was up to the enthusiast to take over from where the factory left off. This is the Cobra II.

body and the 271hp 289ci V-8, the 1965 Shelby Mustang was painted white with two large blue body stripes. In 1966, several additional colors were added and 1,000 Shelbys were even sold to the Hertz car rental firm. As the 1967 Mustang grew in size, the Shelby grew along with it. In addition to the 306hp 289ci V-8 on the GT350, a 360hp 428ci Police Interceptor V-8 powered the GT500. The 428 and 390 V-8s were externally identical so it wasn't a problem installing it in the Mustang engine compartment. It was as fast as any car available in 1967. What's more, the Shelby with its scoops and spoilers looked like no other Mustang or any other muscle car for that matter.

From 1968-70, Ford took over the Shelby operation. The Shelby Mustangs got another bodystyle, a convertible in 1968, and again were offered as a GT350, powered now by the 302ci and the GT500 powered by the 428ci V-8. When the 428CJ engine debuted, it was also made available on the Shelby and called the GT500KR.

With the success of the 1969 Mach 1 and Boss 302, there wasn't much need for the Shelby Mustangs which now, save for the unique bodywork, were almost identical to the production Mach 1. The complete 1969 model run could not be sold in that year; all the unsold cars were fitted with a front spoiler and two hood stripes and sold as 1970 models.

1974-78 Mustang II

For many, the 1974 era represents a low point for Mustangs and performance. Styling on the Mustang II lacked the crisp lines of the original, and what V-8 engines there were, were all low-horsepower versions. There wasn't even a V-8 engine option in 1974. The familiar Mach 1 model was carried over and was

Charlie Kemp raced a 351C powered Mustang II on the IMSA circuit in the 1970s. The Mustang was extremely fast, but unreliable.

Decked out with spoilers and air dams, the 1978 King Cobra projected a strong performance image.

16

available during 1974-78, but it was the Cobra II that was the premier performance orientation on the Mustang II from 1976-78. It consisted mostly of special stripes and graphics which emulated the 1960s Shelby Mustang performance look. Carrying this theme even further was the 1978 King Cobra which came with special spoilers and graphics. Still, with the 302ci V-8 engine available, the Mustang II could be made to perform but it was up to the owner to do it.

1979-92

The current-generation Mustang began with a big splash, even though these Mustangs weren't great performers to begin with. Reflecting Ford's penchant to use the Cobra name wherever possible, the Cobra model replaced the Mach 1 as the premier performance Mustang. The biggest engine available was a two-barrel 302 rated at 140hp but it was the turbocharged 2.3 liter, rated at 132hp, that got all the attention. Ford was trying to wean the performance enthusiast from V-8 power but to no avail. The 2.3 liter proved to be unreliable. Still, there were great strides made in the suspension department as this was the first year that the Michelin TRX suspension package became available.

The 1980-81 period represents the dark ages for the third-generation Mustang. The good-old 302, anemic as it was, was dropped and replaced by a low-horsepower version of the small-block, a 255 incher, rated at 120hp. The 255 didn't have any performance potential because in the process of downsizing it, Ford reduced its weight to the point that the engine, even in stock form, was unreliable.

Whether it was enthusiast pressure or more likely, the introduction of GM's beautifully restyled Camaro and Firebird, 1982 saw the resurrection of the Mustang GT and the 302ci V-8, now called the 5.0 liter. The 302, with a small two-barrel carburetor and single exhaust was rated at 157hp—but it was enough to get Mustang lovers excited once again. The following year was even better. The 302 pumped out 175hp and an attractive convertible joined the line-up. Ford made another attempt to turbocharge the 2.3 liter, resulting in the Turbo GT Mustang. The year 1984 brought more of the same plus a new Mustang model, the SVO. This was a comparatively expensive Mustang designed to appeal to those who preferred European performance sedans. It was a good package but it never got the acceptance that Ford hoped for—the 5.0 liter GTs were quicker and cheaper. Even when the SVO's output was increased to 205hp in 1986 it wasn't enough to save the car. It was dropped after that year.

For performance enthusiasts, 1985 was an important year. It seems that Ford finally made a more credible commitment to the Mustang and performance. With the addition of tubular exhaust headers, a roller camshaft, and a true dual-exhaust system, the 5.0 liter V-8 put out a strong 210hp. Not only that, there

Unlike the first-generation Mustangs, the current Mustangs have tremendous grass-roots popularity. They have become the Chevelle SS and Pontiac GTO of the 1980s and 1990s because they are inexpensive, reliable, and fast.

were suspension modifications made to handle the extra power and to improve handling through the use of the Quadra-Shock rear, larger antisway bars, and the appearance of the Goodyear Eagle GT tires on 15x7in aluminum wheels.

In 1986, the 5.0 liter got a multi-port fuel-injection system. Horsepower dropped to 200 because of a cylinder head change but in 1987, the old head was used once again and with further tinkering in the fuel-injection system, horsepower jumped to 225. The Mustang GT also got a new aerodynamic styling

The first true third-generation performance Mustangs debuted in 1982 with the resurrection of the GT. Even with only 157hp, the GTs gave something for Mustang enthusiasts to cheer about.

As each year passed, the third-generation Mustang's performance got better and better—with stronger engines and more capable suspensions. This is a 1984 20th Anniversary Edition.

Today's Mustang GT provides plenty of power in a civilized package.

Success on the street and success on the track via this 1986 IMSA GTO Roush Racing Mustang. Vaguely resembling the street Mustang, these all-out race cars were powered by four-cylinder turbocharged engines. Paul McLaughlin

A high point for Mustangs was in 1987 when Steve Saleen won the Showroom Stock championship. These cars closely resembled their street counterparts.

package and since 1987, the Mustang has been refined more than anything else.

As you would expect, with the resurrection of the Mustang as a strong street performer, there was a corresponding resurgence on the track. Mustangs and Mercury Capris competed in SCCA's Trans-Am and in the International Motorsports Association's (IMSA) GTO series. A Capri won the Trans-Am series in 1984 and a Roush Racing Mustang won in 1989. These cars may look like Mustangs, but underneath the fancy bodywork they are pure race car, bearing

Roush Racing won the 1989 Trans-Am championship in this Mustang. Paul McLaughlin

Today, Mustangs do well in the SCCA series. Because extensive modifications aren't allowed, it doesn't take a large bankroll to road race a Mustang. This is the car raced by Steeda Autosports, one of the major Mustang performance shops and parts suppliers. Steeda Autosports

20

no resemblance to the street Mustang. They don't even use a V-8—instead, a 2.1 liter turbocharged, intercooled four-cylinder is used which develops over 600hp.

Resembling the street cars are the Mustangs raced in SCCA's Showroom Stock series and IMSA's Firehawk and Bridgestone series. Although these Mustangs aren't as heavily modified as the older Trans-Am cars, they are very close to stock as only minor modifications are permitted. As you would expect, racing against Camaros and Firebirds, the competition is very keen and a Mustang won the 1987 series, driven by Steve Saleen. Since then, Mustangs have performed reasonably well, but without much factory support, it is difficult for them to win against heavily backed GM cars.

Probably where you'll see the most Mustangs raced is on the drag strip. Because of their low cost and high-performance capabilities and potential, the Mustang GT has become the Chevelle and GTO of the 1980s and 1990s. There is great grass-roots acceptance for the Mustang today, something that Ford wasn't able to do with the model in the 1960s. To a lesser extent, you'll see Mustangs on the autocross circuit.

Mustang Engines

289 and 302

By far, the engine that is most closely associated with the Mustang is the small-block Ford V-8. The small-block, however, had its roots in the late 1950s, when the Big Three (Ford Motor Co., General Motors, and Chrysler Corporation) were in the midst of designing a new wave of compacts and intermediates. A large segment of the population didn't necessarily want or need the typical large Detroit sedan—something smaller would do just fine. Spurred by the success of the American Motors Corporation Rambler, Ford, Chevrolet, and Plymouth introduced the Falcon, Corvair, and Valiant, respectively, but product planners also saw the need for something in between, which led to the intermediate-size model. Ford's intermediate, which would eventually go on sale in 1962, was the Fairlane (named after Henry Ford's estate). The problem was that Ford didn't have an engine for the new model.

During the Fairlane's planning stages, there were three distinct Ford engine families: the FE (Ford Engine) series which included the 332, 352, 390, and 406; the MEL (Mercury, Edsel, Lincoln) series which included the 368, 430, and 462; and the Y-block which at that time consisted only of the 292.

None of these engines was adequate for the Fairlane. The FE and MEL series were too big and heavy while the Y-block was not one of Ford's better ideas. The block wasn't strong and the engine had oiling problems. The Fairlane would need a new V-8 and to that end, the small-block V-8 was born.

Displacing only 221ci and putting out only 145hp at 4400rpm with 216lb-ft of torque at 2200, the new engine had some positive features. It was light, 450lb, compact, and strong. Unlike other Ford engines, the small-block's bottom end and oiling system were well thought out and the engine had potential. Ford had to take advantage of its potential almost immediately—the 221 was enlarged to 260ci midway through the model year and by 1963, the 260 was made available on the car maker's compact, the Falcon, as well. Even though the 260 was better, it too, was at best a stopgap measure, until the 289 arrived in 1964.

Besides the mundane versions of the 289, 1964 saw the introduction of the first true high-performance 289. This one was the 271hp Hi-Po 289, as it became known and shortly after the Mustang's introduction, it was made available as an option. The extra power over the 200 and 225hp versions of the 289 that powered most Mustangs was due to a higher compression ratio, a solid-lifter camshaft, and a slightly larger four-barrel carburetor. It was a very satisfying engine. The 271hp 289 was available on 1965-67 Mustangs.

By this time, the 289 had made quite a name for itself as Carroll Shelby used it to motivate his Cobra sports cars. Naturally, when the Shelby GT350 Mustang was born, it too would be powered with the High Performance 289, but Shelby would add his brand of performance on the engine. With the addition of a high-rise aluminum intake manifold, a Holley 715cfm (cubic feet per minute) carburetor, and steel tube headers, the 289 now boasted 306hp. In addition, Shelby marketed a series of Cobra kits that were designed to enable the enthusiast to make similar modifications on regular 289s and even go beyond through multiple carburetion kits, wilder camshafts, modified cylinder heads, and the like. This was the golden age of the 289.

Ford even experimented with the 289. One such experiment was the SOHC (single overhead camshaft) 289. Using a single overhead cam per bank design, this 289 would put out 300hp on a single four-barrel carburetor and would rev to 6500rpm and beyond with ease. The problem was, as it is with today's 302, that the stock cylinder heads and manifold couldn't flow enough air-fuel mixture to take advantage of the extra-rpm capability. Ford had intended to market the overhead cam setup as an over-the-counter kit. Later on, when the 302 was introduced, Ford toyed with the idea of a three-valve overhead cam design, but it never got beyond the mock-up stage as the Boss 302 was already on its way and it could make as much power at considerably less cost.

Another variant was built in small numbers, the Tunnel-Port 302. Used on the 1968 Trans-Am Mustangs, this 302 featured redesigned cylinder heads that had extremely large intake ports, so large that the pushrods were located in tubes in the center of

Although it doesn't look like the special engine it is, the Boss 302 was the ultimate expression of the Ford small-block. Large, 351 Cleveland-type cylinder heads, four-bolt main block, forged-steel crankshaft, special rods, and a mechanical camshaft are only some of its outstanding features. Randy Ream

the intake port. The Tunnel-Port 302 was a disaster, however, plagued with reliability problems.

After the Hi-Po 289 was retired, the 302 became a low-performance engine that powered Mustangs and practically every other Ford vehicle. The last 302 that used a four-barrel carburetor was the one that powered the 1968 Shelby GT350 Mustang. In 1983, the Mustang GT would once again get four-barrel carburetion but in between, all 302s were of the two-barrel variety.

The only exception was the Boss 302 of 1969-70. Ford needed a killer engine for the Trans-Am series and the only way to get the 302 to breathe better was through new cylinder heads. The new cylinder heads, patterned after Chevy's big-block, featured large, canted valves and big ports. Valves measured 2.23in intake and 1.72in exhaust. Along with the heads, the 302's block was beefed up, and to date, remains the only four-bolt main production block. Naturally, an aluminum intake manifold, a big Holley 780cfm carburetor, and a solid-lifter camshaft were part of the package.

The small-block went through a weight-reduction program in 1981. Every component was looked at with an eye toward reducing weight without compromising the 302's inherent strength. Another minor change occurred in 1982 when the 302's firing order went from its previous 1-5-4-2-6-3-7-8 to a firing order that was the same as the 351W: 1-3-7-2-6-5-4-8.

Mention should be made of the 255ci version of the small-block that was available during 1980-82. Its displacement was reduced by decreasing its bore from 4.00 to 3.68in. This engine has little performance potential.

351W and 351C

In 1969, Ford finally introduced a medium-size V-8, the 351 Windsor. It was named after the plant it

With 330hp, the 1971 Boss 351 engine was as quick in street form as most big-block-powered muscle cars of the era.

was made at, in Windsor, Canada. Outwardly, the 351W looks like a larger 302, which in fact, it is. The extra displacement was arrived at by increasing the 302's deck height. The crankshaft's bearing journals were also increased in size. Two versions of the Windsor were introduced. The first was rated at 250hp and used a two-barrel carburetor with a single-exhaust system. A four-barrel, dual-exhaust version was rated at 290hp. The 351W was an interim engine on the Mustang—1969 was the only year for the four-barrel, while the two-barrel version lasted through 1970. The problem was that the 351W is not much of a performance engine. The cylinder heads on the regular 302 are already marginal at best when it comes to airflow, and adding an additional 49ci displacement only compounds the problem.

Whereas the 351W was based on the small-block engine family, the 351 Cleveland (351C), named after the plant at which it was produced, was a completely new engine. It used a new cylinder block, heads, and manifolds and as such, does not interchange with the small-block. The cylinder heads can be made to fit, after some minor modifications.

The Cleveland's claim to fame is its canted-valve cylinder heads. These were made in two versions, the two-barrel and four-barrel. The two-barrel heads came with smaller valves and ports which were considerably larger than those available on the 302/351W. The four-barrel heads were relegated to the

The year 1967 saw the first big-block Mustangs, in this case a 320hp 390.

Not to be outdone, Carroll Shelby installed the 428 Police Interceptor in 1967-68 Shelby GT500 Mustangs.

higher performance 351Cs and featured ports and valving similar to those found on the Boss 302. The 351C production ceased in 1974 but two higher deck variants continued to be produced—the 351M (a modified 351) and 400. These were used on Ford's larger passenger cars and light trucks.

The highest horsepower 351C was available on the Boss 351 Mustang and was called the Boss 351. Following the pattern set by the Boss 302, the Boss 351 got high-compression pistons, a solid-lifter camshaft, and an aluminum intake manifold for a 330hp rating. A somewhat detuned version, the 351 HO rated at 275hp was briefly available in 1972. During the last two years of the first-generation Mustang, the 351CJ powered the high-performance Mustangs.

If you look in the Ford Motorsport performance products catalog today, you'll see 351C type heads available for the racer along with a compatible cylinder block. Interestingly, this block is based on the 351W because it is a better, stronger design.

390, 427, and 428CJ FE-Series

The best–known performance Mustangs of the 1960s are those powered by Ford's big-block V-8s. They represented the easiest way to get a big dose of horsepower and torque for the Mustang.

The 390 was available from 1967-69. While there were performance versions sporting three two-barrel carburetors in the early 1960s, the Mustang came

The 428 Cobra Jet engine, installed in 1968-70 Mustangs, with its tremendous low-end torque proved to be the engine of choice among street racers.

with a more mundane, low-performance 390. The 390 provided effortless acceleration but it wasn't much of a drag engine.

Ford's hot-dog big-block during the 1960s was the 427. Using a different block, the 427 also came with several cylinder heads that could be used on different applications. These were known as the Low, Medium, and High Risers because of the cylinder head porting and intake manifold height. The 427 that was briefly available on the 1968 Mustang was a hydraulic-cammed Low Riser. The 427s were never built in large quantities and consequently they were too expensive for the typical street racer.

The 1967 Shelby GT500 Mustangs got a 428. This was the Police Interceptor 428 fitted with a dual-quad intake manifold. It put out plenty of power and 1968 Shelby GT500s continued to use it until the 428CJ came out.

The 428CJ proved to be the engine that made the Mustang's reputation as a hot street car. A regular production 428 was fitted with 427 Low Riser cylinder heads along with a host of other improvements for an underrated 335hp. It may not have been a glamorous engine, but it got the job done.

Boss 429, 429CJ, and 429SCJ

The most exotic Mustang engine is the Boss 429. As mentioned earlier, the Boss 429 was installed in Mustangs so that Ford could use the engine in NASCAR competition. It used a special cylinder block and aluminum hemi-type cylinder heads along with forged-steel connecting rods and crankshaft. In street trim, the Boss 429 wasn't any better than a 428CJ because Ford didn't make much of an effort to make it a high-performance street engine.

Further versions of the 429 were the 429 Cobra Jet and Super Cobra Jet, which eventually replaced the aging 428CJ in 1971. Based on the production 429, the 429CJ used cylinder heads that had larger ports and valves. These cylinder heads were similar in design to those used on the 351C engines. The 429 Cobra Jet was available only for the 1971 model year.

The 429CJ/SCJ was the last big-block engine to power Mustangs in 1971. It is Ford's most modern big-engine design and the engine, in a somewhat larger displacement (460ci), is still used in trucks.

The 302ci small-block still lives on today with fuel injection and sophisticated electronics.

*Ford resurrected the Cobra name for 1993 with the
Mustang Cobra. The Cobra is a limited edition Mustang
featuring many of the modifications outlined in this book.
It is powered by a 295hp version of the venerable 302ci
V-8.* Ford Motor Co.

*Ford's unique Boss 429 engine was stuffed in specially
modified 1969-70 Mustangs.*

Chapter 2

Rebuilding the 302

Unfortunate as it may seem, the motivating force of your Mustang, the engine, will eventually expire. Usually this is a gradual process. You may start noticing blue smoke coming out of the tailpipes or that the engine doesn't seem to be generating as much power as it used to. Or perhaps you've beat on it too many times and something inside finally lets go. At this point you have to decide what you want to do with the car. If the engine is just tired you may feel it's time to trade it in—which is the typical reaction of most people. If you want to hold on to the car, you'll want to have the engine rebuilt.

If you decide to have the engine rebuilt, you've opened the door to myriad possibilities. You can have the engine rebuilt to its exact condition when it left the factory, but more likely, you'll want to make improvements. These improvements can be a black hole when it comes to cost. One thing always leads to another and another. Look at an engine rebuilding book and you'll soon realize that there are many operations and parts substitutions that you can make. These may not be necessary on a street engine. If you knew how engines are built at the factory you'd realize that they are literally "slapped" together and yet, these engines can take an inordinate amount of abuse. What is even more amazing is the low quality of some of the stock parts, and that they too, can hold up.

Most American V-8 engines, and this includes the 302, are understressed when it comes to horsepower output. Compare the 225hp output of the 302 to, let's say, the 189hp from a 150ci BMW engine. The BMW is putting out 1.26hp per cubic inch while the 302 is loafing along at 0.74hp per cubic inch. And the BMW engine is doing this reliably, as is the 302. There is room in the 302 for power modifications that can be made before it goes into the engine. These encompass the usual intake and exhaust system mods outlined in this book, and the result will be what is called a "mildly modified" street engine.

A "built" engine, on the other hand, can cost anywhere from $5,000 to $15,000. This is due to the cost of the parts themselves—how about $3,500 for a set of titanium connecting rods?—and the labor involved in having the engine blueprinted. Blueprinting means having the engine rebuilt to the specifications originally called for. For example, it is a rare occurrence when the intake ports of a cylinder head actually match Ford's specifications. At the same time, when the engine is assembled it has to be put together within factory specifications. This requires hours and hours of checking and rechecking clearances.

But aren't all engines put together within factory specs? They are, but the factory specs allow for a certain amount of tolerance. For example, connecting rod oil bearing clearance is 0.0008-0.0026in. You may have some bearings on the low side and some on the high side, which is considered acceptable on a street engine that isn't asked to produce a lot of power for a long period of time. However, like everything else, there is an optimum clearance that will make for a stronger running engine. When an engine is blueprinted, all clearances are made as equal as possible to ensure that each cylinder produces exactly the same amount of power.

In this chapter we'll look at basic engine rebuilding fundamentals and make suggestions that are worthwhile for the typical modified "street" engine. I emphasize the word street because some machining operations and parts may not be necessary for a street engine that will only on occasion see the high side of 6000rpm.

Obviously, the typical enthusiast cannot rebuild the engine completely by himself because many operations require the use of specialized equipment. For these, the parts will have to be sent out to the machine shop. However, many preparatory and assembly operations can be made with simple hand tools.

Tools

There is a saying among car enthusiasts that you can never have enough tools. This is true, but it can be surprising how few tools you'll need to take apart and put together an engine.

The 302 is a reliable, well-built engine that will last 100,000 miles and longer, provided it is well maintained and not abused. Under hard usage, however, the possibility that something will break or wear out increases and there is no magical additive that will remedy the situation. Your only recourse is to rebuild the engine. While the engine is apart you can, for a modest cost, install stronger components but on the other hand, it is very easy to go overboard and spend too much on parts that aren't necessary. Ford Motor Co.

Incredible as it may seem, some people don't bother changing the oil and filter. All that crud in the lifter valley is the result of oxidized oil. What little oil there was in the engine didn't do much lubricating. The small-block Ford also has a reputation of being a "dirty" engine.

The first tool you'll need is a shop manual. Not only will critical specifications be listed, but the order in which things should be done will be included. A general engine rebuilding book is good to have, but these won't tell you what you have to do to remove the engine from your Mustang. If you can, invest in a shop manual.

Basic hand tools are required, along with a good torque wrench. The click-type wrenches are preferable because you can torque down bolts a lot faster. You'll also need a harmonic balancer puller and an engine stand in addition to a set of micrometers, a dial caliper, a dial indicator, a piston ring compressor, and a valve spring compressor tool. If you plan to do any porting, a die-grinder with a variety of stones and cutters will enable you to port your heads along with other operations such as engine block deburring and chamfering. You can also invest in other specialized tools, such as an inside micrometer, which can make a rebuild go easier and quicker.

Cylinder Block

The first thing to do after removing the engine from your Mustang is to take it apart. Depending on the rebuild and your budget, it is unlikely that you'll reuse the pistons, camshaft, valve lifters, bearings, timing chain and gears, and oil pump. You'll probably reuse the pushrods, rockers, and maybe the valve springs, and unless there is a damaged rod, the connecting rods.

After the engine is apart, you might as well take it to the rebuild shop that is going to perform the machining operations. They'll have the block and

Sludge coats everything inside the engine. The only way you're going to remove it is to take the engine apart and have it cleaned. The sludge also holds the heat generated by the engine, making it run hotter. Changing the oil often is necessary.

The reason for this engine's failure is obvious, once it's apart. It ran out of oil, causing the pistons to seize. Pistons in this condition make good paperweights.

heads hot-tanked to get them degreased and cleaned. Some may use a jet cleaning booth, in which case long pipe brush cleaners will be used to make sure the oil passages are clean. All bolt holes should also be chased with an undersized tap to make sure they are clean.

Once the block is clean, you'll be able to determine if it can be reused. Every block should be Magnaflux inspected. Magnetic powder is spread on one section of the block at a time while a large U-shaped magnet is moved over it. Any cracks will disrupt the magnetic field and the powder will collect on them, making cracks evident. Every surface of the block should be treated in this manner. You'll want to have additional tests performed, such as a pressure test to determine if there are any water jacket leaks and sonic testing to check for cylinder wall thickness, if you are building a high-horsepower 302.

Even though the 302 block was lightened considerably in 1981, it still performs well enough, except for very high horsepower applications. The block doesn't take kindly to high supercharger boosts or excessive use of nitrous oxide. The beefier four-bolt main SVO block, Motorsport part number M-6010-A4, is necessary for such applications.

The first step after disassembly is to have the block, heads, and other parts cleaned. Hot-tanking or jet-cleaning is how this is accomplished, with the latter method taking a shorter time. If you aren't planning to work on the engine immediately after cleaning, spray all the parts with WD-40 to inhibit rust.

The next step is to have the block deburred. In this process all casting burrs, casting flash, and sharp edges are ground off since they can provide a starting point for cracks. Casting flash may also find its way to the oil pump and clog up the works. Deburring may not be necessary in a street engine, but if you have the time it is a worthwhile operation.

The first major machining operation is align honing and boring. This operation ensures that the main bearing bores are aligned. The main bearing cap mating surfaces are ground to ensure they are flat, and then reinstalled on the block. A boring or honing bar is then placed through the caps, with the end result being main bearing bores that are round and in alignment with each other.

Whereas align boring and honing should be considered necessary in every engine, having the block decked is another operation that is not absolutely necessary in a street engine. Decking ensures that the decks (the surface where the cylinder head is bolted) are aligned with each other and with the crankshaft. Sometimes you'll find that the decks aren't at quite a 90deg angle in relation to the crankshaft. Decking also establishes deck height. Deck height is the distance from the flat (quench) part of the piston to the deck surface on the block when the piston is at top dead center (TDC).

Most rebuilders will have the block deck surface milled slightly to ensure a good sealing surface for the head gaskets.

Most machine shops automatically replace the stock pistons with new 0.030in overbore pistons. To do this, the cylinders are overbored a corresponding amount in two operations—first on the boring machine which removes the bulk of material, and the balance when the cylinders are honed to the final, desired finish which is dependent on the type of piston rings to be used. Most 302s will end up with molybdenum rings which require little, if any, break-in. In this case, the cylinder walls will be finished with

The block should be dry Magnafluxed to see if any cracks are present. This is done by magnetizing the block and pouring a magnetic powder on the block. Some cracks or damaged areas can be repaired, thereby saving you the cost of a new block.

One area to watch for cracks is at the oil passages on the main bearing saddles. The 302's cylinders extend into the block, looking like sleeves. As you can see, they are very thin which is the reason why the 302 block should not be overbored more than 0.060in.

a fine 400 grit honing stone. Chrome-plated rings require a rougher finish. Chrome rings have a very hard surface and a rougher finish traps oil in the cylinder walls to provide lubrication for the rings, but these rings are of little value in a street engine.

Some engine builders use honing plates that are bolted on the deck surface to simulate the distortion caused by the cylinder head on the cylinder. Cylinders honed in this manner will be rounder and produce more power.

At this point, the block must be cleaned with detergent and water to remove the metal dust, chips, and grit on the block and especially on the cylinder walls. It is also important to clean all the oil passages and to spray the entire block with a rust inhibitor. To make sure that there is no abrasive grit on the cylinder walls, use paper towels soaked in automatic transmission fluid to scrub them clean. Use new towels until there are no more grit traces on the towels.

Crankshaft

With the exception of the forged-steel Boss 302 crankshafts, all small-block Ford engines have used cast-iron cranks. The cast crank was lightened in 1981 with smaller counterweights and this, according to Ford, has not proved to be a detriment. The small-block Ford is blessed with a very strong bottom end and crank breakage or oiling problems are not common. One crank that should *not* be used is the one found in the 255ci version. It is hollow and is marginal even for street use.

If the bores don't show much wear, you don't have to overbore the cylinders but most rebuilders will do it automatically by 0.030in for quality-control reasons. This is done in two steps, on the boring machine shown here and when the cylinders are honed.

After the cylinders are bored, the top of the cylinder is chamfered. This is done to ease piston installation later on.

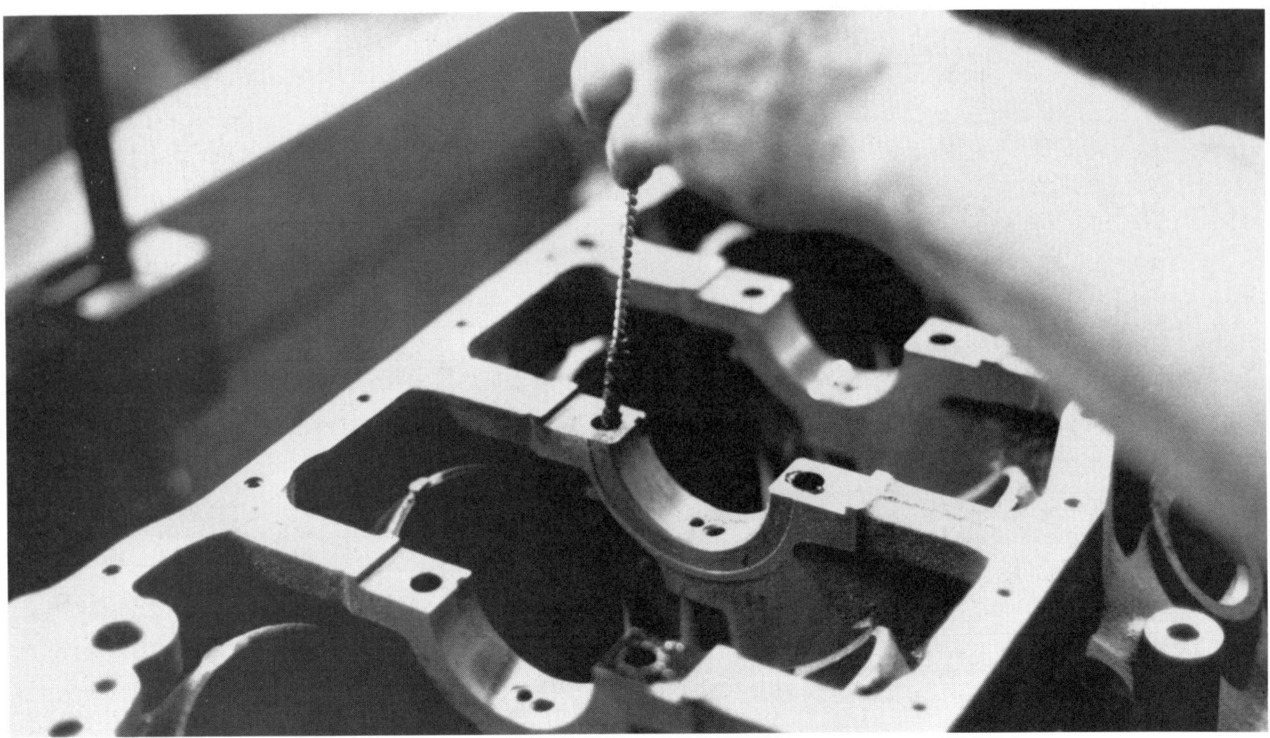

Prior to align honing, the main cap bolts and threads should be cleaned in order to get a correct torque reading. Thread chasers and brushes are used here.

With the main caps bolted in place, they are align honed on this machine. This step ensures that the main bearing bores are perfectly round and in alignment with each other.

There is not much that you can do with the crankshaft besides dropping it off at the crankshaft shop. There they will check it for straightness and cracks. Even one slight crack warrants discarding the crank because cracks can't be repaired.

The journals will be cut undersize, if needed, and they should be micropolished and the oil holes should always be chamfered. That's about all that is needed for a street engine.

Cross-drilling, Tuftriding, and chroming aren't necessary on a street engine. If you are building a high-horsepower motor, then you should plan on getting either a semi-finished or unmachined forging from Motorsport.

Factory crank bearing clearances are listed at 0.0005-0.0015in; 0.0005 is too tight for a performance engine so you should aim for the high end of the tolerance limit. Very high performance engines will typically have larger clearances, 0.0025-0.0035in. A looser fit will result in less friction but also requires an oiling system capable of supplying additional volume to the bearings. Bearing clearances should be checked; Plastigage is easy to use, if you don't have a micrometer. If the bearing clearance is too loose or too tight, you can use undersize or oversize bearings or even bearings made by a different manufacturer to arrive at the desired clearance.

In addition to bearing clearance, you also have to check for thrust clearance which measures the front-to-rear crankshaft motion.

The block's deck surfaces are milled to ensure good head gasket seal. Milling also ensures that the deck surface is straight.

A minor but useful operation is to chamfer all the oil passages to help oil flow. Just as important is to ensure that there aren't any blockages inside the passages.

The final block machining operation is to hone the cylinders. The type of finish is dependent on the type of piston ring used. It is extremely important to thoroughly clean the block after this operation to get rid of all the metal bits and grit that have accumulated. A machine shop will send the block through the jet booth, but if you are doing this at home start off with plenty of detergent and water. Use clean rags soaked in automatic transmission fluid to clean the cylinder bores.

Rods and Pistons

Stock 302 connecting rods are made from forged steel. As such, they are reliable for street use but there are a couple of low-cost modifications that can be made to improve their durability.

First, the stock $5/16$in rod bolts should be replaced. You can use Motorsport's High Strength SVO rod and bolt kit, part number M-6214-A302, or you can have the bolt holes enlarged to accept larger $11/16$in bolts (the size used on the small-block Chevy). This is the kind of modification that will help you sleep at night.

The old 289 Hi-Po and Boss 302 engines came with rods that used $3/8$in bolts. These have been out of production for some time, but you may be able to find a used set. A good alternative is to use the Motorsport connecting rod similar in design to the old Hi-Po/Boss 302 rods, part number M-6200-T100, but use a smaller $5/16$in bolt. These should be replaced with $11/32$in bolts.

As with the crankshaft, the connecting rods should first be checked that they aren't twisted or bent; then Magnaflux to look for cracks. If they pass, the big end should be resized. This is done on a special machine. The process is similar to align honing the main caps. A small amount of metal is removed from the cap to make sure the mating surface is flat, and then reinstalled on the rod. The bore is then made perfectly round on the machine.

New freeze plugs are then installed. The sealer is used to ease installation.

Pay special attention to the rear camshaft plug. This one has a layer of sealer on it. Any leak here after the engine is put back together and running will be a royal pain to fix.

After installing new camshaft bearings, liberally coat the new cam with lubricant and carefully slide it in.

At this point, the 302 block is set on an engine stand. Although it isn't strictly necessary, the stand makes a rebuild go a lot easier and quicker.

The 302's crankshaft, along with the block and heads were lightened in 1981. On the right is a 1981 and later crank while on the left is an older crank. The older crank has larger, heavier counterweights. According to Ford, the lighter crank hasn't caused any durability problems. All 302 cranks, with the exception of the 1969-70 Boss 302, are cast.

Although not necessary on a street engine, you may want to have the side beams polished and shot peened. The reasoning here is similar to having the block deburred—by eliminating the forging line you reduce the possibility for cracks to start.

Regarding piston pin fit, there is no reason to switch from the stock pressed pin to a full-floating configuration. You know that the stock pressed-in pin is not going anywhere when there is a 0.0015in interference fit. Installation is accomplished by heating the rod small end and then the pin-piston assembly is slipped through. When the rod cools, the pin is locked in place.

Factory rod bearing clearance is listed as 0.0008-0.0026in; race engines will typically require more clearance, 0.0005-0.0010in beyond the upper end tolerance limit.

You can spend a lot of money on pistons but again, this is an area where you don't need to go too far beyond the stock cast pistons. Cast pistons are relatively inexpensive, they are lighter than most forged pistons, and they can be installed with less side clearance (because they don't expand as much as forgings) in the cylinder bore, thereby providing better ring seal which means more power. Forged pistons may work fine in high-rpm, high-heat situations but because they are installed with more side clearance, they are apt to be noisy and can increase oil consumption.

A recent development in piston technology is the hypereutectic piston. These pistons are made from a special alloy and are cast at a higher temperature. The result is a strong, light piston that is almost as durable as a forging but without the forged piston's weak points. As you would expect, hypereutectic pistons cost more than regular castings but less than forged pistons.

Considering the octane of today's gasoline, it doesn't make much sense to go for a compression ratio that is more than 9:1 or so, unless you plan to use additives or you're building a race engine. Stick with the stock compression ratio.

The one modification you may want to make before installing the pistons is to have valve reliefs cut a little deeper to compensate for any future higher lift cam installation, or if you are installing a higher lift cam now.

Regarding piston rings, by far the most common rings used today are moly rings. These are made from cast iron that incorporates a molybdenum surface layer. They are long lasting, reliable, and require little break-in. One area that could use some improvement, however, is the oil control ring. The stock low-tension rings are supposed to increase horsepower, but you're better off using TRW or Sealed Power rings which provide better oil control.

You can also gain a few horses by using gapless piston rings. Total Seal Corporation in Phoenix, Arizona, produces a two-piece, double interlocking

36

This crank may not look good but as long as it isn't scored or damaged, light polishing will remove minor surface imperfections.

Although not a Ford crank, this is what happens when the engine is overrevved. The journals will have to be cut down if this crank is to be used again.

The crank's journals are cut on a special machine. If the crank is going to sit around for a while before installation, make sure you spray the journals with WD-40 to prevent any rust formation. After the cutting, the journals are polished.

ring—each ring has a gap, but they occur at different positions so that there is no one gap for gases to escape. They will definitely add horsepower and at a very modest cost.

The finished crank, ready to be installed. All the oil passages have been chamfered in order not to cut the new bearing shells at installation.

Cylinder Heads

All racers put extra-special effort into cylinder head preparation—the cylinder heads, after all, are responsible for all that horsepower you're hoping your 302 will produce. As we have already discussed, the stock 302 heads are lacking when it comes to valve size and porting—both areas are adequately addressed with Motorsport and aftermarket heads. Besides following the usual reconditioning procedures, you can perform some basic porting on the stock heads to improve flow, and remember, even the trick aftermarket heads will eventually need to be rebuilt.

The initial steps to take after removal of the valves, rockers, and springs is to have the heads cleaned, either in the hot tank (not for aluminum heads!) or in the booth. At this point, visually inspect the heads for any cracks, especially around the exhaust seat area. Have the heads Magnafluxed as well.

No matter what you intend for your engine, even if it is going back to dead stock, you should have bronze valve guides installed. The valves in the cylinder head don't just go up and down, the rocker

Two types of rear main seals have been used on 302 crankshafts. Early crankshafts have a raised lip on the journal while later cranks, center and right, do not. Later cranks with a worn journal can be brought up to spec through the use of a sleeve that fits over the journal.

arms exert side-to-side pressures as well, which lead to guide wear. As the guides wear the possibility for the valve not landing squarely on the seat also increases, allowing leaks to occur. Bronze valve guides last longer, require less lubrication than the stock iron guides, allow the valves to be fitted with less clearance, and transfer heat better from the valve to the head. The exhaust valves and seats are subjected to higher than ever temperatures, which contributes to valve seat erosion. The reason for this is that the fuel mixture during part-throttle operation is very lean—good for mileage but creating high combustion chamber temperatures. Exhaust valve and seat failure can also occur if there is a problem with your Mustang's catalytic converters. If they get plugged up, the valve and seat temperature goes way up.

The stock rockers can be refaced and reused, if you are on a very tight budget, but you are better off replacing them, especially if you are installing a new camshaft. You may reuse the stock valve springs, provided they haven't lost any height and tension, but always use new valve keepers. Of course, if you are installing a new cam, it is always a good idea to replace the valve springs.

Assuming that you are going to be reusing the stock valves, you'll gain significant airflow into and

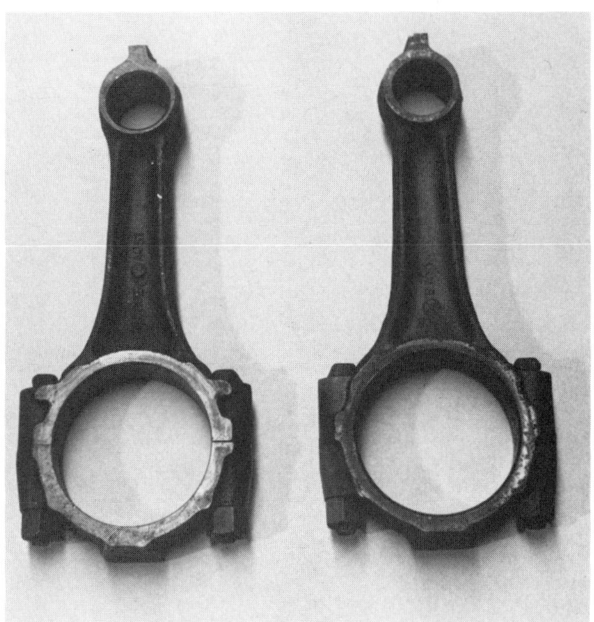

The stock 302 connecting rods are strong enough for a street engine or even some competition applications, provided you change the stock $^5/_{16}$in rod bolts. You can use the SVO high-strength bolt and nut kit, but the $^5/_{16}$in size limits its strength. Have the rod bolt holes enlarged to accept $^{11}/_{32}$in bolts (Chevy small-block bolt size).

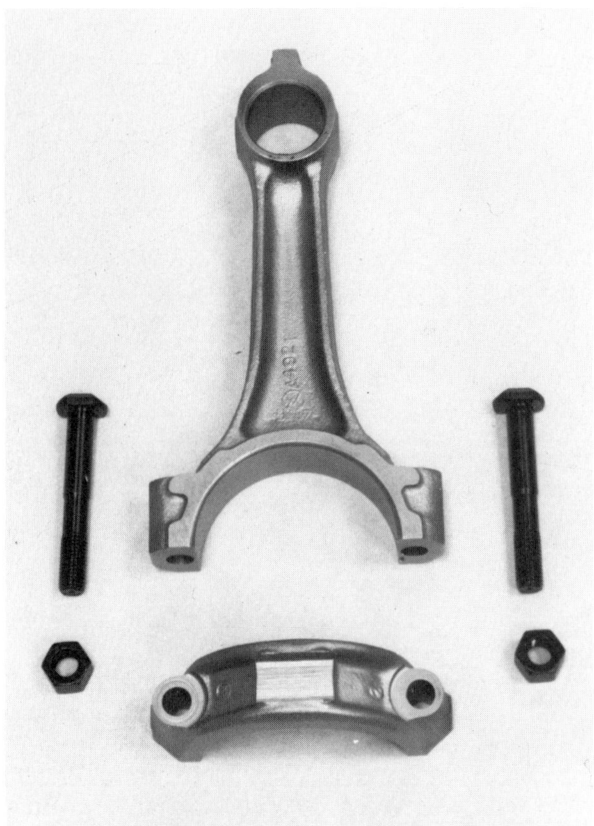

This is the SVO heavy-duty connecting rod (Motorsport part number M-6200-T100) which comes with a specially designed ribbed cap. Even though it comes with high-strength $^5/_{16}$in rod bolts, they should be replaced with $^{11}/_{32}$in bolts. Ford Motor Co.

out of the engine if you have a three-angle valve job performed. The stock heads have seats ground at a single angle of 45deg—good for durability but not for optimizing flow. A three-angle valve job improves flow by smoothing out the flow of gases into and out of the combustion chamber.

It would also be a good idea to do any porting on the stock heads at this point. Refer to chapter 3, which covers the induction system and cylinder heads, for details.

Most rebuilders will mill the head a slight amount for better gasket sealing, usually in the area of 0.0005in. This may or may not be enough to warrant cutting the intake manifold or cylinder head manifold mounting surface to maintain port alignment.

Final Assembly and Break-In

After all the parts have been reconditioned, all that is left is to put them back together. Make sure you have all the parts in one place and that you have all the nuts and bolts that you originally started out with. You can follow the rebuild procedure in the photos, based on a stock 302 at Quality Engine Distributors in Middletown, New York.

When the engine is back in your Mustang's engine compartment, run it at 1500-2000rpm for half an hour to break in the cam. Change the oil and filter immediately, check for any leaks, and then drive the car at moderate, varying speeds for about 500 miles. You'll get varying opinions on this as some will say that with moly rings, you don't need such a long break-in period, and this may be true for nine out of ten cars. Who wants to be the tenth car? Play it safe.

Stock pistons come in two configurations. Shown left is the HO piston with its four eyebrows for valve clearance. If you are installing a high-lift cam or perhaps intend to, this is the time to have the eyebrows enlarged. On the right is a flat-top piston. Pistons are always installed with the indentation toward the front of the block.

Engine Oils

One item often overlooked is the oil that is so vital to your Mustang's engine. You can use a conventional oil and obtain good results as long as you change it every 2,000-2,500 miles, but there is something better available—synthetic oils.

Both synthetic and conventional oils do the same job of lubricating the engine's reciprocating parts, and acting as a coolant, removing heat from hot engine parts. Synthetics just do a much better job. Still, there is considerable apprehension regarding their reliability because synthetics earned a lousy reputation in the 1970s when a major refiner introduced a synthetic oil, Mobil 1. The formulation wasn't quite right and this resulted in engine failures for many.

Today, the situation is much different. Synthetics are totally reliable and offer many advantages over conventional oils. The 1992 Corvette, for example, comes from the factory with synthetic oil. All Callaway Corvettes also specify the use of Mobil 1—any other oil will void the warranty. The best-known synthetics are Mobil 1, Red Line, and Amsoil.

Petroleum-based oils are a complex mixture of hydrocarbon compounds refined from crude oil. Through the refining process, most but not all of the contaminants that exist are removed. In addition, petroleum-based oils also contain wax, not known for its lubricating properties.

Piston pins are installed by heating the small end of the rod and then slipping the pin in. As the rod cools, a tight interference fit results.

The base stock from which synthetics are made are free from contaminants and wax. Mobil 1's base stock is a compound of carbon and hydrogen molecules synthesized from ethylene gas molecules. Mobil calls this synthesized hydrocarbon fluid. Another synthesized fluid is added to this called organic ester.

With the rings installed, piston-rod assemblies are lined up ready for installation in the cylinder block. To prevent any damage to the cylinders or crankshaft, these vinyl sleeves are placed over each rod bolt.

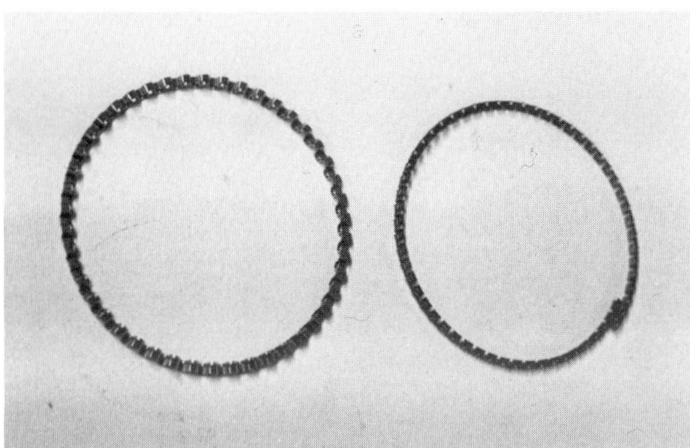

The stock 302 oil piston rings (right) are of a low-tension design which reduces friction but at the expense of increased oil consumption. You can use the stock-type rings, but you may be better off using a regular oil control ring (left) as the increase in power with a low-tension ring is negligible and can be offset by using a good synthetic oil.

The bare cylinder head should be Magnafluxed and visually checked for cracks after it comes out of the jet stream booth. If it passes inspection, the cylinder head's surface is milled to provide a good sealing surface for the head gasket.

Part of Red Line's base stock comes from vegetable oil sources and is modified to improve thermal stability, while other materials are added to complete the final product. Amsoil uses a combination of seven different base stocks in producing its final product.

Synthetic oils provide considerably higher viscosity ratings at critical areas without the use of viscosity improvers. A synthetic 10W-40 will generally have higher viscosity at high temperatures than a conventional 20W-50. The reason for this is the base stock from which the synthetic is constructed.

A major advantage of synthetics is their ability to remain stable at high temperatures without breaking down or oxidizing. Petroleum-based oils will boil away under high temperature. These oils, depending on viscosity, have a thermal breakdown between 350 and 400deg Fahrenheit. This is important because the upper cylinder area of an engine will see temperatures in the 600deg range. Thus, a petroleum-based oil will begin to break down or oxidize almost immediately. Oxidation occurs when the hot oil is exposed to oxygen which then leads to the formation of organic acids that will combine and form varnish deposits. These deposits coat the metal, reducing the ability to transfer heat and accelerating engine wear. Other by-products of oxidation include tar, sludge, and thickening of the oil.

Besides its resistance to viscosity loss at high temperatures, synthetics also have much stronger film strength. Film strength is the amount of pressure needed to force out a film of oil between two flat pieces of metal. A good petroleum-based oil measures at 500lb, while most synthetics are around the 3,000lb level. This is important—because of its inherent higher film strength, there is much less blow-by past the rings and thus less oil contamination.

While a petroleum-based oil will boil away as temperatures increase, a good synthetic, such as Red Line, will lose only about 4 percent of its weight. At higher temperatures, 475deg F. and above, conventional oils will volatize completely, while synthetics will still be lubricating at 700deg.

This probably is the reason why conventional oils have to be changed so often. Eventually, all the oil in the crankcase will oxidize and break down. The oil does get saturated with contaminants, but contaminants that are the by-product of the oil's own decay and not totally due to those produced by combustion. Synthetics don't need to be changed as often, but this is a point that elicits much skepticism.

Mobil used to advertise 25,000 mile change intervals and even their current literature states 25,000. However, their current position is that even though the oil can go 25,000 miles, to ensure a margin of safety, the oil can be changed sooner, depending on how the car is used. The same applies with Red Line. Red Line recommends oil changes between 12,000 and 18,000 miles, depending on the type of service and the degree of blow-by gases contamination. This means that with an older, looser engine, and if considerable stop-and-go driving is expected, oil drain intervals in the 10,000-12,000 mile range are recommended with filter changes every 5,000 miles. New-car owners should follow the manufacturer's warranty requirements.

Yet another benefit of synthetics is their ability to lower oil temperature in the crankcase. It is a well-known fact that oil not only lubricates, but it also serves as a coolant medium, drawing heat away from the engine's reciprocating parts. However, as temperatures rise, petroleum-based oils have a tendency to bead on the metal surface while synthetics will wet the entire surface, showing affinity for the hot metal rather than itself. The lower oil temperature has the obvious effect of extending engine and oil life. Synthetics will reduce oil temperature by 20-30deg.

All this translates to better mileage because the oil is "slipperier," but more important is the increase in horsepower. A synthetic is good for an extra 5-10hp, as much as a set of "shorty" headers.

In addition to synthetics, also consider using an oil cooler. A good oil cooler will reduce oil temperature by 20deg, thereby extending oil life.

A deep-sump oil pan is a must on any performance engine. If you think about it, the 5qt capacity that is standard on the 302 may not be enough for high-performance use. When the engine is running,

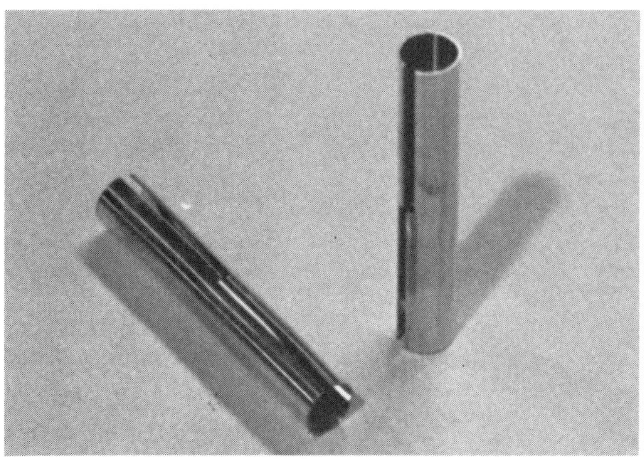

Bronze valve guides should always be installed. Their cost is modest and they will outlast any other reconditioning method.

you have 1qt in the filter, another quart in the oil passages on the way to the bearings, and perhaps another on the way down to the oil pan. This doesn't include all the oil that is thrashed up by the spinning crankshaft, leaving about 2qt (or less) in the oil pan. Under hard acceleration or cornering, the oil pump pickup may become uncovered—your engine won't run on air. A larger capacity oil pan is a worthwhile addition.

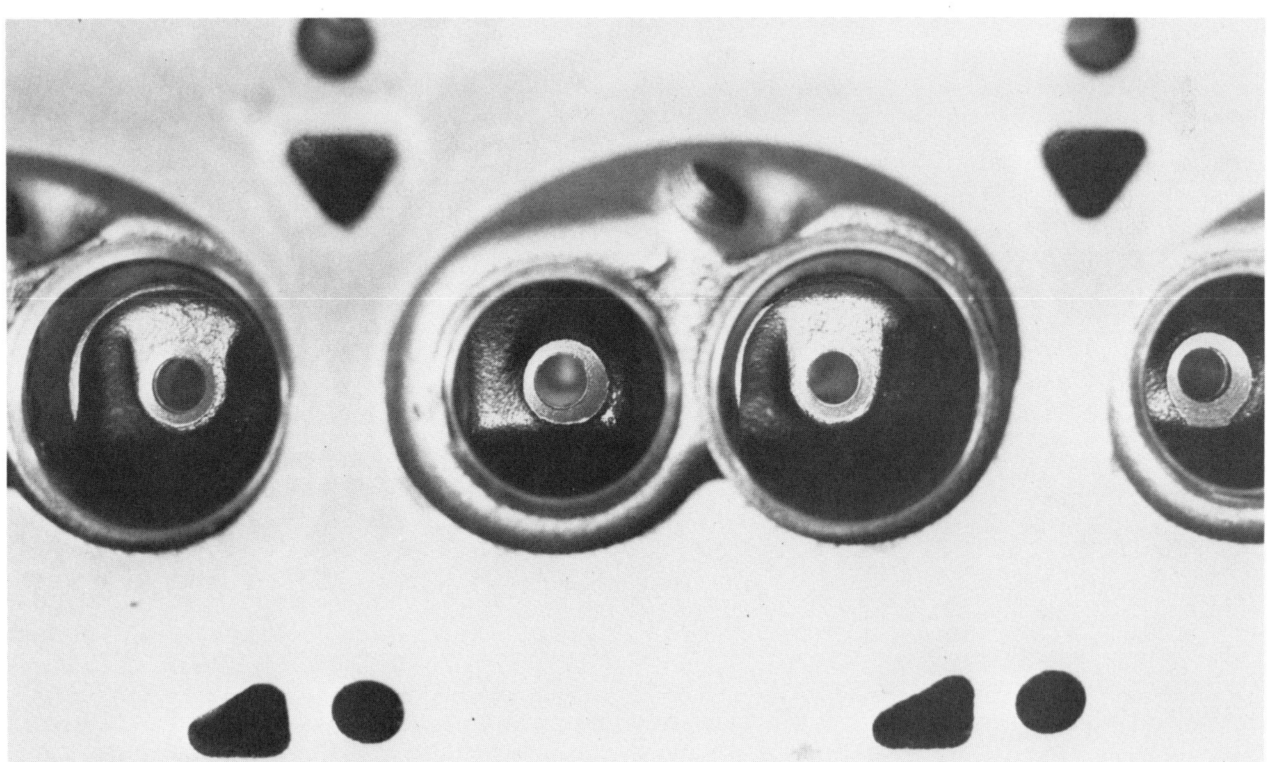

As you can see, the bronze valve guide insert is very thin, but even so, it is superior to the stock cast-iron guide.

You can reuse the original valve springs, provided they are up to stock specifications. Here they are being checked on a special valve spring machine. If you are installing an aftermarket camshaft, you should install the springs that came with the cam kit.

After the valve job has been performed, the valves are lapped. Lapping will show if the job has been done correctly or not and also ensures a good seal.

The main bearing shells are installed at this point. Make sure that they are lubricated before you place the crankshaft on them. If you are going to use the Plastigage method of measuring bearing clearance, this is the time to do it.

Install all the caps and torque them down to specifications. Then remove them to check bearing clearance. If there is too much or too little clearance, try switching the bearing shells or use another set. Don't forget to check the crank thrust clearance with a dial indicator. After the caps are installed, spin the crank to make sure that it turns freely.

The next step is to install the piston-rod assemblies. Turn the crank at bottom dead center for each cylinder and using a ring compressor, lightly tap the piston in. Before you start, make sure that you oil each cylinder.

Once the piston is in place, turn the block over and install the rod end caps. If you didn't use a micrometer to check bearing clearance, use Plastigage.

You can check rod side-to-side clearance with a feeler gauge. Hopefully, it will be within specs.

Once the pistons are all in place, install the timing chain and fuel pump eccentric. This engine is using a stock-type nylon gear assembly, as it is a warranty rebuild.

The nylon timing gear (left) is not recommended, however, as the teeth can shear off. If you are on a tight budget, use at the very least, a timing chain setup that uses a cast-iron gear.

Next, bolt down the oil pump. The stock oil pump uses an aluminum housing. A cast-iron pump is more reliable, however. Grit or metal particles can eventually chew up the soft aluminum housing. This will lead to pump failure, but also adds aluminum particles to the circulating oil.

The oil pump pickup bolts onto the oil pump—one of Ford's better ideas, as some other engines use a pressed-in pickup which can work itself loose.

The reconditioned heads are installed on the block. Follow the torque-down sequence in the factory manual.

Coat the lifters with oil and drop one in each lifter bore. The 302 engines using a roller cam must use guide plates and a guide plate retainer which bolts down in the lifter valley. Slip each pushrod in, and install the rocker arms. If you are using the stock rockers, all you have to do is tighten them down.

With the installation of the timing chain cover and crankshaft dampener, this engine is ready to be painted and delivered to the customer, which in this case was a Ford dealer.

A deep-sump oil pan is a good idea for a high-performance application, provided you have the ground clearance. Motorsport offers a variety of pans. Ford Motor Co.

Chapter 3

Induction System and Cylinder Heads

Getting the most from your engine largely depends on how much air-fuel mixture you can get into it. The traditional method of improving the induction system has been to install a larger carburetor and a more efficient intake manifold. This seems fairly simple, but in some cases it has been a source of endless problems, not to mention magazine articles over the years. One of the problems, or let's say characteristics, of the induction system is that it is the most visible of any modifications that one can make. Consequently, there has been lots of romance associated with the induction systems—but what *looks* good doesn't often *run* well on a street machine.

Carburetion

The 1979-82 V-8 powered Mustangs came with a two-barrel intake manifold and carburetor. From 1983-85, in the quest for more power, Ford went to a larger four-barrel, a Holley flowing 600cfm.

In the past, Ford performance engines came with aluminum high-rise intake manifolds. These are basically refined dual-plane manifolds that follow stock configuration but have taller, larger passages for better engine breathing. Dual-plane types have also been known as the Cross-H or 180deg design, which was originated by Ford in the early thirties. With this type, each half of the manifold feeds half the cylinders, and the two halves are not connected. It is called a 180deg design because the engine draws alternately from each manifold half as it moves through the firing cycle. The dual-plane manifold provides excellent throttle response and low- to mid-range power. However, it tends to become restrictive at high rpm.

The other single four-barrel or X-type design that has been used successfully is the single-plane manifold. Here, all the manifold runners are connected to a common chamber of plenum and are fed by a single carburetor. With their simple design, single-plane manifolds really came into their own when the Edelbrock Corporation refined its design to provide superior performance over the dual-plane design. These manifolds have been developed and refined to such an extent that they match the low- and mid-range response of the dual-plane manifolds while surpassing them at higher rpm. Most, if not all, of the newer single-plane manifolds look very much alike. Usually, it is best to follow the manufacturer's recommendations according to your intended usage.

How much better are the new-generation single-plane manifolds over the dual-planes? Edelbrock made a series of tests (see chart) when it introduced its Torker 289 for the 289/302 engine in the early 1970s. The manifolds used in the test were a stock two-barrel Ford unit; Edelbrock's dual-plane high-rise type, the F-4B; and the Torker 289. The engine was a blueprinted 302 with a Ford solid-lifter cam, Accel distributor, stock compression, and dyno headers.

The stock two-barrel intake seems to hold its own up to 3500rpm; from then on, the power increase slows down considerably. With the simple addition of a Holley 500cfm two-barrel, there is a 23hp increase at 5000rpm.

The 1983-85 302 HO engines came with a 600cfm Holley carburetor. The Holley is not controlled by an EEC computer, however, as these Mustangs did not come with one. With the exception of additional emission equipment and electronic ignition, this 302 isn't too different from a comparable 1960s' style small-block. Something that you don't often see these days is a non-air-conditioned Mustang.

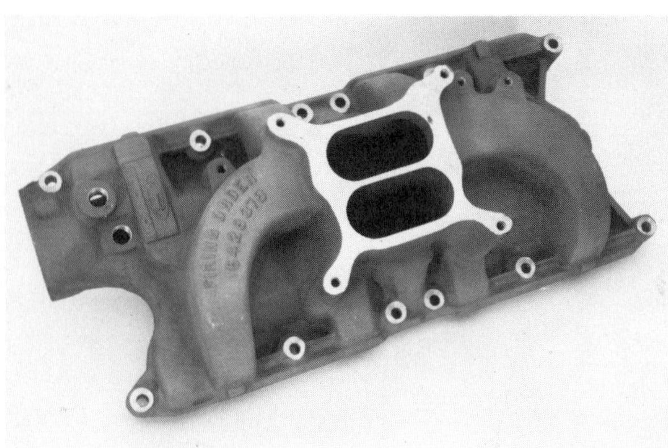

The Motorsport A321 four-barrel intake manifold provides a healthy boost in power over the stock single-plane manifold. Its design is very similar to the old Cobra dual-plane, high-rise intake used on Shelby Mustangs. Ford Motor Co.

The F-4B high-rise with the 725cfm Holley peaks at 5000rpm. It is likely that this particular manifold would do better with a smaller 600cfm carburetor.

The Torker 289, even with the 650cfm two-barrel, outdoes the F-4B with a Holley four-barrel. The less-restrictive nature of the single-plane design is evident, as the 302's power peak is reached at 5500rpm, probably where the cam peaks as well. The best combination is with a 600cfm Holley, proving that bigger is not always better.

The Torker 289 is good for at least a 30hp increase over the dual-plane intake, and with a four-barrel, more than 70hp over stock. This is a tremendous return on a very simple investment. Bear in mind that these results were obtained with a blueprinted, modified 302. You can't expect the same results on a dead-stock 302, although you're bound to see a healthy improvement.

Edelbrock's line of manifolds for the 302 has expanded since then to include the Performer series of manifolds.

Only two two-barrel versions of the 302 were produced between 1979 and 1982. The 1979 version was rated at 140hp while the 1982 produced 157hp. Both came with a single-exhaust system. Although you will see some benefit in the installation of an aftermarket Holley two-barrel carburetor, you are

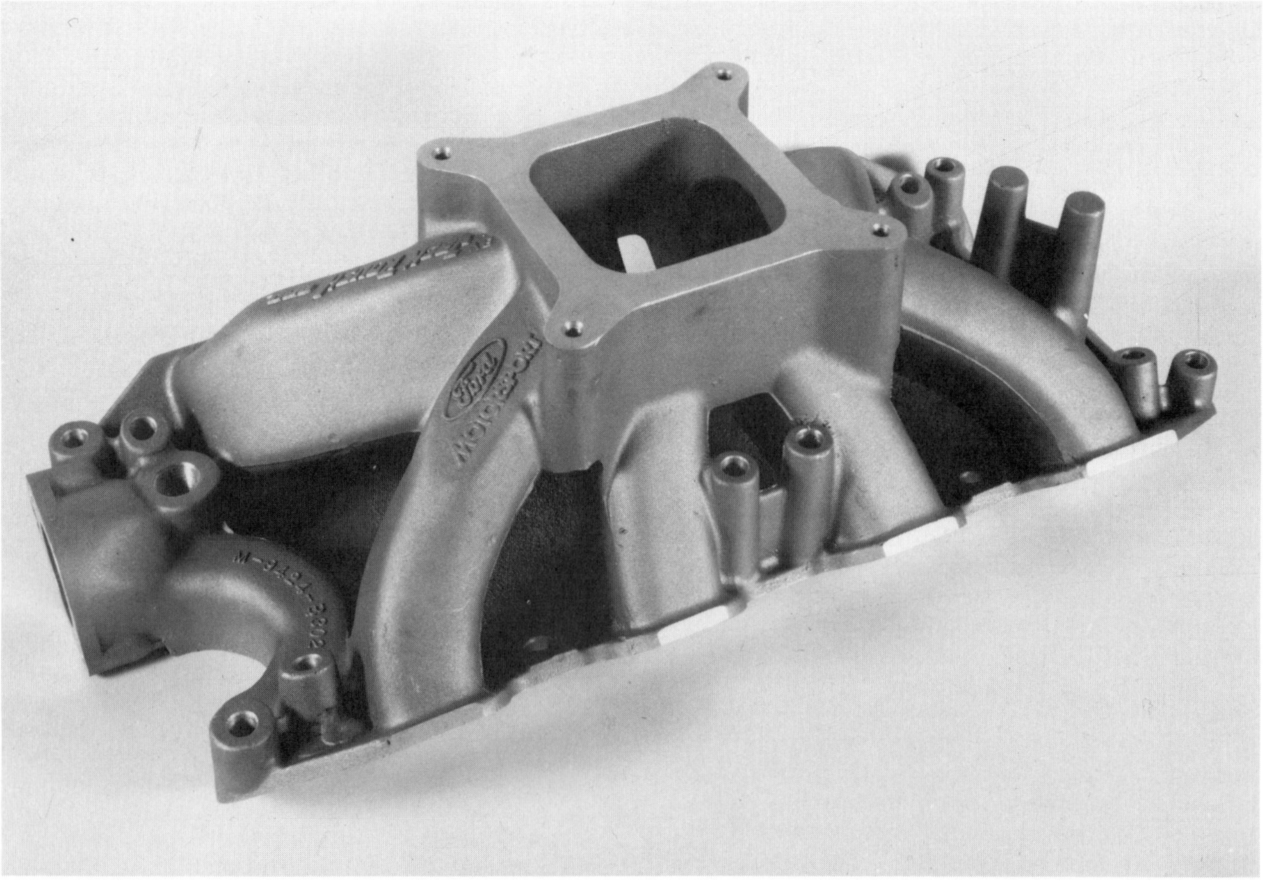

This is an all-out single four-barrel manifold for 302 engines with Cleveland-style cylinder heads. Large, isolated runners are designed for high-rpm operation and to keep the incoming fuel mixture as cool, and therefore dense, as possible. This is definitely not a manifold for the street. Ford Motor Co.

Edelbrock Torker 289 Intake Manifold vs. Various Ford Intakes

This test was conducted on a blueprinted 302 engine with a Ford High Performance camshaft, Accel distributor, and dyno headers.

RPM	Stock 350 cfm 2-bbl & Manifold HP	Stock manifold & 500cfm Holley 2-bbl #4412 HP	Edelbrock F-4B & 725cfm Holley 4-bbl, #4118 HP
2500	126	135	122
3000	153	166	149
3500	174	189	180
4000	188	207	213
4500	204	224	233
5000	206	229	245
5500	201	228	244
6000	188	—	236

RPM	Torker 289 & Holley 725cfm 4-bbl #4118 HP	Torker 289 & Holley 650cfm 2-bbl #6425 HP	Torker 289 & Autolite 600cfm 4-bbl HP	Torker 289 & Holley 600cfm 4-bbl #6619 HP
2500	129	113	119	128
3000	159	150	144	157
3500	188	180	175	187
4000	222	210	209	218
4500	256	240	242	251
5000	270	254	259	264
5500	267	251	258	274
6000	—	—	—	261

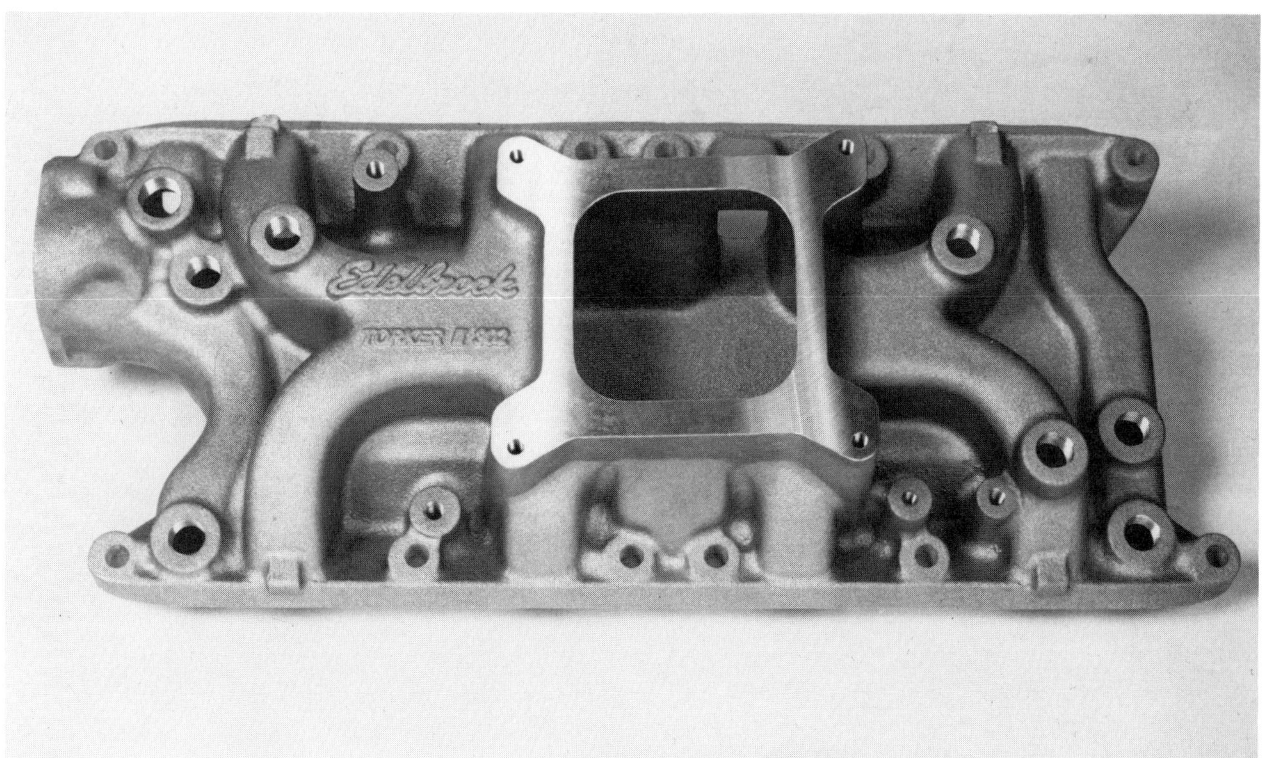

The Torker 302, with its 1500-6500rpm operating range, requires the use of a stronger-than-stock camshaft, ported heads, and a less-restrictive exhaust system. Edelbrock Corp.

much better off replacing both the stock intake and carburetor. If you have a 1983-85 carbureted 302, you have a little more flexibility; the stock Holley four-barrel is optimally sized from Ford, flowing 600cfm. You can experiment with jet changes and vacuum secondary spring opening rates—the typical carburetor hot-rodding tricks that are very well detailed in HP Books' *Holley Carburetors and Manifolds*.

A fairly recent innovation from Holley has been the Quarter-Mile-Dial electronic fuel bowl system.

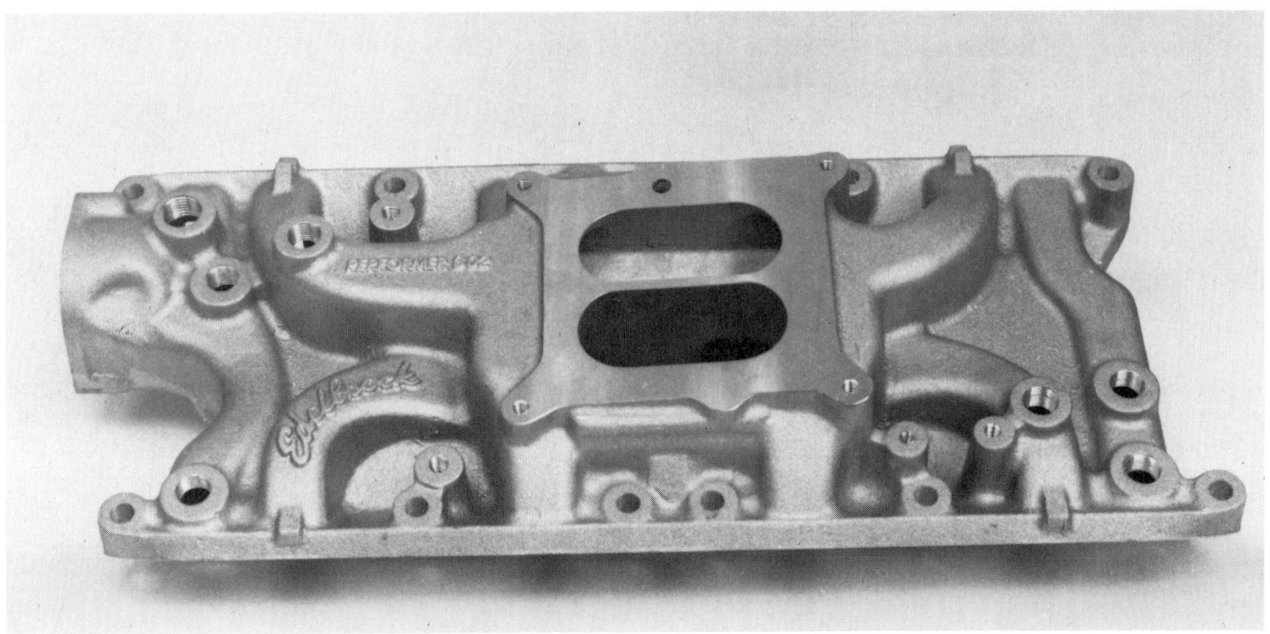

Edelbrock's Performer 302 gives up a little on the low end but makes more overall power at other rpm levels than the Motorsport A321. It is designed to function between 1000-5000rpm, and is a good choice for a stock engine. Edelbrock Corp.

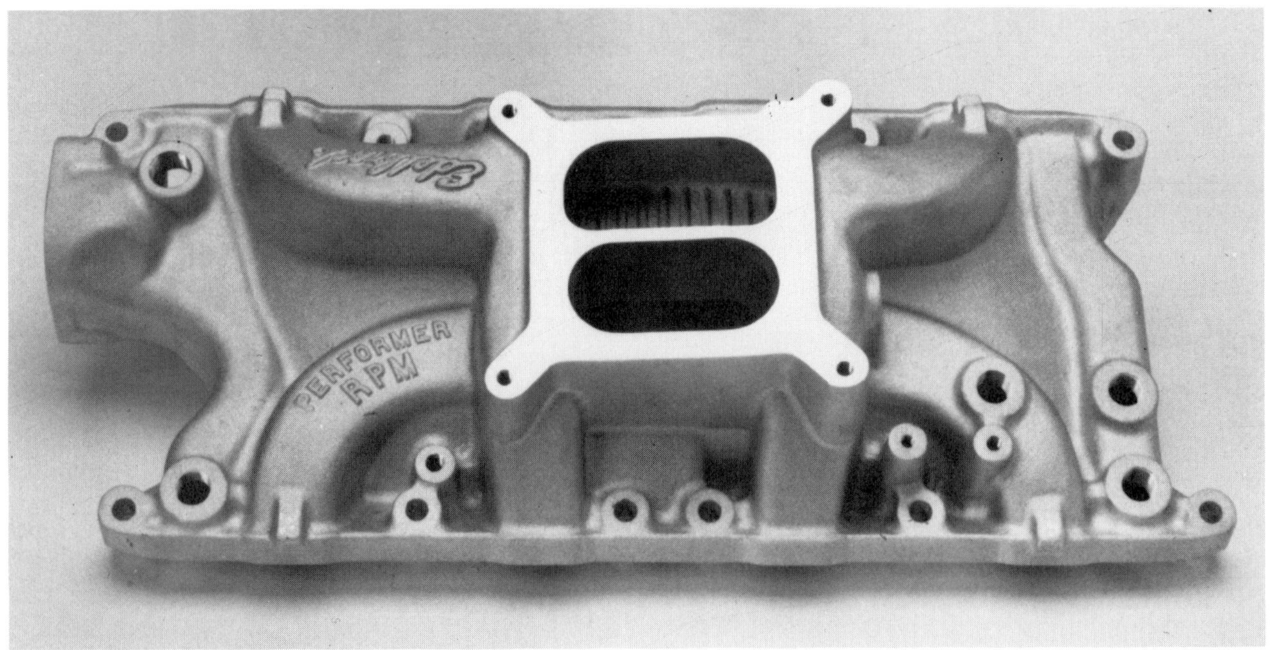

Edelbrock's Performer RPM produces more power than the Performer 302 but gives up a few horses on the bottom end. It is designed to work in the 1500-5500rpm range and is ideal for an engine that's been modified with headers and a mild cam. Edelbrock Corp.

Through the use of a dash-mounted control you can electronically change the fuel mixture from ⅓ to 10 jet sizes. This is a real time saver and you are even able to adjust the air-fuel ratio between the primary and secondary side of the carburetor to compensate for any intake manifold distribution peculiarities. The bowls can be retrofitted on existing carburetors, or you can buy brand-new carburetors with bowls included.

In my opinion, if you decide to replace the stock carburetor, there is nothing better than one of Holley's double-pumpers. These carburetors have a mechanical secondary operation and use two accelerator pumps. For best results, though, you should consider additional modifications such as a stouter camshaft, freer flowing cylinder heads, and exhaust system mods. Holley part number 0-4776 flows 600cfm, number 0-4777 flows 650cfm, and so on to 850cfm. Which is best for your 302? Again, it depends on which other modifications you have made. A slightly modified engine will work well with a 600 or 650cfm unit while a more modified engine may tolerate a larger carburetor.

Another point worth considering with carburetors is whether to retain vacuum secondary operation or switch to a mechanical secondary carburetor, a category that includes Holley's double-pumpers. The secondary two-barrels on a vacuum secondary controlled carburetor open up upon engine demand—therefore it is difficult to overcarburete with such a unit. With mechanical secondaries, an oversize carburetor will result in bogging (hesitation) when the throttle is floored, not to mention poor fuel economy.

With most aftermarket carburetors you'll find that your engine will not ping if you disconnect your EGR (Exhaust Gas Recirculation) valve. That is because they are calibrated for maximum power— meaning that they may be on the rich side.

But maximum power output is not the primary aim of the stock carburetor (or fuel injection for that matter). The primary goal is to meet federal emission standards; after that has been accomplished, driveability, ease of starting, maximum power, and other considerations come into play. In an ideal situation, there would be an air-fuel ratio of 14.7:1 if all the fuel in the combustion chamber would be perfectly mixed and burned. This rarely happens, however. For an engine to make maximum power, all the air that went into the combustion chamber has to be used up and to ensure that this happens, an excess of fuel has to be introduced. In addition, sometimes extra fuel is introduced to cool the engine. Naturally, this does not make for a clean, nonpolluting engine.

The opposite occurs for a carburetor calibrated for maximum fuel economy. In this situation, to get the most out of the fuel that is in the combustion chamber, an excess of air has to be introduced, resulting in air-fuel mixtures as high as 18:1. The excess air ensures complete fuel combustion.

Since the early 1970s, EGR valves have been used to recirculate a portion of the spent and partially spent exhaust gases into the combustion chamber to reduce emissions, usually to the tune of 10 percent. The valve opens only at part-throttle openings, such as when the vehicle is cruising. Obviously an engine doesn't run on spent gases, but these gases enable the engineer to lean out the carburetor further for better fuel economy because they help to cool the hot combustion chamber. Lean fuel mixtures increase combustion chamber temperatures dramatically. Thus the use of the EGR valve on a basically stock engine can be beneficial, but if you are looking for maximizing power output and have made the appropriate changes in your induction system, then an EGR valve is unnecessary.

Like all the other parts of your engine, the manifold and carburetor you choose will work best when they are compatible with the rest of your engine—specifically the camshaft, exhaust system, and the rear-axle gears you are using. There is no point in overfilling the cylinders if you can't get the spent gases out quickly enough.

Recommendations

As for specific intake manifold recommendations, according to Ford, if you have a mildly modified street engine, the old standby, Motorsport part number M-9424-A321, will give you more power than stock. In comparison to Edelbrock's Performer, you'll have more low-end power with the A321 but the Performer will make more overall power throughout the rpm range. The A321, after all, is basically the

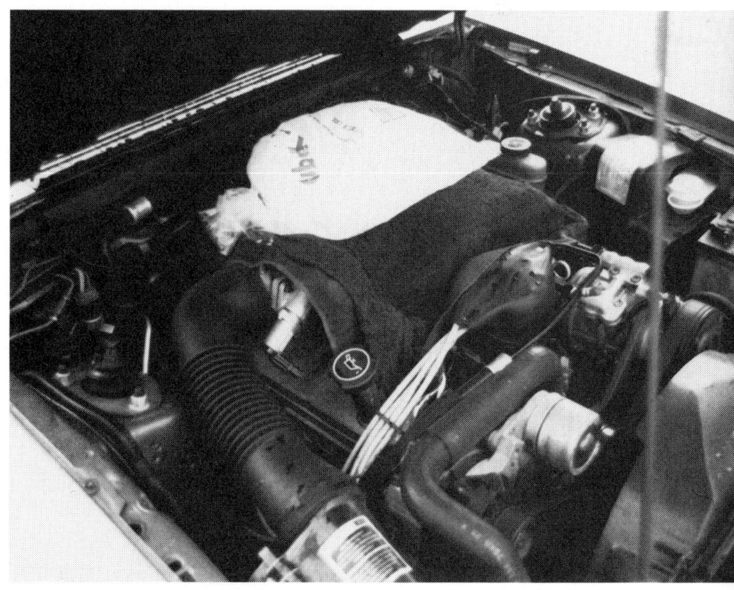

A common sight at the drag strip: A bag of ice is placed on the intake manifold to cool it down in between runs. A cooler manifold will help keep the intake air cooler, resulting in a denser and therefore more powerful fuel mixture. Every little bit helps!

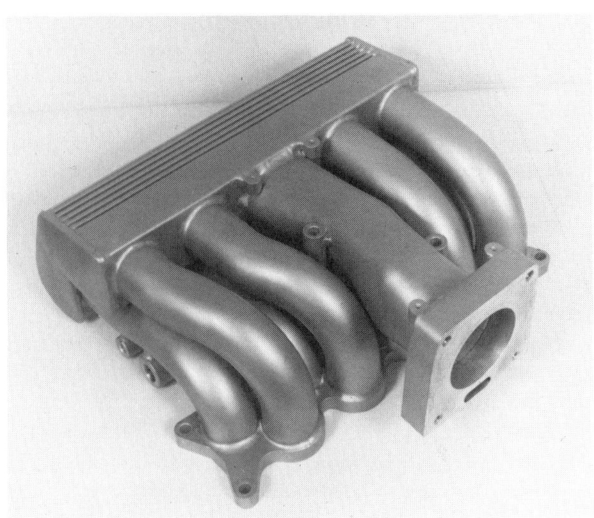

This is the tubular upper half of the Motorsport performance EFI intake. It weighs 8lb less than the stock manifold, and the throttle opening measures 2.75in or 69.85mm. If you install a larger than 69.85mm Mass Air Sensor you should have the throttle opening enlarged. Although you'll see a power increase with even the stock cylinder heads, this manifold is designed for engines using heads with bigger ports and valves. Ford Motor Co.

same Cobra manifold that came on the 306hp 289s that powered the early 1965-67 Shelby Mustangs. It is also very similar to Edelbrock's F-4B used in the Torker 289 manifold test. The stock four-barrel carburetor or an aftermarket unit flowing in the 600-650cfm range is acceptable for a hot street application or even a Mustang that will see some drag strip or road racing action. Ford's part number M-9424-D302, a single-plane manifold, follows the same basic configuration as the production manifold but it does produce more upper-end rpm power due to its larger passages.

Beyond what you can get from Ford, there is Edelbrock's Performer RPM and the Torker II 302, both of which require a more modified engine in order to realize their full potential. These manifolds can be made to work on the street, as can other more exotic intake types such as two four-barrel or three two-barrel multiple-carburetor manifolds. However, it is not just a matter of bolting them on but carefully selecting and matching the rest of your engine's components so that they all work together to maximize output while retaining as much as possible in driveability. To fully take advantage of a manifold that breathes better at higher rpm requires at the very

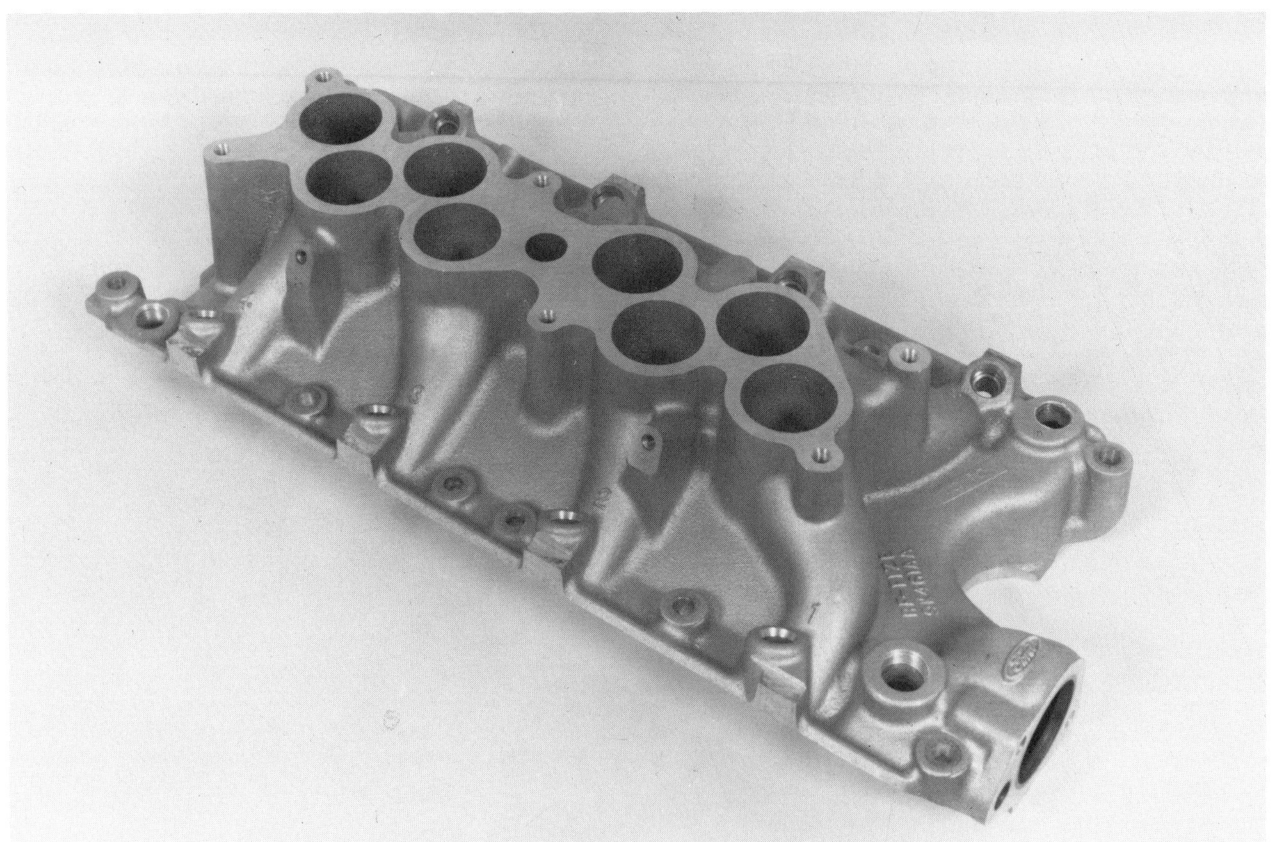

The bottom half of the Motorsport performance EFI intake. Texas Turbo Engineering makes a spacer that fits between the two halves of the manifold to help keep the intake *mixture cooler. You can't use the bottom half with the stock upper half, and vice-versa. Ford Motor Co.*

least that the camshaft and cylinder heads allow for the extra flow.

One advantage the carbureted 302s have over the fuel-injected engines is that you don't have to worry about an EEC (Electronic Engine Control) computer. The Holley-equipped 302s are not controlled by any computer system.

Electronic Fuel Injection

Whereas the use of a four-barrel Holley carburetor represented 1960s technology adapted to the harsh (emissions-wise) reality of the 1980s, it was at best a stopgap measure. To get more power from the 302 and still meet emission regulations while maintaining the driveability and fuel economy that a street car requires, meant the use of a fuel-injection system.

A fuel-injection system is inherently more efficient than carburetion—however, it is also more complex. As air is pulled through the carburetor, fuel is also pulled and mixed into this air stream which is then distributed to each cylinder via the intake manifold. In a fuel-injection system, rather than the fuel passively mixing in the air stream, fuel injectors squirt a predetermined amount of fuel into the air stream just as the intake valve begins to open. Fuel-injection systems can be mechanically or electronically controlled; all current fuel-injected engines use electronically controlled systems.

It is often an overlooked fact, but the first fuel-injected Mustangs were introduced in 1984—in fact, four engines were fuel injected: the 2.3 liter Turbo GT, the 2.3 liter SVO, the 3.8 liter V-6, and automatic-equipped 302 HO engines. The Turbo GT and SVO engines used a Speed Density multi-port system while the 3.8 liter and automatic 302 HO engines used a throttle-body system.

All current electronic fuel-injection (EFI) systems can be divided into three types by the method used to measure the airflow that the engine is using. Based on this airflow measurement, an electronic computer (in this case, Ford's EEC-IV) calculates the amount of fuel that has to be injected into each cylinder and then sends an appropriate electronic signal to the injector, allowing it to open.

The first system, used on throttle-body fuel injection, is relatively simple—it uses throttle position and engine rpm as the basis for airflow calculations.

The 1984-85 automatic-equipped 302s got a throttle-body fuel-injection system which is regulated and controlled by the EEC-IV computer. The throttle body resembles a two-barrel carburetor, sharing the same bolt pattern and using the same intake manifold. Two fuel injectors are housed in the throttle body; the injectors point downward, spraying fuel into the throttle-body valves and into the intake manifold. An electric high-pressure fuel pump, located in the fuel tank, supplies the throttle body with fuel and a fuel pressure regulator maintains a constant pressure of 39psi (pounds per square inch). Compared to other systems, throttle-body systems have very few sensors and are more user-adjustable.

There is not much that you can do to increase the performance of a 302 throttle-body injection system. It is possible to substitute a throttle body from a larger Ford engine but there again, the restrictive nature of the intake manifold will limit power.

To improve power on a throttle-body system, you should use an aftermarket intake manifold, such as Edelbrock's Performer, with a two-to-four barrel carburetor adapter for the throttle body. All the benefits of the improved manifold should be evident with throttle-body injection.

In 1986 the Holley four-barrel carburetor was replaced by a multi-point, pulse time, mass airflow fuel-injection system. For measuring airflow, it used a Speed Density system. The Speed Density system is by far the most common one used on today's fuel-injected engines. It was used on 1986-87 and 1988 49 State (all but California) 302 HO engines. Through the uses of a Manifold Absolute Pressure Sensor, a Volume Airflow Sensor, a Manifold Air Temperature Sensor, a coolant temperature sensor, and a throttle position sensor, the density and fuel requirements of the engine are calculated by the EEC-IV processor. All the information gathered from these sensors is compared to a preprogrammed table stored in the computer which is based on the volumetric efficiency of a stock engine. As long as the computer "sees" sensor readings that are recognizable, the engine runs fine.

The Motorsport high-performance 65mm throttle body allows for more airflow. Larger throttle bodies are already available from the aftermarket. Ford Motor Co.

The third way of measuring airflow is through an air meter, such as the Mass Air Flow system. The 1988 California-bound engine and all engines from 1989 were equipped with Hitachi air cleaner-mounted Mass Air Flow units. The only difference from a Speed Density system is that a Mass Air Flow system measures all the airflow that goes into the engine through an airflow sensor built into the air intake system.

The Mass Air Flow sensor (MAF) used on the 1989 and later engines uses a heated platinum wire to measure airflow. This wire is heated to about 100deg higher than the incoming air. As the incoming air rushes over the wire, it cools the wire. To maintain the same temperature, additional voltage is fed to the wire. Based on these voltage fluctuations, a signal is sent to the EEC-IV control unit and from this, the correct fuel mixture and ignition curve is calculated. The MAF measures four attributes of the incoming air which allows for more precise fuel delivery: volume, air temperature, barometric pressure, and humidity.

Volume: As more air flows through the sensor, such as during acceleration, the incoming air will cool the wire. As more voltage is fed to the wire to maintain its temperature, the EEC-IV increases fuel flow accordingly to the injectors.

Air Temperature: Colder air will cool the wire and colder air is also more dense. The additional voltage sent to the wire will signal the EEC-IV unit to increase fuel flow as needed, and vice versa.

Barometric Pressure: As weather (and altitude) changes, barometric pressure changes as well. Lower barometric pressure causes the intake air to be less

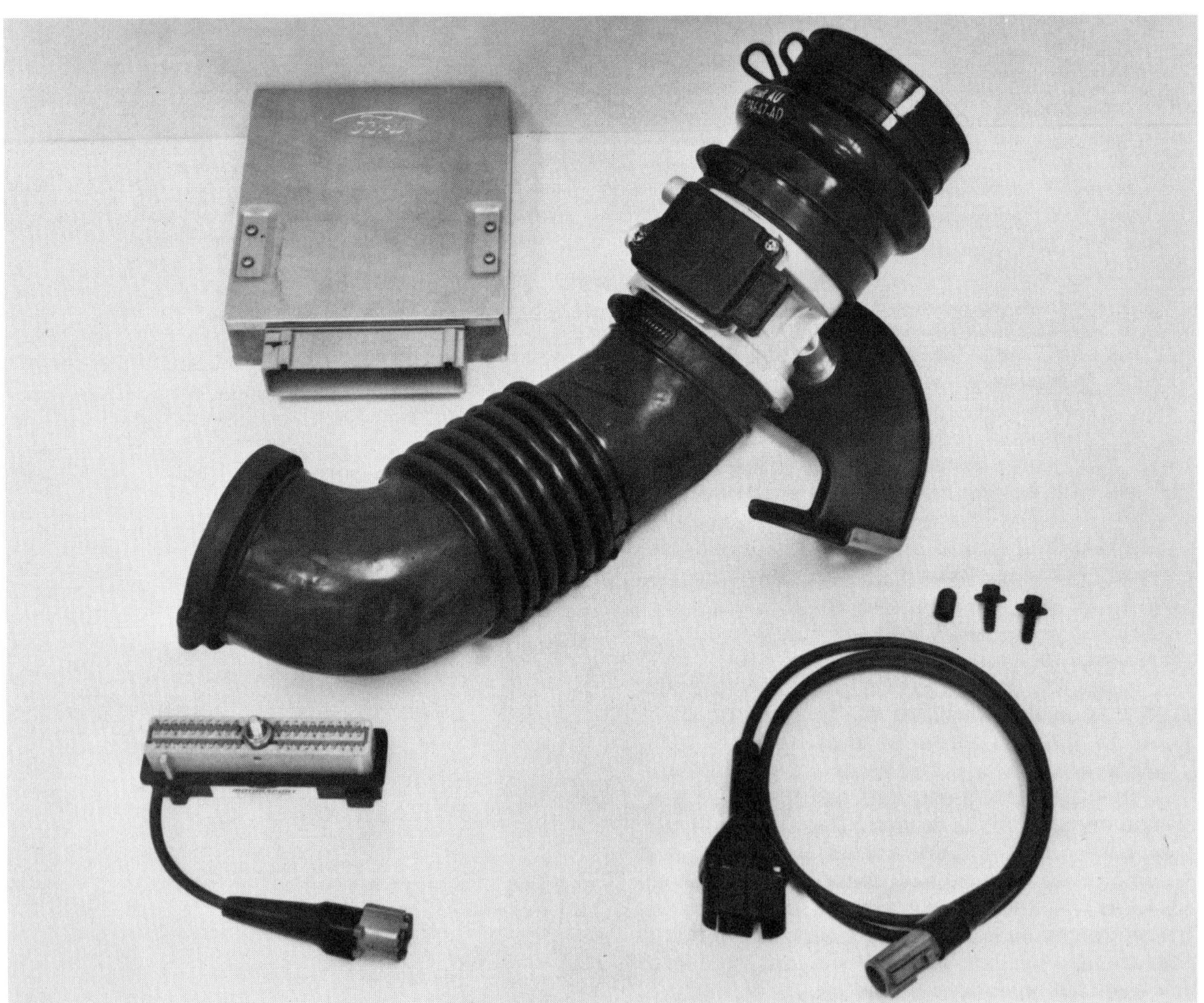

The Motorsport Mass Air conversion kit for Speed Density-equipped 302s. By providing a direct airflow measurement it enables the EEC-IV computer to provide correct fuel flow and spark advance, thereby maintaining good idle and driveability. This is especially important if a different camshaft, cylinder heads, or headers have been installed—something the Speed Density system isn't designed to cope with. Ford Motor Co.

dense, which means that it will have less of a cooling effect on the wire, and vice versa. Once again, the EEC-IV will respond to compensate for any barometric changes to maintain correct fuel flow.

Humidity: Humidity decreases air density and the EEC-IV compensates for any humidity changes.

The Mass Air Sensor measures all these characteristics simultaneously—allowing for very accurate airflow measurements, which translates to better engine performance. It also has a self-cleaning feature. After the engine is shut off, the wire will be

The Professional Flow Technologies Pro-M 77mm Mass Air system flows considerably more air than the stock unit. Unlike installing a larger carburetor, a larger MAS system doesn't reduce performance at low rpm. Because it is less restrictive than the stock MAS, the Pro-M is good for a 15-20hp increase on a dead stock engine. Professional Flow Technologies

The Pro-M installed. Installation is extremely easy. Unlike installing an oversize carburetor, a larger mass air system won't hurt low-end performance or reduce mileage. Professional Flow Technologies

There is no point in installing a larger throttle body if the EGR spacer isn't equally as large. The Motorsport spacer measures 67mm and there is enough metal for enlarging it slightly if used with a larger throttle body. Ford Motor Co.

heated red hot for about one second, to burn off any dirt that may have covered the wire and would cause inaccurate readings.

The primary advantage of a Mass Air Flow over a Speed Density system is that the airflow system allows for additional engine modifications without the usual driveability problems associated with a modified engine using a Speed Density system. For a better understanding of how both systems work, read the following section on open and closed loop computer operations.

Open Loop and Closed Loop

The EEC-IV computer operates in two modes— open and closed loop. The engine operates in the open loop mode primarily when the engine is started. This translates into a spark curve that is slightly more advanced and a richer fuel mixture to keep the engine running. The engine also runs in open loop mode when certain sensors have failed. As the coolant temperature approaches 160deg Fahrenheit, the computer gradually backs off on the timing and mixture.

In the closed loop mode, the computer analyzes all incoming data to achieve a chemically correct or stoichiometric fuel mixture which has an air-fuel ratio of 14.7:1. As mentioned earlier, this is the ideal situation where all the fuel is, in theory, perfectly mixed and ignited in the combustion chamber.

The primary sensor used in both open and closed loop modes is the oxygen sensor located in the exhaust system. The oxygen sensor measures the amount of oxygen in the exhaust. Because it is a transducer, the oxygen sensor converts the oxygen content into an electrical impulse—which the computer is programmed to recognize. For example, if oxygen sensor output is 0.1 to 0.33volt, then the engine is running too lean as oxygen is present in the exhaust. Conversely, if the reading is 0.8 to 1.1volts, then the engine is running too rich as no oxygen is found in the exhaust.

Of all the sensors used, the oxygen sensor takes precedence over the others as far as the computer is concerned. The computer is programmed to base all its subsequent decisions on these readings. Thus it doesn't pay to try to fool the computer by disabling certain sensors, as the oxygen sensor will note any changes in the exhaust and instruct the computer to compensate—which is to bring the system back to acceptable emission levels.

The ability to compensate is built into the system—not to thwart the hot rodder, but to enable the system to adjust for aging sensors and any

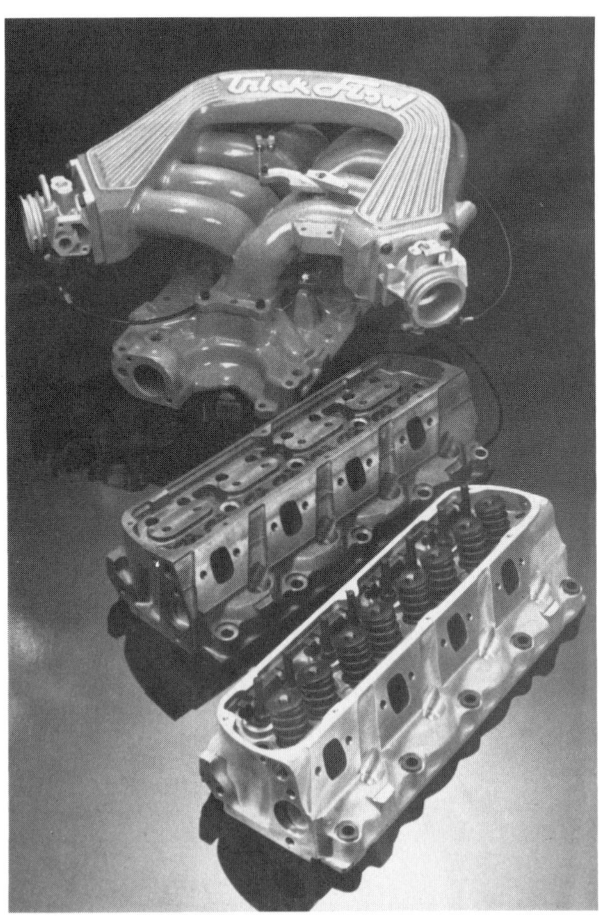

Dual-quad intake manifolds were the hot ticket in the 1960s—today we have dual Mass Air Sensor manifolds. These "trick" manifolds are for racing only and are a complete overkill on a street engine. Synchronizing both sensors is difficult. Will-Burt Automotive

An assortment of Mass Air Sensors (MAS), EGR spacers, and throttle bodies. Down the left column are the stock 55mm MAS, 60mm EGR spacer, and 60mm throttle body. The 55mm MAS effectively limits the intake tract to 55mm. In the center (top to bottom) is a 61mm MAS, 65mm EGR spacer, and throttle body, while on the right (top to bottom) is a 70mm MAS with 68mm EGR and throttle body. Steve Collison

manufacturing tolerances of the entire system. The computer has a correction table in its memory for each sensor and it automatically adjusts the system according to these correction factors.

The problem occurs when the computer doesn't recognize the incoming data from the oxygen sensor, such as in a Speed Density system that has a nonstock camshaft. The computer tries to match the incoming information with the data in its memory—something that can't be done since it isn't there. As the computer searches for the correct setting, the engine will idle erratically and incorrect timing and fuel mixture conditions can occur as well. As long as the engine is stock, the closed loop mode works perfectly well with the Speed Density system.

By adding information from the airflow sensor in a Mass Air Flow system, the computer can compensate for any anomalies encountered in a mildly modified engine. Thus, idle quality and driveability are once again possible in a dual purpose Mustang.

However, in both Speed Density and Mass Air Flow systems, at wide-open throttle (WOT) the EEC-IV computer is programmed to maximize power, irrespective of any parameters relating to emission quality. Thus the EGR valve is closed, ignition timing is maximized, and the fuel curve is calibrated for maximum power.

Speed Density vs. Mass Air

It would follow, then, that in order to maximize performance on 1986-88 Speed Density Mustangs with a modified engine, a Mass Air Flow system is required. This can be accomplished by Motorsport's Mass Air conversion kit, part number M-9000-A51 for manual-equipped Mustangs and M-9000-B50 for automatics. The kit consists of a new EEC-IV computer and jumper wire harness and a stock 55mm Mass Air Flow sensor with appropriate hoses, clamps, and brackets. Without a Mass Air Flow system, a Speed Density system will lose streetability and performance—especially when a nonstock camshaft is installed—because of the Speed Density's "after the fact" engine management, as described earlier.

Opening up the stock Mass Air Sensor is not recommended for two reasons. First, it is easy to damage it beyond repair, as has been done here. Second, it will throw the sensor's calibration off, resulting in a leaned-out fuel mixture. Steve Collison

Auto Specialties' 71mm Mass Air Sensor can be used with the stock Mustang system or the Motorsport 65mm throttle body and EGR spacer. Auto Specialties Inc.

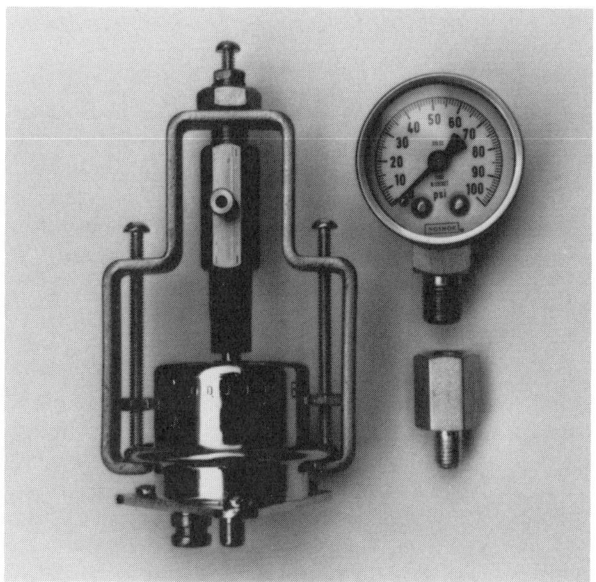

For highly modified engines an adjustable fuel pressure regulator is necessary. This one can be adjusted to 55psi. Auto Specialties Inc.

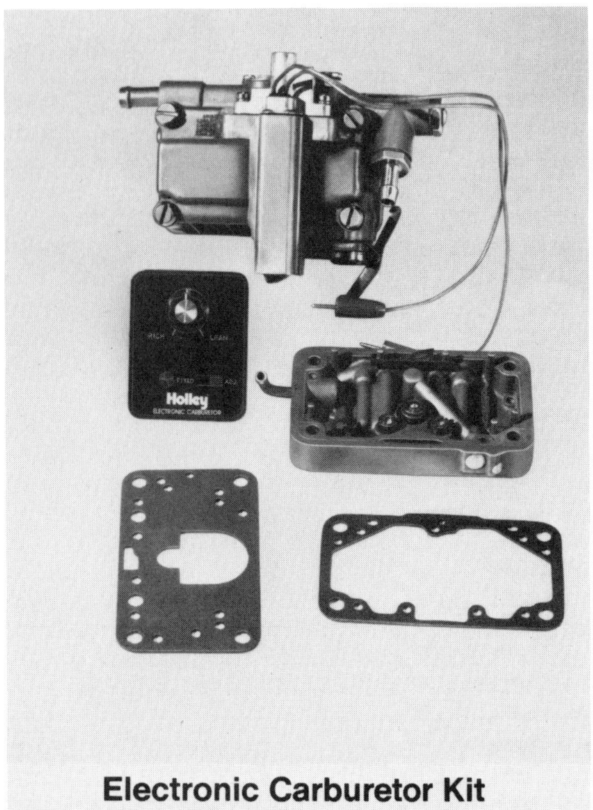

Electronic Carburetor Kit

With Holley's electronic fuel bowl conversion kit, you can adjust jet size from the driver's seat on a carbureted Mustang. The kit has a range of about ten jet sizes. Holley Replacement Parts Division

This is the Saleen SC performance intake manifold and Mass Air Sensor kit for the late-model 302 engine. It includes an upper and lower intake assembly, a 77mm Mass Air Sensor, a water-jacketed EGR spacer, 65mm throttle body, and K&N air filter. Saleen Performance Parts, Inc.

Fuel-Injection Modifications

Compared to carburetors, there isn't much available yet in the way of intake manifolds or most other fuel-injection accessories and components.

One area where there is considerable activity in the aftermarket is with larger Mass Air Sensors, EGR spacers, and throttle bodies. All of these are designed to let more air into the engine, but by themselves won't provide for an increase in power. Compared to a carburetor, the air entering the 302 has a more tortuous route to follow: air first enters the air filter box, then follows the intake ducting through the Mass Air Sensor, throttle body, and EGR spacer (if it is a Mass Air system). The air then flows through the intake runners and into the intake manifold and finally through the intake ports. It is not a system that promotes velocity, and the possibility of turbulence through the use of mismatched components is a real danger.

The 1989 and later Mustangs came with a 55mm Mass Air Sensor and a 60mm throttle body—the effective intake tract is therefore 55mm as the Mass Air Sensor limits airflow. There are plenty of larger aftermarket units available including those offered by Professional Flow Technologies in Madison Heights, Michigan. Their Pro-M meters will measure up to 77mm, with larger units in the works. Incidentally, Ford Special Vehicle Operations has just started offering the same unit under part number M-12K579-A32, while Steeda Autosports of Pompano, Florida, has an 80mm unit. (See Appendices for details.)

An interesting claim made by Professional Flow Technologies, which has been borne out by dynamometer tests, is that simply installing the 77mm Mass Air kit will result in a 15-20hp increase over stock. The reason for this is that besides flowing more air, the 77mm unit has much less of a pressure drop—meaning that it is considerably less restrictive than the stock Mustang Mass Air unit. Because of poor design, the factory air meter has a pressure drop in the order of 12-24in, which translates to a 5-7 percent drop in horsepower because the engine just can't breathe well enough.

The current Ford Motorsport catalog lists a 65mm throttle body, part number M-9E926-A302, and 67mm EGR spacer, part number M-9H474-A50. If you use these with the stock intake manifold, the plenum opening will have to be opened up to match. Naturally, you'll have to use a Mass Air Sensor that measures 65mm or larger. As mentioned earlier, the 77mm unit is also available.

There is no point installing a larger throttle body without installing a complementary EGR plate and Mass Air Sensor—the effective opening will be the smallest of the three. They all should match.

By themselves, a larger throttle body and related componentry generally will not result in an increase in power (except over the stock unit because of its inherent restrictions) as all they are doing is letting more air in the engine. The limiting factor in how much air can be used is the intake valve itself—how long it stays open and how well the intake port in the cylinder head is shaped. In other words, to take full advantage of a larger throttle body, EGR spacer, and Mass Air Sensor, you'll need cylinder heads with larger valves, bigger ports, and a more radical camshaft.

As a guidepoint, the 65mm Ford throttle body is adequate for engines designed to produce 300hp, as are the stock 19psi fuel injectors. For engines with more radical modifications, larger throttle bodies are required. Larger-than-stock injectors are a waste on an engine that is not expected to produce more than 300hp.

Still, if you are going to install a larger Mass Air Sensor kit, you might as well install the largest one available, such as the Pro-M meter. The extra airflow potential won't hurt as would an oversize carburetor.

Besides a larger Mass Air system, it would be wise to install the SVO EFI manifold kit number M-6001-A50, which consists of an upper aluminum tubular manifold that is 8lb lighter than the stock piece and a matching cast-aluminum lower manifold. The runners measure 1.65in and the throttle opening is 2.75in. Although the SVO manifold cannot be used with the complementary stock manifold, it is designed to be used with production fuel rails, sensors, and wiring harness, making its installation a snap. The manifold itself is worth a 21hp increase.

High-Performance Cylinder Heads

The 302 engine has many strong points: it is compact, light, and yet strong enough to produce a considerable amount of power. If it has one weak area, it is the cylinder heads, and more specifically, the exhaust port. It must be remembered that this engine was designed in the late 1950s and it embodies that era's thinking when it comes to porting. Typical of most Ford engines of that era, the intake ports are fairly decent. They are large and provide a straight shot to the intake valve with minimal, if any, obstructions. You can get a fair amount of fuel mixture in, but you must also provide for its exit. The stock 302's exhaust port, while it may have been adequate for an engine displacing 221ci (the original size of the engine), is way too small for an engine displacing 302ci.

Before you decide on a set of cylinder heads, there are certain facts to keep in mind with the late-model fuel-injected 302. First, the 302 in stock fuel-injected form is designed to make power at relatively low rpm, considering the rpm potential this engine has. It's easy to look at the flow figures and decide that the heads with the most flow at the highest lift are the ones to get. Big-port heads achieve their high-

Something you don't see everyday is a cylinder head from the 255ci version of the small-block. Note the minuscule intake ports. Obviously, this head should not be considered for any performance application.

With the exception of the 1986 HO, all 302s come with this type of combustion chamber. It has a large, open chamber which is designed to produce low emissions.

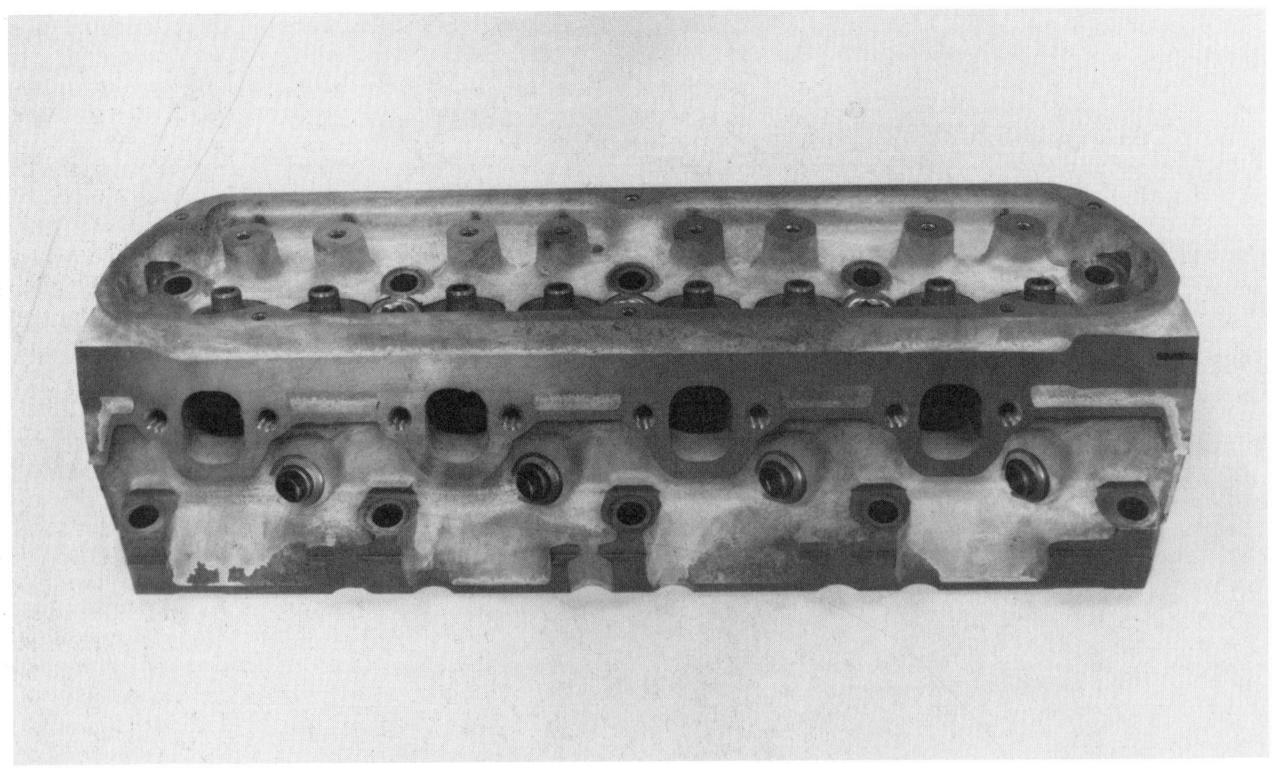

This is the Motorsport GT-40 cast-iron cylinder head. It accepts 1.84/1.54in intake/exhaust valves, stock rocker arms, and has much better porting. It also accepts all stock emission equipment. In terms of overall cost, it is the least expensive aftermarket head you can install. Ford Motor Co.

flow figures at high rpm and at high camshaft lifts—usually beyond the range of the stock 302's camshaft. In other words, a set of heads with big ports and valves will probably be a waste for a mildly modified street car. And you don't want a set of heads that sacrifice low- to mid-range flow for upper-end flow. In choosing between two comparable heads, always pick the one that has better exhaust flow. Finally, there is also the matter of cost to consider. With the exception of the GT-40 heads, all the other aftermarket heads are designed to accept screw-in rocker studs and guide plates—a necessity if you are planning to build a revving 302 but not necessary on a street car using the stock or a slightly stronger camshaft. All the aftermarket heads also use larger-than-stock valves (stock valves measure 1.78in intake, 1.45in exhaust), requiring the purchase of new valves. It is easy to get sucked into spending more than necessary—for example, do you need the lighter weight of stainless steel valves on an engine that won't rev over 6500rpm? Probably not.

Two basic cylinder heads have been used on the current generation 302s. With the exception of the 1986 HO head, all cylinder heads have a large combustion chamber. In 1986, Ford went to a kidney-shaped combustion chamber on the HO (which also comes on the base versions of the engine). This design shrouds the valves and impedes flow and according to Ford experts, this head should not be used in any performance application. From 1987, Ford went back to the open chamber design.

The least expensive road to higher flowing cylinder heads is to have your stock heads ported. You can achieve noticeable results by having the intake ports matched to the intake gasket and having the same thing done to the exhaust ports. In addition, have the large Thermactor hump in the exhaust port ground out. The intake and exhaust valve guide bosses are also on the large side and should be reduced in size.

Another modification that will yield beneficial results is to grind away the ridge that is left by the factory's machining operations beneath the valve seats. By grinding away this ridge, flow isn't impeded.

These modifications, along with a good three-angle valve job, will increase flow but you'll get better results if you opt for new cylinder heads. There are many available. Let's look at what Ford has to offer.

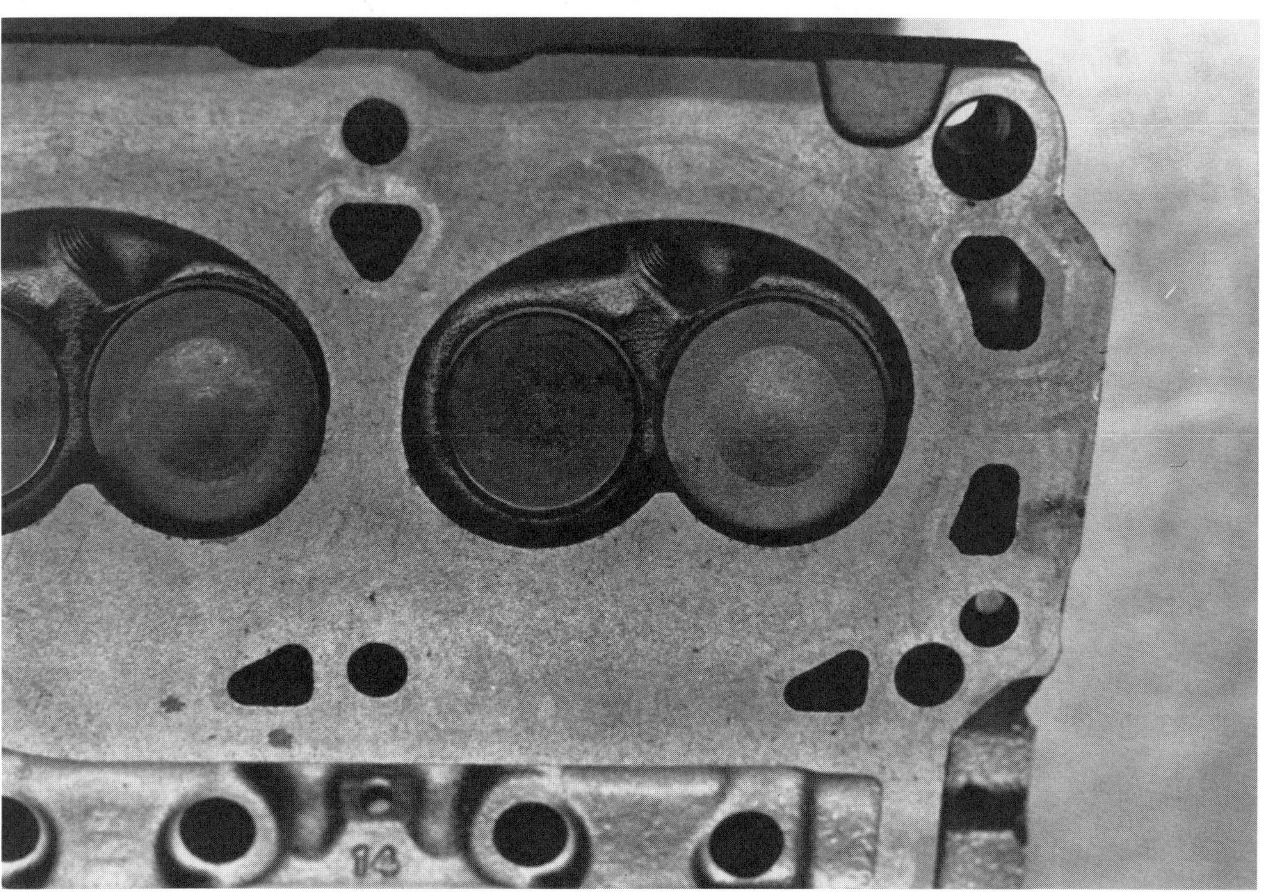

All 1986 HO heads (and later base 302 heads) came with this kidney-shaped combustion chamber. They aren't recommended for high-performance applications due to increased valve shrouding which impedes airflow. In 1987, Ford went back to the open chamber heads.

If you have a grinder and aren't afraid to use it, reduce the size of the valve bosses and the ridge left by the factory machining operations that are just below the valve seats. These simple modifications will help flow.

The biggest obstruction to exhaust flow is the large Thermactor (air pump) boss that protrudes into the exhaust port. This should be ground down. The exhaust port should also be matched to exhaust gasket size.

The heads that require the least amount of work to replace are the so-called GT-40 heads, part number M-6049-L302. They are called GT-40 because they incorporate many of the features used on the Ford GT-40 long-distance race cars of the late 1960s. The heads are cast in iron and are designed to take 1.84/1.54in intake/exhaust valves (same as the 1969-70 351W heads), and the stock rocker arms. A nice feature of these heads is that they come with exhaust valve seat inserts to prevent exhaust valve seat wear. The stock heads have induction-hardened seats (no inserts) which means after a valve job, there is less "hardness" left in the seat. They are also compatible with all stock emission devices.

The big deal heads for the 302 from Ford are the aluminum heads, Ford part number M-6049-J302, which flow considerably better than the GT-40 heads. They are designed to accept 1.94in intake and 1.60in exhaust valves along with stud-mounted rocker arms. Whereas the GT-40 heads are a direct replacement for the stock heads, the J302, as they are known, do not provide for an exhaust crossover passage or EGR—which means that if you intend to use them on the street, the factory EEC-IV computer may not be able to keep the engine's emission levels within acceptable levels.

Dart Windsor cast iron heads are available bare or fully assembled. As you would expect, these heads have much larger intake and exhaust ports, larger valves, 2.02/1.60in intake/exhaust, and they accom-

The reason for the Dart II head's exceptional flow properties is the revised porting, especially on the intake side. The bigger ports will flow more air but like everything else, there is a compromise as they only start to create more power above 3000rpm. The Dart head is shown on the bottom. Steve Collison

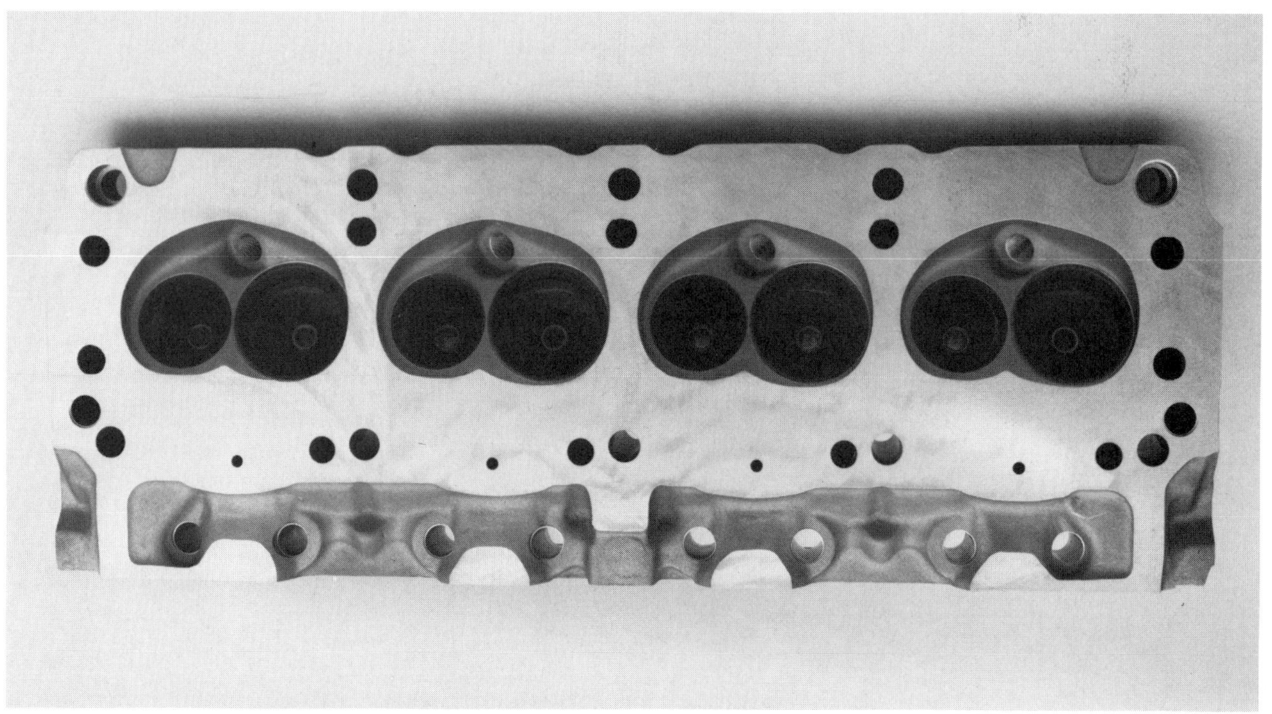

The best cylinder head from Ford is the J302 aluminum head. According to Ford, these heads are good for a 30hp increase over the production heads. Since they do not have an exhaust crossover or provision for EGR, using them on the street may not be a good idea. They are designed to accept threaded rocker-arm studs. Ford Motor Co.

The Dart II Windsor cast-iron head for the 302 from World Products. The exhaust ports are a major improvement and the heads by themselves, according to World, are good for a 57hp increase over stock at 5000rpm. The heads accept 2.02/1.60in intake/exhaust valves and require the use of screw-in studs, pushrod guide plates, and rockers. World Products, Inc.

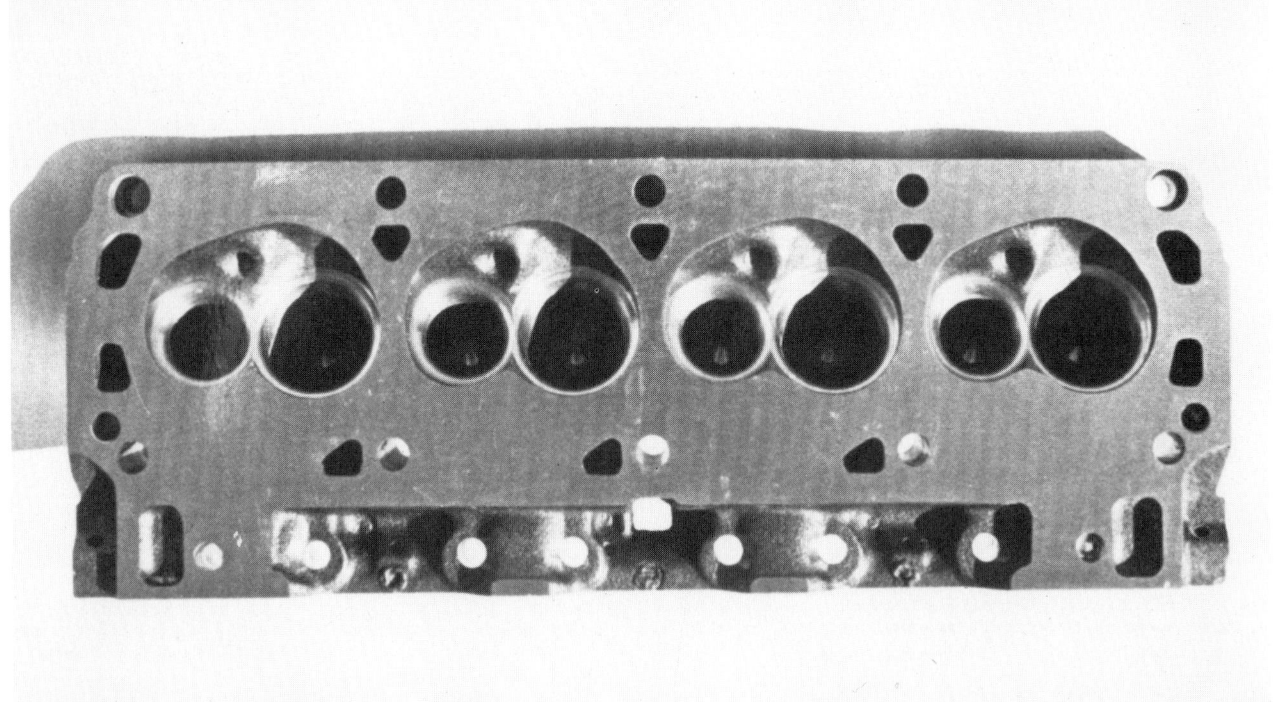

The Dart head's combustion chamber shows there is barely any room left for larger valves; spark plug location has been relocated as well. Steve Collison

modate all stock emission systems. In addition, the Windsor heads can accept even larger intake valves, measuring 2.10in, and they are set up to accept adjustable rocker arms with screw-in studs. A nice feature of the Windsor is that there is a steel exhaust valve seat insert so the heads can run on today's unleaded gasoline with no problem. According to World Products, Incorporated, of Ronkonkoma, New York (see Appendices for details), these heads are worth 57hp over the stock heads.

World Products now also offers the Windsor Jr. heads, which have smaller ports and combustion chambers and can only accept 1.94/1.50in valves. These are suitable on engines where you don't plan on changing the stock camshaft or induction system.

The Trick Flow heads are also highly regarded and you can get them in either cast iron or aluminum—aluminum will result in a 40lb weight savings. Standard valve sizes are 1.94/1.60in intake/exhaust, with optional valves available to 2.125/1.65in (2.08in intake on the aluminum heads) and of course, the ports are larger and flow considerably better than stock. The standard valve guides are magnesium bronze and the guides are already machined for Teflon valve seals. Both heads are designed for an adjustable valvetrain and both are set up to connect to all stock emission devices. And like the Dart heads, valve seat inserts are installed so they will run on unleaded gasoline.

Kenny Brown's Project Industries Gold Heads take a different approach (see Appendices for address). Brown feels that although the aftermarket heads currently available make good race heads, because of the EEC-IV computer, the typical Mustang can't take advantage of their superior flow capabilities. The Gold Heads, available on an exchange

Trick Flow cylinder heads come in either iron or aluminum. They can accommodate intake/exhaust valves up to 2.125/1.65in, use adjustable valvetrain parts, and accommodate all the stock emission equipment and accessories. This is the iron head. Will-Burt Automotive

World Products Windsor Heads vs. Stock Heads

A 1985 302 HO short-block was fitted with a Motorsport camshaft, part number M-6250-B303. The carbureted induction system consists of a Weiand 7515 single-plane intake manifold and Holley part number 4778 700cfm double-pumper carburetor. EFI consists of a stock system. The exhaust system for both engines consists of shorty-type headers.

Stock Heads

| | Carburetor | | EFI | |
RPM	HP	Torque (lb-ft)	HP	Torque (lb-ft)
3000	147	259	160	280
3500	173	260	188	282
4000	202	265	212	278
4500	225	263	234	273
5000	244	257	246	259
5500	254	243	237	227

World Products Windsor Heads

| | Carburetor | | EFI | |
RPM	HP	Torque (lb-ft)	HP	Torque (lb-ft)
3000	152	268	164	286
3500	182	273	199	299
4000	218	286	229	300
4500	248	290	250	292
5000	281	295	261	274
5500	305	291	257	245
6000	312	278	—	—

Chart courtesy Super Ford Magazine.

In both cases, the carbureted 302 produces more power than fuel injection, but only above 5000rpm, which points to the inherent restrictions built into the stock EFI intake tract. The World Products heads, by themselves, produce more power than the stock heads.

basis, are reworked stock heads with larger, 1.94/1.60in valves and superior porting. They accept stock valvetrain components, or they can be modified for adjustable rockers.

There is one other possibility to consider if you are seeking better cylinder heads and that is to install a set of 351 Cleveland heads. Installing a set of the four-barrel heads has the effect of duplicating the Boss 302 engine of 1969-70 vintage. These heads feature extremely large ports and valves which measure 2.19/1.71in—perhaps too large for a street engine. A better choice is to get a set of 351C/351M/400 two-barrel heads, which have somewhat smaller ports and valves that measure 2.04/1.65in intake/exhaust. They do flow significantly better than the stock 302 heads. Although there are several carburetor intake manifolds available from B&A Ford Performance Incorporated, in Fort Smith, Arkansas, for this application, there is no fuel-injection manifold yet on the market, although Texas Turbo Engineering, Incorporated, of Houston, Texas, is working on one. It is an involved swap requiring machine work, new hardware, and new pistons.

There is always an "ultimate" cylinder head and at this time it is an aluminum thirty-two-valve head manufactured by Arao Engineering of Chatsworth, California. The Arao cylinder head has four valves per cylinder—two intake, measuring 1.60in and two exhaust valves measuring 1.40in. The interesting thing about this head is that it is designed to work with the stock camshaft and pushrods. Both intake and both exhaust valves are actuated by a single pushrod from the stock location. Each rocker consists of two valve levers and one pushrod lever. Because of the additional valve area, the Arao heads will outflow any currently available head at any lift and rpm and they fit the 302 block with a minimum of alterations. The heads are also designed to work with currently available intake and exhaust manifolding. (See Appendices for further information on manufacturers.)

Fuel-Injection Conversion Kits

Several fuel-injection conversion kits are currently available for carbureted Mustangs. Best known is Holley Performance Parts' Pro-Jection universal fuel-injection conversion, which provides improved driveability, throttle response, fuel economy, and increased power. This is a retrofit throttle-body system designed for noncomputerized engines. They are made in several configurations. For a street engine there is Model 3200, part number 502-2, which flows 670cfm. It is a two-barrel system designed for

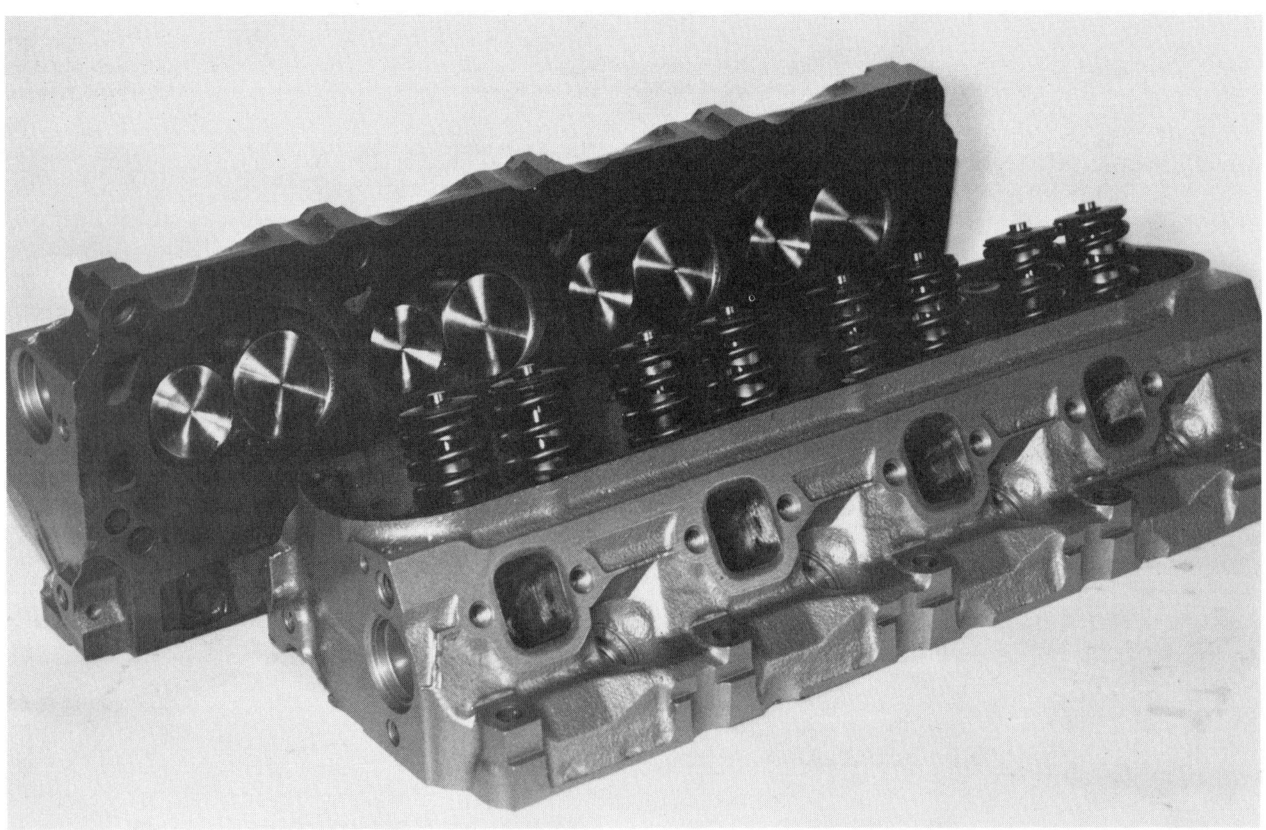

Kenny Brown Gold Heads are stock heads that have been ported and modified with larger valves to produce almost as much power as one of the aftermarket heads. One advantage they have is that they accept all stock valvetrain components, thereby reducing cost. According to Kenny Brown, they outflow the GT-40 heads.

engines under 360ci and can sustain a 320hp output. Model 3400, part number 504-1, is a 900cfm four-barrel system designed for V-8 engines that produce between 300 and 600hp. Both kits require a four-barrel intake manifold and both come with the following:

• Dual 80lb per hour Holley-designed fuel injectors (four with Model 3400, part number 504-1)
• Adjustable fuel pressure regulator
• Electronic Control Module (ECM)
• Inline fuel pump
• Wiring harness
• Adjustable fast-idle solenoid

The electronic control unit is user-adjustable to provide air-fuel settings for the choke, accelerator pump, and for power output at various rpm ranges. Besides requiring a four-barrel intake manifold, a return fuel line is necessary but otherwise it is a simple bolt-on installation. Naturally, a high-performance intake manifold will provide the same sort of power gains as it does with a carburetor. Holley's tests have shown that this system is good for a 2-3mpg (miles per gallon) gain and is about 0.50-0.75sec quicker in the quarter mile.

For the all-out racer, Holley offers throttle-body systems that flow up to 4,400cfm.

The Digital Fuel Injection company also has a throttle-body system that works on the 302. It uses GM throttle-body bodies and along with a computer, the system comes with an oxygen sensor to maximize fuel economy. The system is more complex than Holley's, but it is completely tuneable with a User Interface Module in which the fuel mixture can be adjusted at idle and at WOT (wide-open throttle). The unit can also be custom calibrated with Digital's CALMAP calibration software. You'll need an IBM-compatible computer to do this.

If you can afford it, you'll be better off with a throttle-body conversion kit over a carburetor setup.

Ram Air Systems and Air Cleaners

Although it sounds like a great idea, a ram air system where a scoop is used to channel air into the

Kenny Brown's Gold Heads are ported stock heads. The port entrance is close to the stock opening with the major part of the porting done inside the port. This definitely should not be attempted by anyone who hasn't any experience in porting heads. The most that the typical Mustang owner should attempt is just to match the ports to the intake gasket. These heads are also fitted with 1.94/1.60in intake/exhaust valves. Project Industries

This is what the reworked exhaust port looks like on the Kenny Brown Gold Heads.

You can also install 351 Cleveland heads on the 302. Canted valves and large ports and valves are what make these heads great. This is the two-barrel head, which is plenty for the 302. These Australian versions have the smaller four-barrel type combustion chamber. The swap requires new pistons, head bolts, and some minor cylinder head modifications.

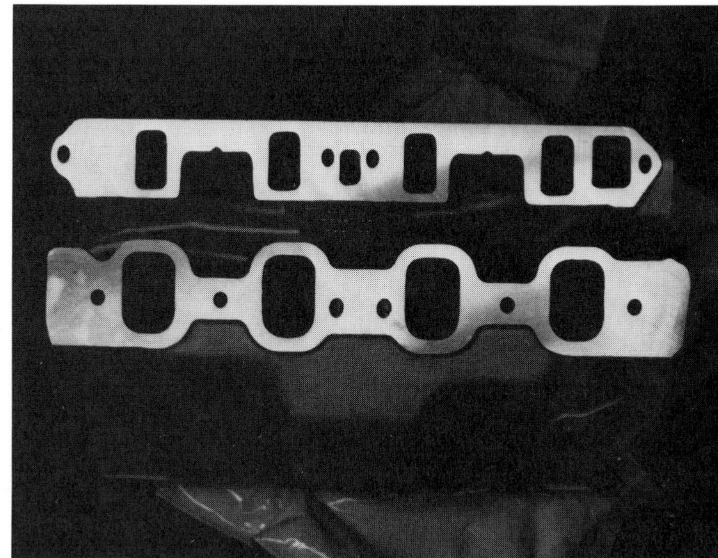

One of the reasons why the old 351 Cleveland heads flow so much better than the 302 is port size. These are the larger, Boss 302 type (bottom).

Ford doesn't make any intake manifolds to accommodate the 351C heads on the 302, however, B&A Ford makes several. This is a dual-plane high-rise type. B&A Ford Performance Inc.

intake system doesn't result in a large increase in power. There is 1.2 percent increase at 100mph, 2.7 percent at 150mph, and 4.8 percent at 200mph. So you have to be moving very fast in order to see any gains from ram air. But you may say that cars do produce more power with a ram air system and this can easily be verified on the drag strip. This is absolutely true, but it isn't due to ram air; rather to the fact that the air fed into the intake system is considerably cooler (denser) than the underhood air.

Typically, the air entering the carb has been heated by passing through the radiator and over the hot engine. An engine taking in hot air will produce considerably less power than one taking in cold air. For every 7.2deg in temperature drop the engine will produce 1 percent more horsepower. Thus if the outside temperature is 70deg F., the underhood temperature 150deg, and the engine is producing 300hp with underhood air, it will produce 345hp with outside air, assuming the fuel mixture is adjusted (enriched) to compensate for the cooler air.

That is why you'll find that even lowly 2.3 liter Mustangs have a flexible hose attached to the air cleaner which feeds the carburetor cooler, outside air. Cold-air systems should never be disconnected but instead should be made more efficient and less restrictive. The Ram Air systems made by Kenne-Bell Performance Products or Texas Turbo are the best of

both worlds—they provide a slight ram air effect while supplying cooler, denser air to the intake tract via a scoop located under the front valance panel.

Carbureted engines use air cleaners; EFI engines use air boxes. Both stock systems are restrictive. Their first priority is to quiet intake noise. The stock air cleaner used on the 302 has twin snorkels—while two snorkels are better than one, the air cleaner doesn't let the carburetor flow its full 600cfm. The best system would be one that combines the benefits of the stock fresh-air intake with the beneficial effects of an air cleaner that uses a less-restrictive element, preferably an open-element design. Fuel-injected cars should use the Kenne-Bell or Texas Turbo Ram Air systems described earlier.

This chart compares a Motorsport EFI GT-40 intake manifold top and bottom (part numbers M-9424-A51 and M-9K461-A50) to a stock intake. Tests were performed on a stock 5.0 liter V-8 at Special Vehicle Operations in Allen Park, Michigan.

| | Stock Intake | | GT-40 Intake | |
| | | Torque | | Torque |
RPM	HP	(lb-ft)	HP	(lb-ft)
3000	170	294	167	292
3500	200	300	197	294
4000	220	288	224	303
4500	228	266	244	284
5000	229	239	248	261

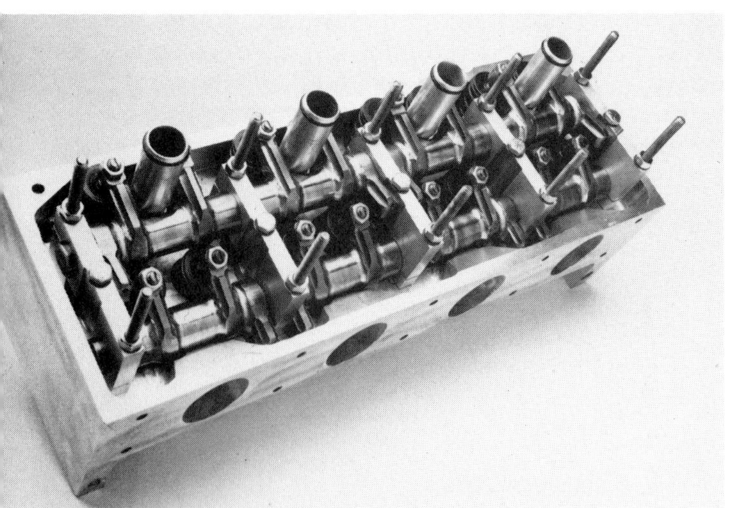

The Arao head is made from a billet aluminum forging. The additional valve area makes for considerably more flow at any lift and rpm level. Because of this, a short-duration camshaft can be used for excellent low-end response. Arao Engineering

Both intake and both exhaust valves are operated by the stock pushrods, with each pushrod actuating two levers. This simple design allows the use of the stock camshaft and the use of all currently available intake and exhaust manifolding. The only modification required to install the heads on the block is the hand notching of the top inside corners of the block for clearance of the exhaust pushrods. Arao Engineering

Holley's Pro-Jection kit is a comparatively low-cost way to convert a carbureted 302 to throttle-body injection. The system includes a 900cfm throttle body, wiring harness, electronic control module, and fuel pump. This is the four-injector version, good for engines producing 300-600hp. Holley Replacement Parts Division

The old inverted air cleaner lid modification updated to work on a carbureted Mustang. By turning the air cleaner lid upside down, you are letting more air into the air cleaner, thereby reducing restriction.

Fuel-injected engines can benefit just as much from a ram air system as carbureted engines. However, the true benefits are not from the negligible ram air effect but from

feeding the engine cooler, denser air. This is a kit from Texas Turbo Engineering. The intake mounts beneath the front valance, as shown. Texas Turbo Engineering, Inc.

This enterprising racer has temporarily removed the right headlight in order to direct air into the intake tract of his homemade ram air system.

Carbureted 302s will benefit from the use of a large, unrestrictive air cleaner assembly. The stock air cleaner, even with its two inlets, limits airflow making the carburetor flow less than its 600cfm capacity. The only drawback with this particular setup is that the engine doesn't benefit from ingesting cooler, denser outside air.

Chapter 4

Camshaft and Valvetrain

There is nothing like the rough idle a hot cam makes. You're letting the world know that you mean business; however, there is no reason to change the stock cam in your 302 if all you are interested in is a strong-running engine that produces around 300hp. That sort of power is enough to get you a low-thirteen-second quarter-mile time and you can do this without sacrificing any of the stock engine's driveability and mileage. Changing the camshaft will alter performance and affect the intake and exhaust system, relative economy, and driveability of your Mustang. It is not something to be taken lightly; a mistake made in choosing the camshaft will not only result in a poor-running street Mustang, but will also create additional work to get the car back into proper street-running condition.

The stock cam found in most Ford engines was designed for smoothness and low-end power to provide long, trouble-free performance. Changing to a performance cam will move the power-producing band up the rpm range of the engine. The problem in selecting a cam is figuring out how far to move up the power curve without hurting low-end performance and mileage. The goal should be to choose a cam that will increase power over stock without losing the economy of a stock cam. How much power should a cam change provide? A good target is an increase of about 10 percent.

Two areas in cam design affect the engine's power curve: lift and duration. A cam with more valve lift will generally produce more power than a cam with less lift. However, there are practical mechanical limits to increasing the amount of lift. For street use it is around 0.500in. Anything more than that has a tendency to accelerate valvetrain component wear. Also remember that the stock ports and valves are small, meaning that increased lift may not do anything until their capacity has been increased to take advantage of the extra lift. Everything is interrelated. The big advantage of increased lift is that it produces more power, without hurting driveability and fuel economy to a large extent.

Duration is the length of time, measured in degrees, that the valves are left open to allow the fuel mixture to enter and leave the combustion chamber. Obviously the longer the duration, the more mixture that enters and the more power the engine will produce. Beyond a certain point, longer duration will mean more power but at the expense of low-end performance. The duration of a given cam is only optimized at a certain rpm or rpm range. If the intake valve opens at top dead center of the intake stroke, by the time the column of air-fuel mixture in the intake tract gets moving to enter the cylinder, the piston will already be on its way down. The fuel mixture is always lagging behind. Thus the intake valve has to be opened earlier, especially as the engine revs faster. Not only that, the valvetrain can't open the valve instantaneously and what is even more amazing is that the whole intake stroke process takes only 0.01sec—at 3000rpm. At 6000rpm, the fuel mixture is lagging even farther behind. To get complete, or more

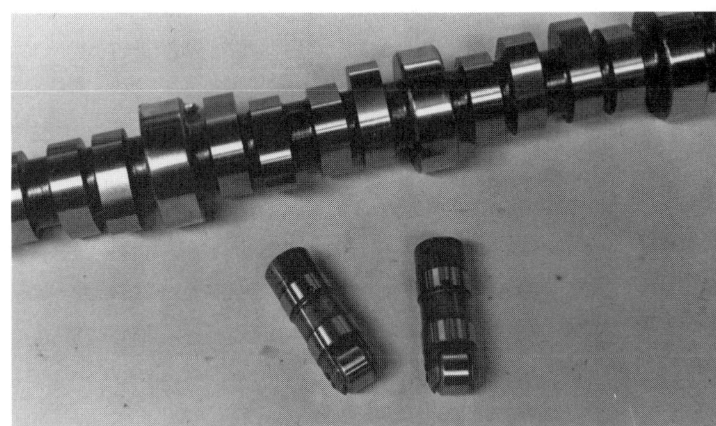

Roller camshaft and roller hydraulic lifters, by themselves, are worth an extra 30hp due to reduced frictional losses. All 1985 and later 302 engines have them. Because the camshaft is made from steel, a steel distributor drive gear is required if you decide to use a roller cam in a pre-1985 block; otherwise the stock gear will quickly wear out.

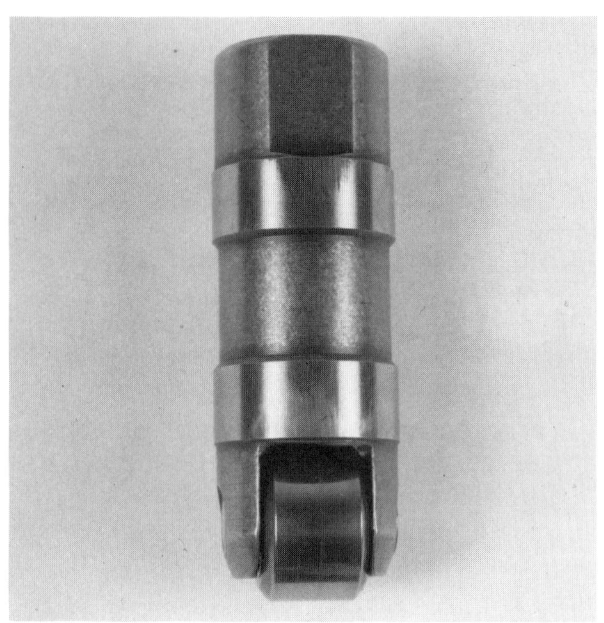

Ford roller hydraulic lifters require the use of a block that has taller lifter bosses. You can use regular flat-tappet lifters on a roller lifter block, but you can't use the hydraulic roller lifters on pre-1985 blocks. Ford Motor Co.

complete cylinder filling at that rpm, the valve would still have to be open when the piston is on its way up during the compression stroke—which obviously it can't do. That is why race cams have lots of duration to increase cylinder filling, but that long duration kills the low end. The thing to do, therefore, is to find a cam that combines reasonably high lift with duration short enough to allow good low-end performance. Also remember that EEC-IV equipped cars aren't programmed to run with long-duration camshafts. The computer will only tolerate cams that have slightly more duration than stock. Unless you want to invest in an aftermarket (expensive) electronic control system, you're limited to using a stock or nearly stock cam.

Also consider overlap and its effect. The overlap period occurs when both the intake and exhaust valves are open at the same time. It would seem that by having both valves open simultaneously, the intake mixture would become diluted, thereby diminishing power output. However, if the exhaust valve is left open after the piston has passed top dead center (and the intake valve is opening), the exhaust gases will continue to flow out anyway and their flow will actually help pull more intake mixture in. Like

If you are installing a new camshaft, it is always a good idea to replace the original valve springs and retainers. If you are on a tight budget, however, you can retain the stock springs provided they are up to specs. You'll find that most camshaft kits contain all the necessary parts designed to complement the camshaft.

duration, a camshaft has to be designed to take advantage of this overlap period and like duration, the more overlap, the higher the rpm you need to turn the engine to take advantage of it.

You can determine overlap by a cam's lobe center angle which is the distance, in degrees, between the centers of the intake and exhaust valves. The greater the angle, the less overlap. A street cam can have angles in the 112-120deg range. If you look at the roller cams available from Motorsport, you'll note that both the B302 and B303 cams have exactly the same lift and duration figures; the only difference between the two is that the B303 has a smaller lobe center angle which means that it will produce more upper-rpm power because it has more overlap.

Most aftermarket cam manufacturers have a wide selection of cams that can also provide more lift with duration figures similar to stock Ford cams. They also have hotter cams that increase duration in small, incremental steps. Each manufacturer lists in its catalog what is best for your particular application according to the modifications already made on your engine. Remember that the hotter the cam, the greater the necessity of complementing that cam with the rest of the engine—meaning larger carburetor, exhaust headers, and so on.

It used to be that you couldn't compare a stock Ford cam with those offered by aftermarket manufacturers because Ford used "advertised" duration to describe cam events while the aftermarket used duration measured at 0.050in lift. The cams listed in the Motorsport catalog now have duration figures measured both ways, making comparison easy. A practical limit for street operation is duration figures in the 230-240deg range (measured at 0.050in lift).

Duration at 0.050in Cam Lift (deg)	RPM Range
200	1000-4000
210	1300-4500
220	1500-5500
230	2300-6000
240	3000-7000
250	3800-7500
260	4200-8000

Hydraulic Roller Cams

In the 1960s, the high-performance engines usually came with a mechanical- or solid-lifter camshaft. Today there is no point in choosing a mechanical-lifter camshaft over a hydraulic cam. A hydraulic cam is maintenance free and easier on the valvetrain. Anti-pump-up hydraulic lifters can provide a top rpm of 7000 or so, more than enough for the street and on an EEC-IV equipped car that has a built-in rev limiter, that cuts in at about 6200rpm.

A major innovation, at least as far as camshafts go, occurred on 1985 and later 302 engines. They came with hydraulic roller lifters. Previously, roller lifter camshafts were pretty much a race-only occurrence. The advent of the hydraulic roller lifter combines the benefits of a roller lifter with the lack of maintenance of a hydraulic lifter. Roller lifters roll over the cam lobes which means they are much more reliable in high-speed, high-load applications. Roller lifters also enable the cam grinder to design cams with very high lifts and fast-opening ramps—qualities that are lacking in the stock 302 roller cam. However, roller lifters also reduce internal friction, thereby making additional horsepower. The roller cam used in the 302 is worth 30hp more than the comparable flat-tappet hydraulic cam used in previous years.

The roller camshaft is made from steel rather than the typical cast iron used on flat-tappet hydraulic and solid-lifter cams, so it is more expensive. In addition, the roller cam can only be used on special cylinder blocks that have higher lifter bosses. You can use regular flat tappets with a roller lifter block, but you can't use the hydraulic roller lifters on a regular block, at least not the stock Ford roller lifters. The pushrods are also shorter to compensate for the longer length of the roller lifters. Don't forget to switch your distributor's drive gear to a steel gear (see chapter 6 on electronics and ignitions), otherwise the stock gear will quickly wear out.

By using a cam kit manufactured by Crane Cams Incorporated, however, you can use the hydraulic roller cam on blocks that weren't originally designed to accept the roller cam. The kit consists of a special retainer, similar to the stock Ford plate. (See Appendices for source information.)

The stock 302 roller cam has an advertised duration of 266/266deg intake/exhaust and 0.444/0.444in lift—a fairly tame grind. The Motorsport catalog lists two roller camshafts for the 302, part numbers M-6250-B302 and M-6250-B303. Both have the same duration and lift specifications—284/284deg advertised duration, 224/224deg duration at 0.050in lobe lift, and 0.480/0.480in valve lift. The difference between the two is *lobe center angles*. As stated earlier, the lobe center angle is the angle between the centerline of the intake lobe and the centerline of the exhaust lobe. A smaller lobe center angle will produce more top-rpm power while a higher lobe center angle will produce a better idle and a wider power band at the expense of some high-rpm power. Both of these cams are compatible with the EEC-IV computer as long as the Mass Air Flow system is used, and Ford states that this cam is good for a significant increase in power over 4000rpm.

Roller Rocker Arms

There seems to be a lot of romance associated with roller rocker arms. They look great—even though you can't see them once the valve covers are on—and they are a definite plus when it comes to high-lift camshafts because they will reduce side-to-side valve stem wear. Aluminum or any good after-

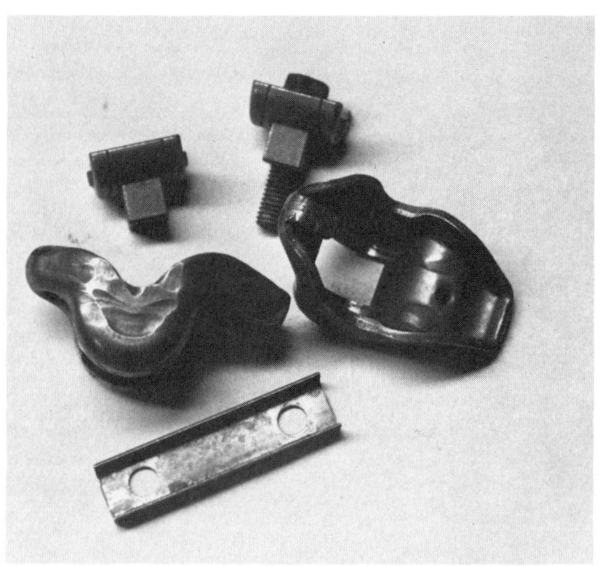

The 1977 and later small-blocks came with pedestal-type rocker arms which are nonadjustable. All you do is bolt them down tight. If you have installed a high-lift cam, you may have to use shorter pushrods or go to adjustable rockers.

market roller type rocker should be installed on a street engine, but not solely for the reasons mentioned above. Stock rockers are worth replacing because they are built to such loose tolerances that you'll find their actual rocker ratio is often less than specified. Aftermarket rockers are built to much closer tolerances, which usually results in a horsepower increase—and *that* is the reason you'll find magazine articles and cam manufacturer ads espousing aftermarket rockers. Since 1977, 302 engines have used stamped-steel rockers with sled-type fulcrums and bolt directly on the cylinder head. They are not adjustable. If you aren't modifying your engine with a high-lift camshaft, there is no need to replace the stock rockers. However, the Motorsport catalog does list an improved-strength, stock-type rocker, part number M-6564-A302. If you are in a rebuild situation, you may want to consider these.

If you *must* have roller rockers, you can use aluminum roller rockers that are a direct replacement for the stock rockers—meaning you don't need rocker arm studs or pushrod guide plates. They are available under part number M-6564-BS51 (with a 1.60:1 rocker arm ratio), and M-6564-ES51 (with a 1.72

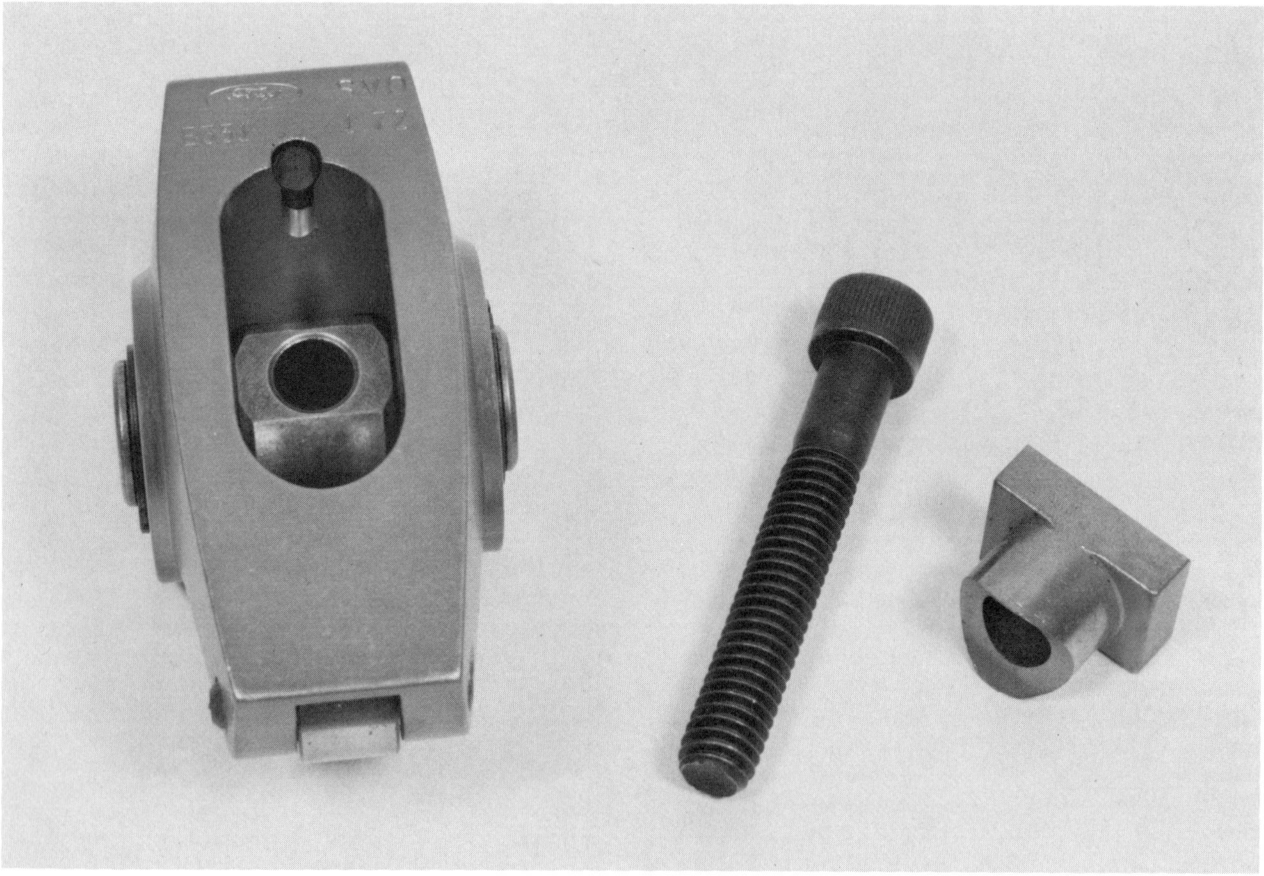

If you want to install roller rockers on the stock or GT-40 heads without resorting to guide plates, new hardened pushrods, rocker studs, and pedestal machining, then these Motorsport bolt-on rockers are for you. They come in either a 1.60:1 or 1.72:1 rocker ratio. The 1.72:1 is shown here. Ford Motor Co.

ratio). These rockers won't fit under the stock valve covers of the 5.0 liter EFI engine, but they do fit under the 5.0 liter HO diecast aluminum valve covers of the Motorsport chrome cover, part number M-6582-D302, provided that the baffle from the right-hand cover is removed. The polished aluminum cover, M-6582-E302, will clear these rockers, but will not fit under the EFI manifold.

The stock rocker arm ratio is 1.60:1, meaning that the rocker arm multiplies the cam lobe lift by a 1.60 factor. Thus a cam with a 0.300in cam lobe lift has a valve lift of 0.480in. A 1.72:1 rocker will provide 0.516in of lift at the valve on the same cam. Going from a 1.60 to 1.72 rocker ratio, though, will reduce the rpm at which the valves float. To maintain the same valve float speed, you must increase valve spring pressure by 10 percent.

The stock rockers will not work on most of the Motorsport and aftermarket high-performance cylinder heads, with the exception of the GT-40 heads. In this case you'll have to invest in a set of stud-mounted rocker arms, screw-in rocker studs, guide plates, and

To install stud-mounted rockers, the rocker arm pedestals have to be lowered and tapped for screw-in studs. This is an early 289 Hi-Po head which came with adjustable rockers. If you are building a street engine operating with the stock EEC-IV computer, then you don't need to have your heads machined for adjustable rockers because it won't let you rev the engine high enough to take advantage of a high-lift, long-duration cam.

In a high-output, high-rpm application, stud-mounted roller rockers are the way to go. These rockers reduce side loading to the valves, especially important when heavy valve springs are used. They are available from many sources. These are 1.60:1 rockers from Motorsport. Ford Motor Co.

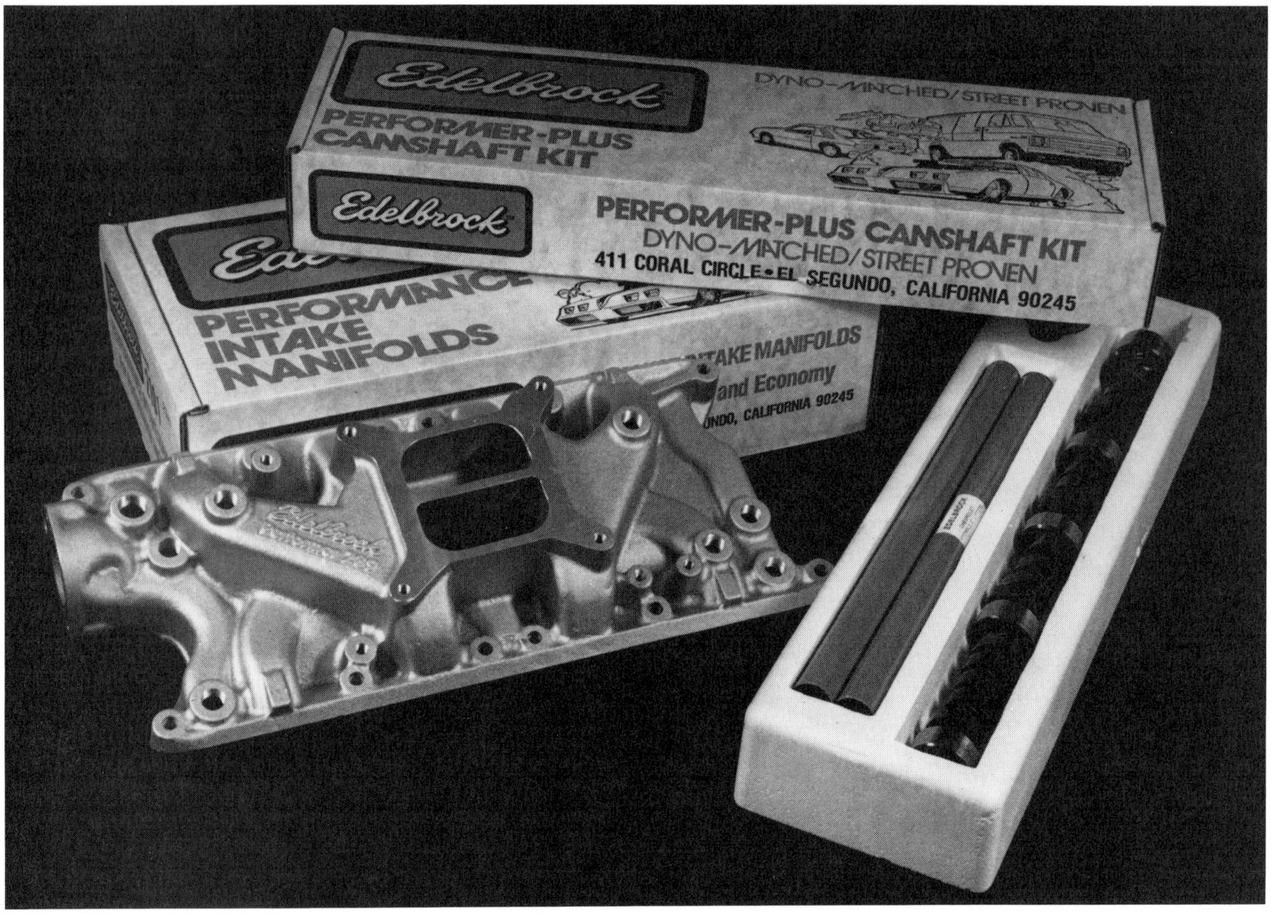

It is important that the cam you choose be matched to the rest of your engine. Edelbrock has invested a lot of dyno time to find out which camshafts work best with their manifolds. Edelbrock Corp.

For competition engines, Motorsport has this nifty belt-drive camshaft drive system. It comes with a nine-position multi-index crankshaft sprocket. For the street, a full-roller or cast-iron heavy-duty timing chain assembly is sufficient. Ford Motor Co.

hardened pushrods. You will then have an adjustable valvetrain.

To use adjustable rockers with the stock or GT-40 heads, the rocker pedestals will have to be machined and tapped for rocker studs.

Crane also makes a kit to convert to adjustable rocker arms. It uses the stock bolt-down holes to mount a rocker stud, and nylon guide plate to achieve adjustability. The kit includes sixteen studs and guide plates and you'll also have to purchase a set of rockers. As these studs are on the thin side, they aren't recommended for a competition engine but they will work fine on a street or mildly modified engine. The advantage of this kit is that you don't have to remove the heads from the engine or machine the pedestals down.

The stock spring retainers are a two-piece steel design which promotes valve rotation. They are fine for a street engine, but for a more serious application you may want to consider a single retainer. Never use aluminum or even anodized aluminum valve spring retainers on the street, unless you don't mind having bits of aluminum circulating with the engine oil. The valve springs can chew up the retainer. Stay with steel retainers, which are good enough to 7500rpm. Even though they are heavier, they are far more reliable and their slight weight disadvantage is of little consequence on a street engine. If you are installing a high-lift cam, you may also need shorter pushrods to maintain correct rocker arm geometry. Be sure to ask the cam manufacturer. Always follow the recommendations of the cam manufacturer when it comes to valve springs.

One final point concerns timing chains. If your 302 has the nylon timing gear, be sure to replace it. Although it is lighter and quieter, its reliability is questionable in a performance engine. A full-roller timing chain and sprocket is best but at the very least, use a timing chain that uses iron gears.

Valve Springs

While the camshaft lobes open the valves, it is the springs that close them—and this has to be done just as precisely and accurately. Rev an engine too high and the inertia effect on the valve springs may be too much so that the lifters won't be able to flow the cam lobe's contour. The result is valve float. Besides making the valves float, such a condition leads to further weakening of the springs—a 10 percent loss in tension means that the valve springs should be replaced. But a more serious consequence to valve float is the real possibility of the valves "kissing" the pistons, even if you have clearance notches on the pistons.

Common sense would dictate that to cure this problem one should install very heavy springs. This will work, but at the expense of increased valvetrain wear. You will also have to install stronger pushrods and roller rockers to ease the strain on the system. What is needed is the lightest tension spring that will get the job done—and in this case you must follow the cam manufacturer's recommendations.

Most high-performance springs consist of a spring with a counterwound inner damper coil. Racing camshaft kits will also include a smaller inner spring which enables the engine to rev higher.

To install heavier springs, the heads will require machining to reduce the size of the valve guide so that the inner spring will fit, and to increase the size of the valve spring seats to accommodate the spring's larger diameter.

Valves

You can install a larger carburetor, or a performance fuel-injection manifold, or a hotter cam, but if the valves in your engine aren't big enough to let all that extra mixture in and out, it is all a waste of money. The stock Ford 302 cylinder head is not known for its large valves; in fact, they are quite small, measuring 1.78/1.45in intake/exhaust. All 289 and 302 heads manufactured since 1963 come with valves of this size.

You can advance or retard camshaft timing with this nine-position crankshaft sprocket. Generally, advancing the cam increases mid-range power at the expense of the top-end while retarding the cam helps upper-rpm output. The 302 will run better with the cam advanced 2-4deg. Ford Motor Co.

The 302 uses single springs on both valves with a two-piece retainer designed to rotate the valves. They are adequate for a street engine, but most cam manufacturers recommend that you switch to a single steel retainer for high-performance use.

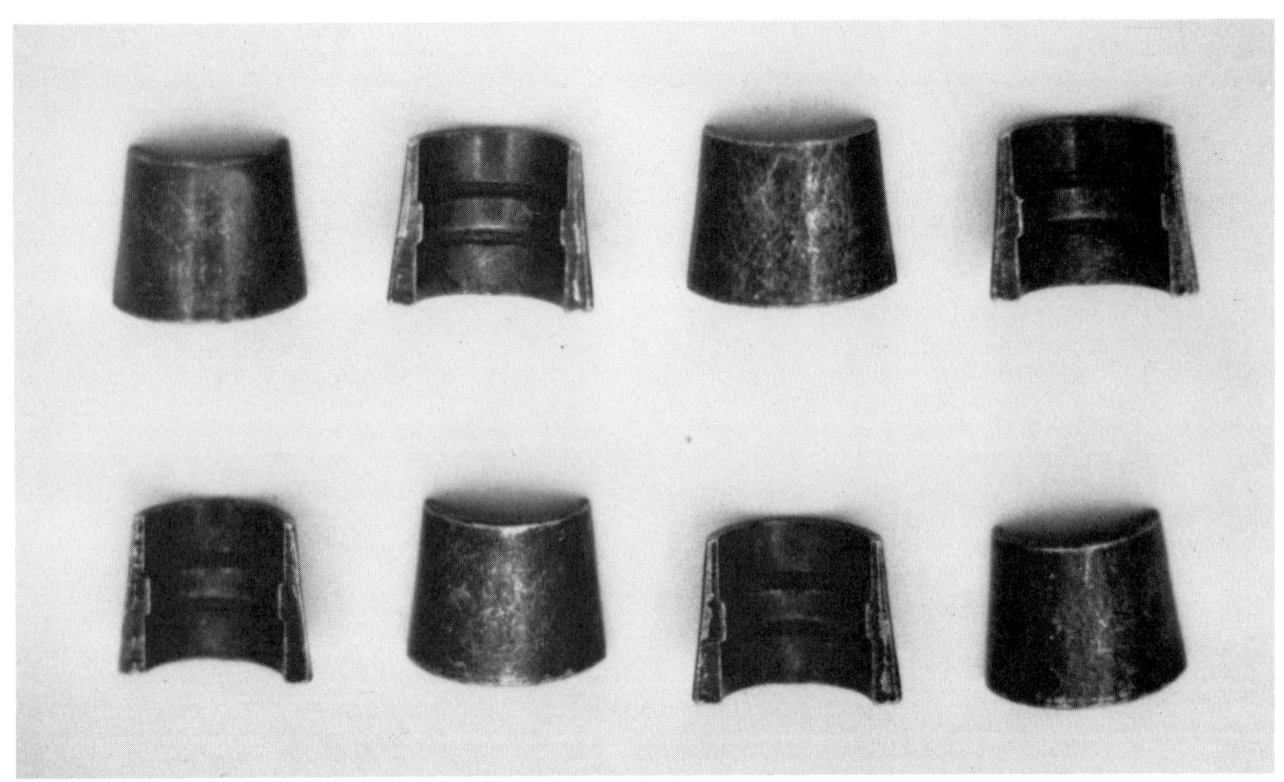

It doesn't pay to skimp on any portion of your valvetrain. These small keepers are the only things that prevent the valves from falling into the combustion chamber. Always use high-quality steel keepers. Ford Motor Co.

If you have aluminum heads, then you must use steel valve spring seats underneath the valve springs. Otherwise, they'll chew up the head. Ford Motor Co.

You can get around this restriction by installing cylinder heads that come with larger valves; all aftermarket heads have larger valves. The GT-40 head has 1.84/1.54in valves, which are the same size as the 1969-70 351 Windsor heads. You could install these valves on the stock head, but you are better off putting in even larger valves.

The least expensive way to do this is to install Chevrolet small-block valves measuring 1.94/1.60in intake/exhaust. These are readily available and relatively inexpensive. They have the same stem diameter as the Ford valves and the valve spring keeper grooves are in the same location, but the valve is not quite as tall as the stock Ford valves. Still, they will work, but you must ensure that correct valvetrain and rocker arm geometry is maintained.

One consequence of larger valves is that the valves will be closer to the combustion chamber walls which shroud the valves and thus restrict flow. In order to take advantage of larger valves, the combustion chamber will have to be modified by enlarging it to remove restrictions around the valves. This will result in a lower compression ratio. Also remember that in order to run unleaded gas, the stock valve seats were induction hardened. You'll either have to install hardened valve inserts or use a lead additive, otherwise the valve seats will quickly wear away. Considering the cost of new valves and the seat inserts, you may be better off buying a set of aftermarket heads. Everything you do on an engine is a trade-off—you just can't get away from it.

Recommendations

As stated earlier, the stock cam, mild as it is, is good enough for 300hp provided the rest of the engine is built correctly. The 1992 SAAC Mk 1, for example, is rated at 295hp using a 65mm Mass Air Flow system, GT-40 heads, and shorty headers. It has high thirteen-second quarter-mile acceleration, 22mpg stock driveability, and it passes all emission regulations.

Changing a cam should be attempted only after you first have optimized the intake and exhaust system of your Mustang. Passing an emissions test as part of renewing your registration is becoming a reality in more and more states each year. Too often a new cam will make your engine fail.

You can use the Motorsport B302 or B303 roller cams for more upper-end power without having to compromise the stock electronics and according to Ford, your engine should still be within stock emission parameters.

Very high rpm engines require correspondingly stiffer valve springs. These are dual-springs with a dampener. High-rate springs like these will accelerate valvetrain component wear and shouldn't be used on a street engine. Orion Industries

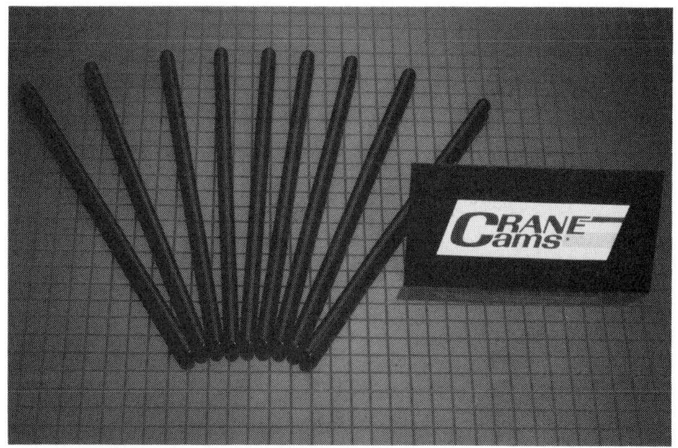

Heavy valve springs will almost always require that you use new, stronger pushrods since the stock ones will bend the first time you rev the engine over 5000rpm. These chrome-moly pushrods are from Crane Cams. Crane Cams Inc.

Chapter 5

The Exhaust System

A lot has been written about exhaust systems over the years, about different types of headers and mufflers, and the benefits of each. Unfortunately, ignorance still abounds when it comes to exhaust system dynamics, and much of what has been written only compounds the problem. The result: most performance exhaust systems aren't delivering what their manufacturers claim. Unfortunately this also once again applies to exhaust system components for current Mustangs.

After all, aren't headers and the rest of the exhaust system there to reduce back pressure, allowing the really important power-producing parts of your engine to get on with their jobs? Nothing is ever that simple—the more you know, the more you'll realize how complex headers and exhaust tuning can be. It is not just a matter of slapping on a set of headers and expecting miracles. In many cases, the installation of headers will do little to boost power.

Headers, like everything else in the engine, must be chosen with the understanding of how they work and how they'll complement the rest of your engine's components.

Headers

Through a process called scavenging, headers let spent gases increase an engine's output. Specifically, scavenging is a process where a fast-moving column of gases actually extracts additional gases from a cylinder. When the exhaust valve closes, the gases in the header tube don't stop, they keep moving—possessing considerable momentum. This movement actually creates a small vacuum (a lower pressure area) under the exhaust valve. When it's time for the exhaust valve to open again, this lower pressure area extracts or scavenges exhaust gases from the engine. As exhaust gas speed increases, so does the scavenging effect. This means that the header tubing size must be small enough to maintain high-exhaust velocity but at the same time, large enough so as not to restrict the engine at high rpm.

Thus a header with the correct tube diameter will show higher speeds and lower elapsed times (ET) on the drag strip. On a street car, a performance increase will be seen throughout the rpm range. But if the tube diameter is larger than it should be, you'll experience a power loss due to reduced exhaust gas velocity. In fact, tubing that is only ⅛in larger than it should be for a particular engine combination may not even improve a car's street performance! The same car will probably show an improvement on the drag strip as the header is disconnected from the rest of the exhaust system, but this will be due to reduced back pressure and not due to header scavenging.

It's the old thinking that bigger is better. Bigger exhaust tubes are thought to be better. But bigger is definitely not better in this case. Enthusiasts have always warned of the results of choosing an over-

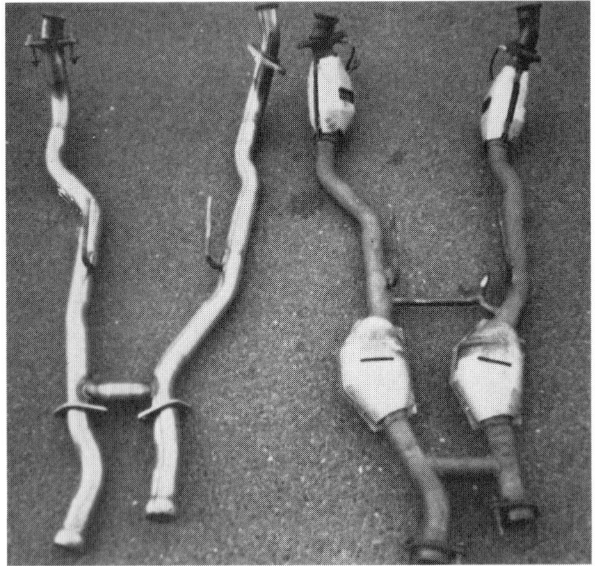

Restrictions are obvious in the stock exhaust system (right) with its four catalytic converters. The off-road system on the left is a lot better, but its many curves tend to reduce flow. Exhaust system modifications have traditionally been the first area to attack in the search for more power. A free-flowing exhaust system lets the engine produce all the power it was designed to. Steve Collison

sized carburetor, but rarely are warnings issued with the same sort of urgency when it comes to headers. And the car companies are just as susceptible to bigger-is-better thinking. You can look at the current Motorsport catalog and see photos of a lot of nice headers, but the reality is they won't do much for the typical street-driven Mustang. If you look at the "headers" that have been standard equipment on Mustangs since 1985, you should notice that they look very similar to the high-performance exhaust manifolds found on Ford's 1960s 427 engines.

Another point to consider when it comes to tubing size, especially as it applies to the drag strip, is that a maximum-*power* header is not necessarily the same as a maximum-*performance* header. On the strip, you are looking for the highest average power output during the time spent going down the strip. Certainly a big-tube header will produce more power at a higher rpm (see graph) but when the rpm drop during shifting, there is a horsepower loss resulting from the diminishing exhaust velocities. With a smaller tube header, maximum output is less, but low- and mid-range power is higher because the smaller tubing encourages better scavenging. Looking at the accompanying graph you'll see that as long as Area A is smaller than Area B, the use of a smaller tube header will result in a faster car.

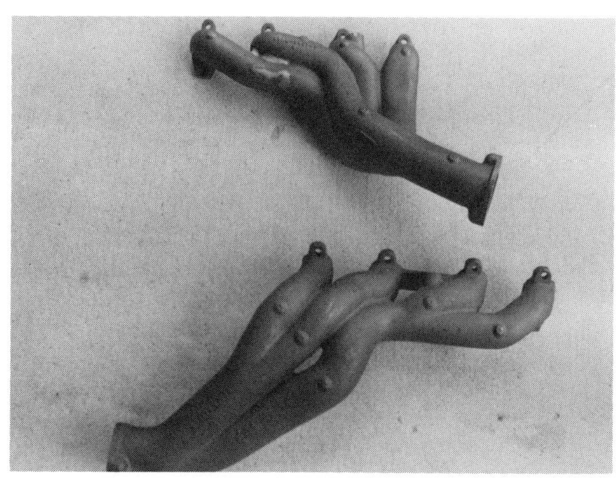

A set of factory cast-iron headers for the old 427 big-block. It is interesting to note how similar in design they are to the current factory tube headers for the 302.

Another so-called truth you probably read about is that you'll have to enrich your fuel system on a carbureted application after installing headers. Did you ever ask yourself why? The only time you have to enrich the carburetor is if you've installed a header with an oversize tube diameter. A larger tube diame-

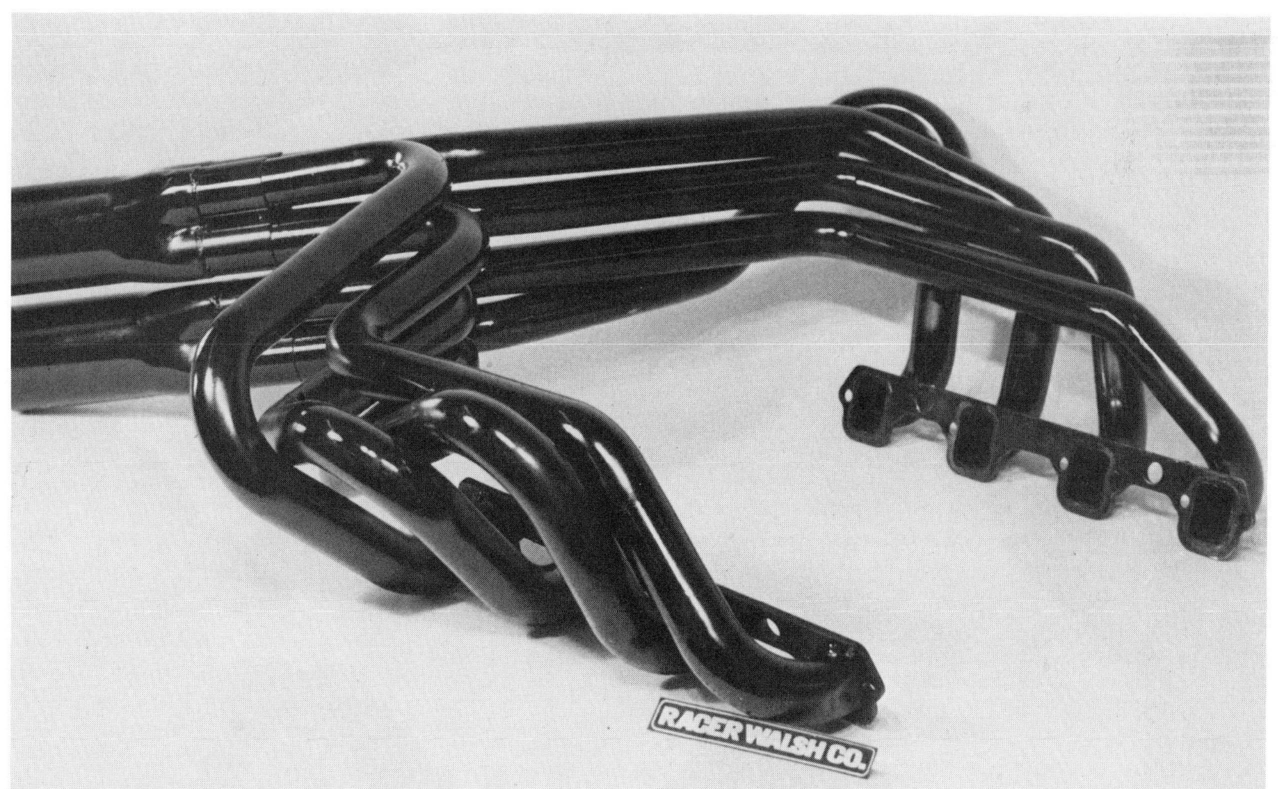

This race-only header is known as a 180deg design because some of the pipes connect to the opposite collector to take advantage of even exhaust sequence scavenging— an exhaust pulse occurs at every 180deg crank rotation. Racer Walsh Co.

ter not only reduces gas velocity, but also reduces the signal to your carburetor, thereby letting your engine run lean. A correctly sized header will not need this sort of adjustment and, in many cases, will actually cause the engine to run too rich. On fuel-injected engines, the oxygen sensor will notice any variation in oxygen content in the exhaust and adjust the fuel mixture accordingly.

Thus on the street, big-tube headers are of no value because they will reduce low- and mid-range output. At the top end, the restrictions inherent in the car's exhaust system nullify any advantage. And the same thing can occur on the track. Too large a tube diameter will only reduce overall performance.

If this is correct, then why do many header manufacturers only sell headers with oversize tubes? Although some manufacturers list smaller tube headers in their catalogs, the sad truth is that customers *want* big-tube headers because they believe that's the best way to go. Ever try to tell someone that his car will go faster with smaller headers? Old beliefs die hard.

How often have you heard that headers improve power by reducing or eliminating back pressure? Back pressure is another way of saying restriction. By following this logic, it would seem that a bigger header would eliminate back pressure. As we have just seen, this sort of thinking doesn't apply with headers. It is far more applicable when choosing mufflers and tailpipes, where large-diameter pipes and mufflers do make a difference.

Headers can also be "tuned" to help cylinder filling during the intake cycle. When the exhaust valve is open, a positive sound-wave pulse is produced and travels to the end of the header tube. There it reflects back up the tube as a negative wave pulse. Assuming that the header tube length is correctly matched to the engine, the negative wave will reach the cylinder when both intake and exhaust valves are open (during overlap). As the negative wave collapses when reaching the cylinder, it reduces the pressure in the chamber, allowing more air-fuel mixture to enter—and thus more power.

The length of the header tube determines at which point in the rpm range the beneficial effects of exhaust tuning occur. The shorter the tube, the higher the rpm range where additional power will be made, and conversely, the longer the tube, the lower the rpm. To take full advantage of exhaust tuning, a manual transmission-equipped car should have header length that lets the headers tune at approximately the middle of the rpm range. An automatic-equipped car

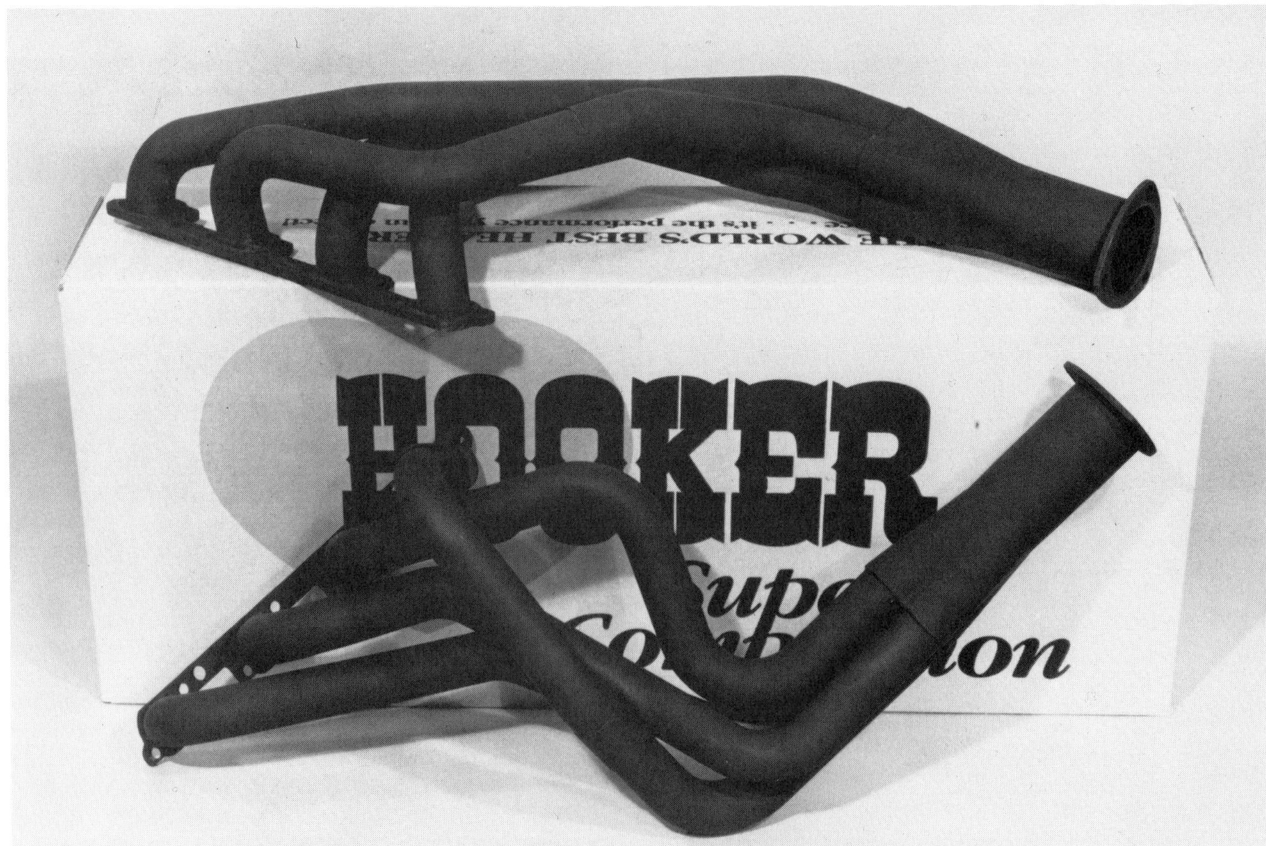

Hooker's headers for the Mustang have a 1¹/₂in tube diameter with 27in long tubes. These are ideal for a street Mustang and outperform the shorty-type header. Longer collectors help to boost low-rpm torque. Hooker Headers

88

with the same engine should have header tubing that is 4-6in longer to boost lower and mid-range rpm, which is important for an automatic on the drag strip.

If exhaust tuning is to be of any value, the header tubes must be of equal length. If they are not, it will become difficult to properly tune an engine because the tube variations will cause one cylinder to run richer and another leaner. It is difficult to achieve perfection here, given the limitations of engine compartments, but for maximum power output, tube variation should not exceed plus or minus 1in. If a header is advertised to have 36in tube length, all the tubes should at least measure between 35 and 37in. Problems will show up if tubing variations start to exceed 1in, and if a header has a variation of 10in or more (some have as much as 21in!) the headers will show a negligible power improvement. If you are a racer, you will want to have true equal-length headers.

Shorty Headers

You'll find a major problem with the current crop of shorty-type headers that most aftermarket suppliers offer, including Ford. You can just look at these and see that the tubes aren't by any stretch of the imagination equal. An equal-length header will run circles around an unequal-length header.

There is even an equal-length shorty available. That is an improvement, but you should also remember that the longer the header tube, the lower the rpm at which horsepower is maximized. The shorter the tube, the higher the rpm. For good street performance, header tubes should be between 32 and 36in long.

The only benefit that a shorty-type header may have is when it is compared to the stock headers that have been available on 1985 and later 302 engines. The stock pipes are pretty crimped, while most shorty headers feature smoother, bigger tubes. And the shorty headers are a direct replacement, thereby allowing the use of catalytic converters. But their cost effectiveness versus power increase has to be considered in light of their cost. Kenny Brown of Project Industries, through extensive dyno testing, has found that the typical shorty is worth only about 7hp over stock.

Another point to consider are collectors. Most collectors measure between 4-12in but 98 percent of the time, a longer collector produces more power. As

For racing or for a highly modified 302, you can use these $1^{5}/_{8}$in tube headers from Racer Walsh. Collector size is easily adjustable as different collector ends can be slipped in. Racer Walsh Co.

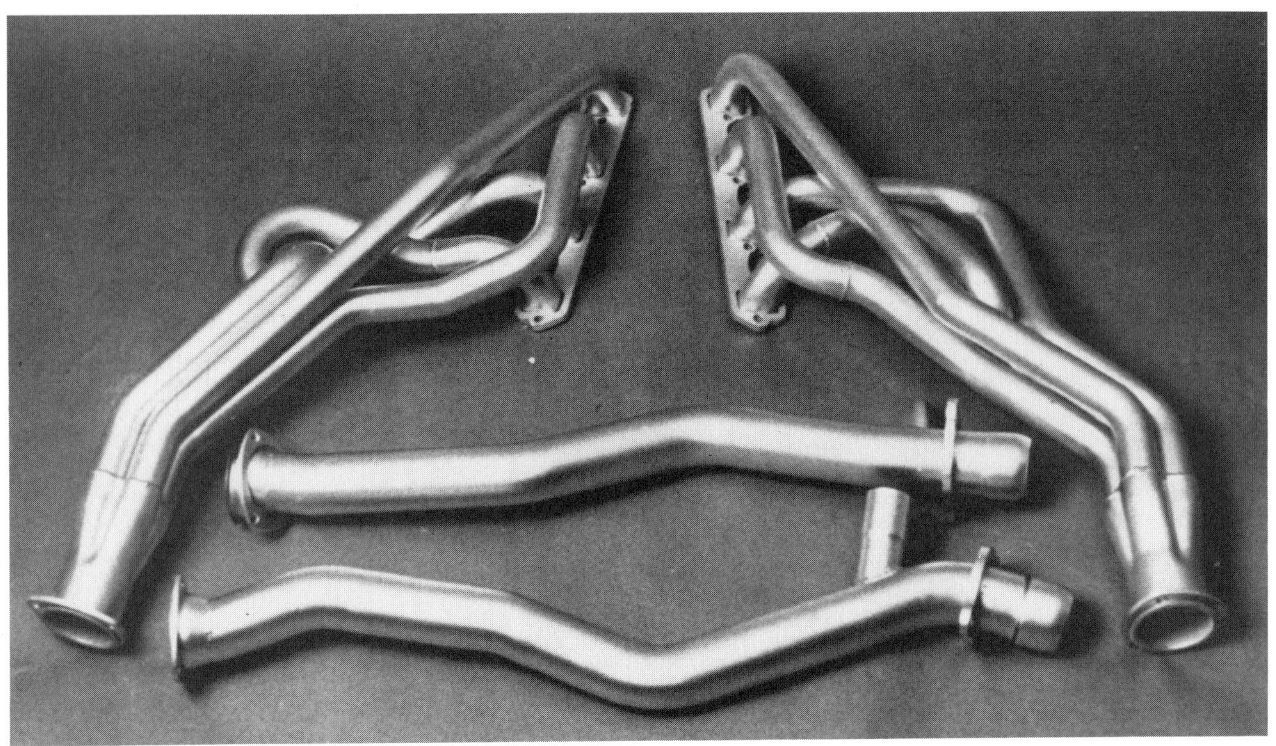

Texas Turbo Engineering has this Street Monster Header kit which incorporates a 2¹⁄₂in off-road exhaust system. This kit is suitable only for highly modified 302 engines *that are capable of propelling Mustangs in the low-12sec range. Tube diameter is 1⁵⁄₈in. Texas Turbo Engineering, Inc.*

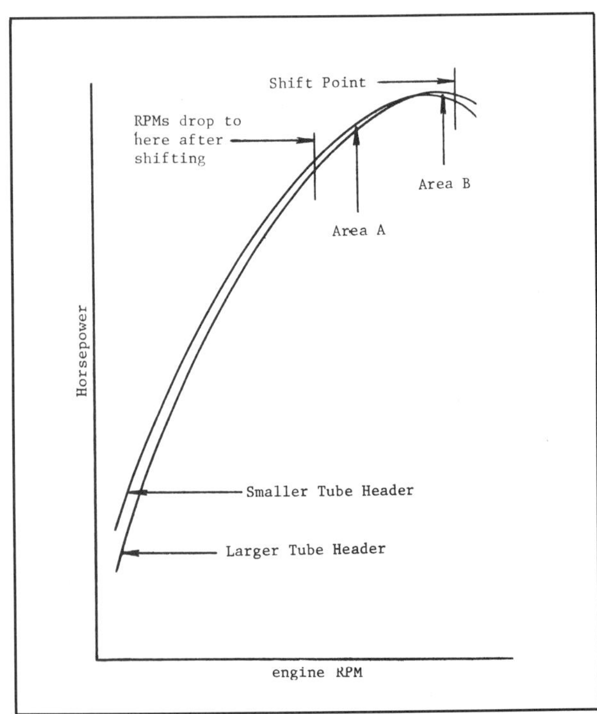

A smaller tube header may not produce as much horsepower at high rpm, but by producing more low- and mid-range power than a big-tube header it will produce a higher average output, thus outperforming the big-tube header on the strip. Headers by Ed, Inc.

much as 0.3sec reduction in ET can be realized by just the simple addition of a 12in collector. This is because a collector creates a free-flowing secondary scavenging area.

For the person interested in more power the replacement of the stock headers is beneficial. Any of the shorty types are not recommended at all. Yes, they are slightly better than the stock headers, but considering their cost, a full-size header is the way to go because it will make much more power. There are two sets available in the Motorsport catalog, both having a 30in tube length and pipe diameters of either 1⁵⁄₈ or 1³⁄₄in. Neither is recommended, however, because the tube diameter is way too big for a street engine.

If you look at the enthusiast magazines, you'll often see dyno tests of various brands of shorty headers over the stock headers. The results that I have seen over the past two years only state how much power they'll increase at the engine's highest rpm, and at best, this is a rather negligible amount. A big-tube shorty header may increase top-end horsepower, but what the magazines often fail to show you is that they'll reduce power in the all-important low- to mid-rpm range, which is so critical on the street.

The stock or mildly modified 302 does not respond well to tube diameters larger than 1½in and you'll see a definite decrease in power. If you have modified your engine so that the car will run in the twelve-second range or lower, then a 1⁵⁄₈in tube or larger will be necessary, but a larger than 1½in tube will cause a power decrease in the typical modified street engine.

Although there are several good headers available with equal-length tubes, most are suitable for racing only. One of the few manufacturers that offers an equal-length street header for the 302 is Hooker Headers (see Appendices). Tube diameter is 1½in, while length is 27in. Hooker made the 27in length specifically for a street-type engine because the stock engine runs out of breath at around 5000rpm, so the shorter tube length is designed to help the engine breathe better in this range. A 12in collector extension can be used to broaden the torque curve with these headers.

No matter how good your headers are, most of the benefits they provide will be nullified if the spent gases have to go through the stock catalytic converters and mufflers, especially at higher rpm.

Exhaust Pipes

As we have seen, headers are complex. It can be difficult to choose the right header that will work best with your particular combination, but the rest of your car's exhaust system is very simple by comparison. Here, the bigger-is-better philosophy does work. For example, you should try to fit the largest possible exhaust and tailpipes that have a minimum of bends.

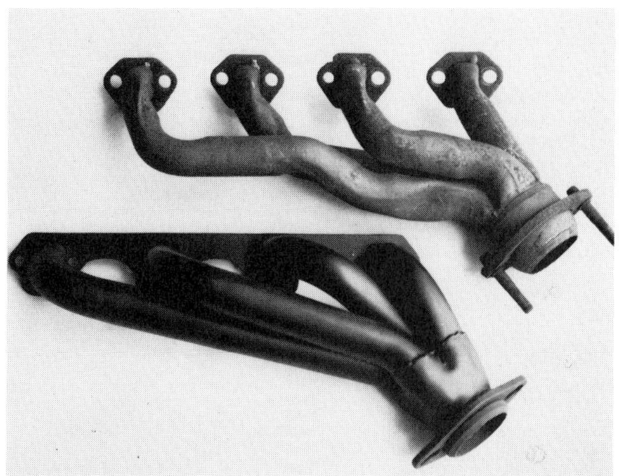

A stock 1985 header (top) compared to a shorty-type header. The smaller tube diameter and many crimps restrict flow of the stock unit while the shorty provides better flow, resulting in a 5-10hp increase. Steve Collison

The optimum size seems to be 2½in inside diameter, but a street engine can do just fine with a 2¼in system.

Mustangs built up through 1984 came with a single-exhaust system that used two outlets to simu-

The shorty headers available from Motorsport. They have a 1⅝in tube diameter and are made from stainless steel. A large tube diameter is suitable for a highly modified engine. Ford Motor Co.

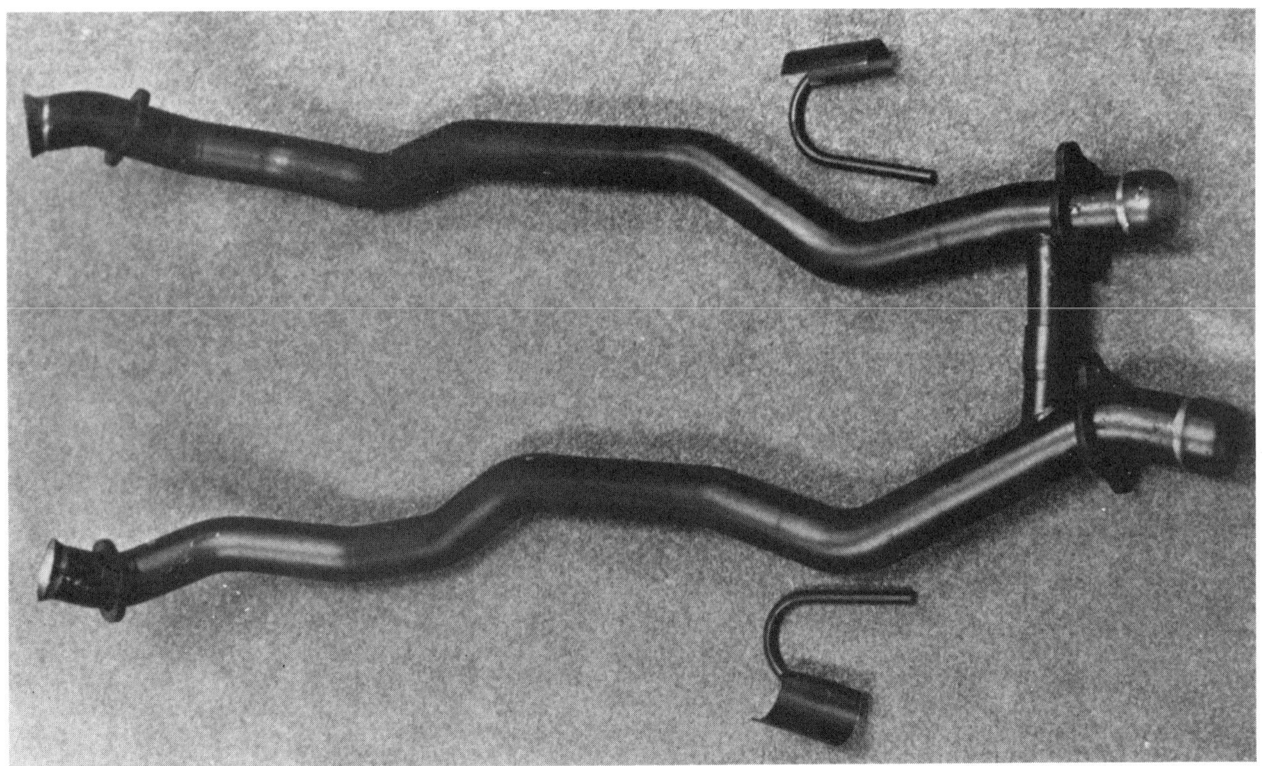

These off-road pipes are from Texas Turbo Engineering. They measure 2¹/₂in in diameter which is larger than the 2¹/₄in off-road pipes from Motorsport. The pipes come with an oxygen sensor fitting and a balance tube. Adjustable hanger brackets make installation easy. Texas Turbo Engineering, Inc.

late a dual system. The 1985 and later engines had a true dual-exhaust system, which is partly responsible for their higher power. Even so, the stock dual-exhaust system with its four catalytic converters is very restrictive. To get the most from your engine, you can replace the catalytic converters with one of the many off-road exhaust system kits that are available. The Motorsport kit is made of stainless steel (and is therefore more expensive) and is not a direct replacement for the street system since it isn't designed to hook up to the stock mufflers, although it can easily be made to. Walker Manufacturing makes a direct replacement kit, but the extra bends add up to some additional restriction over the Ford system. Texas Turbo also offers a 2¹/₂in system that includes adjustable brackets for easier installation. Most of these kits are designed to work with the stock headers, and by themselves will make a significant improvement.

Most of these off-road exhaust pipes have a built-in crossover tube, a definite plus. This improves low-end torque and helps to keep noise level down.

Catalytic Converters

All this brings up the subject of catalytic converters. Ford catalytic converters flow better than those found on Chrysler or GM cars because they have a honeycomb design. Catalytic converters are very effective in removing pollutants, but they *do* have drawbacks. The biggest problem with converters is that they are restrictive. You can install aftermarket modified converters which increase flow, but be warned, they are expensive. Second, catalytic converters need to see exhaust gases that are the

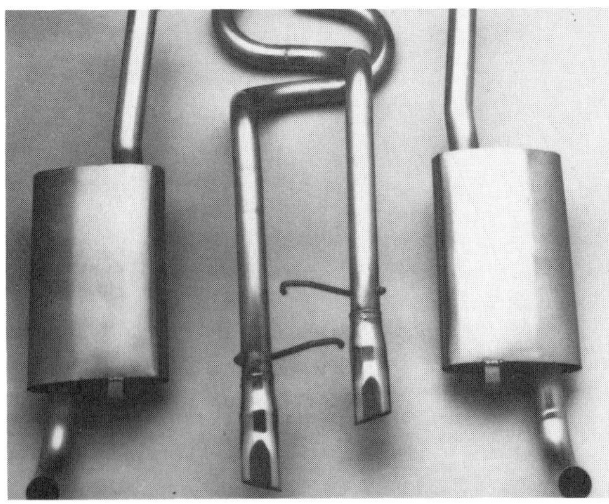

A high quality and efficient replacement system for the catalytic converters is available from Boria. It comes with a million mile warranty because it is made from stainless steel. Boria Performance Industries

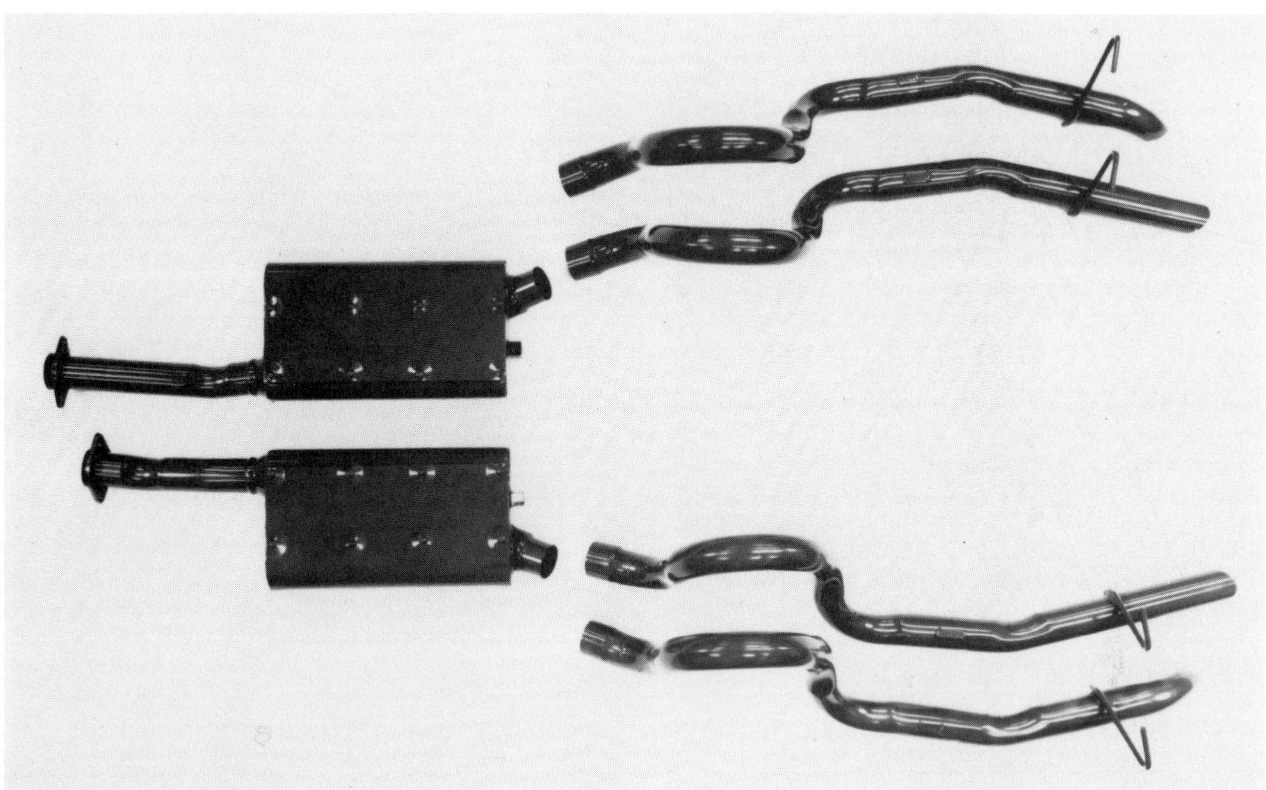

The Flowmaster exhaust system incorporates two Flowmaster mufflers and can be ordered with tailpipes that exit straight through or downward. Tests have shown that a Mustang equipped with Flowmaster mufflers will produce more power than without any mufflers at all. Flowmaster Incorporated

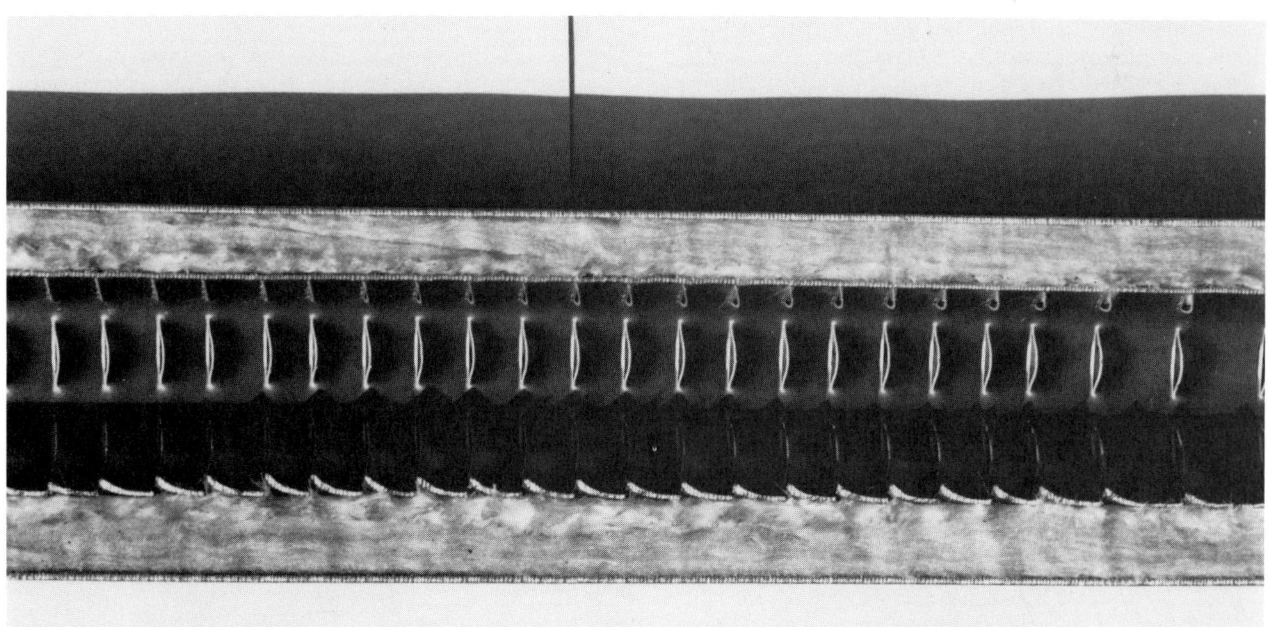

In a glasspack muffler, the fiberglass absorbs sound through the slats cut in the center pipe. A good turbo-style muffler is not only quieter but less restrictive. Slat openings in this type muffler should face the rear for less restriction. Other types of glasspacks have holes cut into the tube that face outward and are less restrictive. Thrush Inc.

result of combustion of an air-fuel mixture in the 14.7:1 range, which is controlled by the engine's EEC-IV computer. This is a fairly lean air-fuel ratio. If you've modified your fuel-injection system or carburetor to provide a richer mixture for more power, then the effectiveness of the catalytic converter is greatly reduced.

Another point to remember is that catalytic converters are extremely sensitive and over time, can clog up. A misfiring spark plug or the choke sticking in your carburetor in the morning is enough to make a converter useless. And as they get older, they clog. You'll often see cars that check out fine in terms of oil consumption, compression, emission systems, and the like but are down on power. If they also tend to run hotter than normal, you can be sure that the cause is bad catalytic converters. This restriction in the exhaust system will cause burned exhaust valves, and it can be particularly damaging to a turbo-charged application as the extra heat will fry a turbocharger.

Mufflers

The last point to consider when choosing a new exhaust system is mufflers. You can forget the stock mufflers because they are too restrictive. Stock mufflers are designed to meet noise regulations, while performance is a secondary consideration.

Most of us go through a glasspack phase. These mufflers have a straight-through design which uses fiberglass to quiet exhaust noise. Made in various lengths (the longer the quieter), there are important internal differences between various brands. The least restrictive are those that don't have the internal louvers protruding into the exhaust flow.

Glasspacks, however, are hard to live with and over the past fifteen years or so, the big deal in street mufflers is the so-called Turbo muffler. The most efficient of these mufflers are very loud; some are better than others. Some of the best-flowing include

Cyclone's Sonic 2½in, Walker's Dyno Max 2½in, Supreme's Super C 2½in, and Thrust Incorporated's Turbo 500. All of these mufflers work well, are much better than the stock mufflers, and have a very high cubic-feet-per-minute flow rating, as measured on a flow bench.

But is a flow bench an accurate way to measure muffler efficiency? In a flow bench, there is a smooth, constant source of pressure or vacuum. But in actuality, exhaust flow is pulsing in nature. These tests are easy to perform but they are all based on the principle that the best possible performance is obtained with an open system, whether it is open headers or just an open, straight-through pipe.

Mufflers made by the Flowmaster Corporation of Santa Rosa, California (see Appendices), however, produce more power than open headers or straight pipes! This goes against the grain of commonly accepted logic. When the exhaust valve opens there is a pulse of exhaust gases, energy, and sound energy, which travels at almost 1,000fps (feet per second). Directly behind this pulse is a low-pressure area. As the pulse travels down the exhaust system, it loses speed and any obstruction will slow the pulse even more. The low-pressure area behind the pulse helps to pull the next pulse through the system, and the greater the low-pressure area, the faster the pulse moves. This also pulls more fuel mixture into the cylinder. Flowmaster has been able to utilize the sound and pulse energy contained in the exhaust to create a low-pressure area greater than the one created by the pulse alone. Previously unproductive sound energy is changed to productive additional low pressure behind the pulse—like a booster.

In a conventional muffler, the unwanted sound energy is absorbed with fiberglass, ceramic filters, baffling, and back pressure, all of which produce a quiet exhaust system. But the penalty is lost power and airflow. In a Flowmaster muffler, the sound energy is neither absorbed nor impeded, creating power that did not exist before.

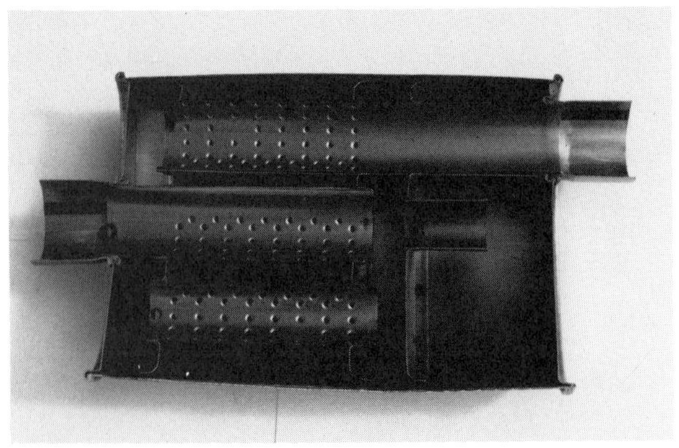

This is what should be avoided in a muffler. Note the restrictive inlet and outlet tubes. You can't see inside a muffler, but you should always check inlet and outlet tubes to make sure there isn't any restriction.

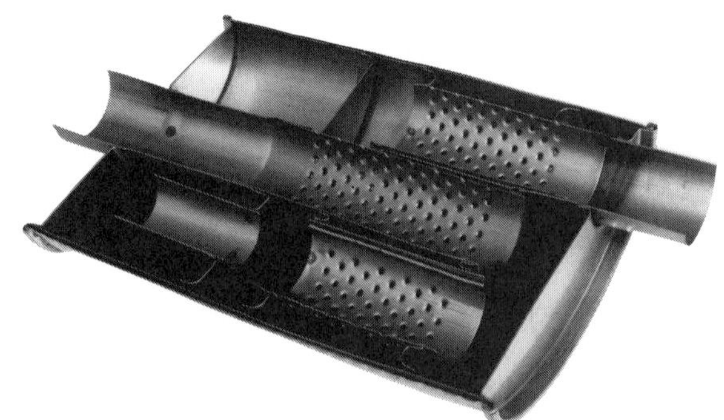

Thrush's Turbo 500 series mufflers have larger inlet and outlet tubes that do not neck down—which means more power. Thrush Inc.

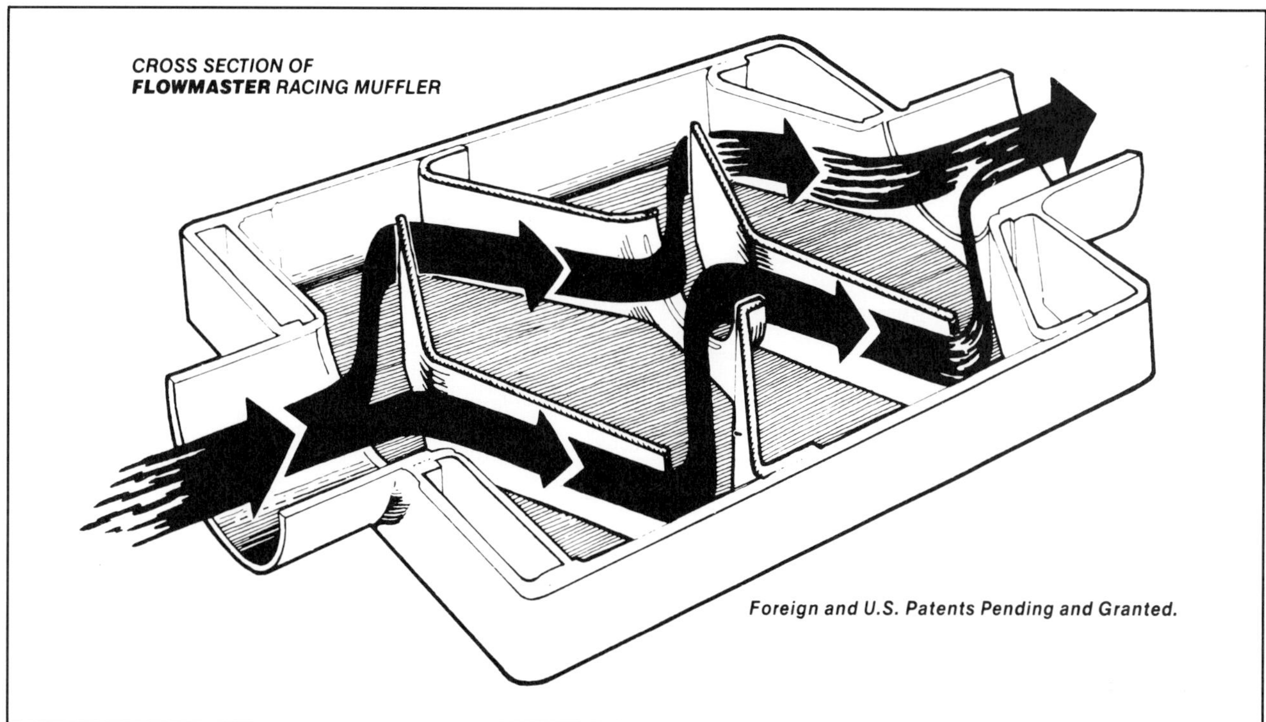

A look inside the Flowmaster racing muffler. Street units follow the same principles, but are not identical. The result is a muffler that actually adds horsepower while most conventional mufflers merely allow the engine to produce most of the power it was designed to deliver. Flowmaster Corp.

Power was increased through the use of Flowmaster part number 42553 mufflers on a 1989 Mustang LX at the rear wheels. Tests were performed by Performance Associates.

	Horsepower		Torque (lb-ft)	
Rpm	Baseline	Flowmaster	Baseline	Flowmaster
2500	105	110	221	231
3000	125	135	219	236
3500	140	150	210	225
4000	145	160	190	210

So, the Flowmaster is more than just a muffler in the conventional sense. The dyno test results on a 1990 Mustang GT performed by Performance Associates show a maximum increase of 15hp at the rear wheels and 27lb-ft of torque over the baseline mufflers, which in this case were Walker glasspacks, already more efficient than the stock Ford units.

Exhaust Tuning and Superchargers/Turbochargers

If you've ever seen blown dragsters, you've probably noticed that they have very short, straight, or slightly curved exhaust pipes, called zoomies. There is no collector, with each exhaust port having its individual pipe. And because in a supercharged engine the force feeds the cylinders, header scavenging is of no value at all—in fact, there is no header or exhaust scavenging in a supercharged engine. Therefore collector size, tube length, and tube diameter are of no importance in a supercharged engine. All you need to use is headers that are large and free flowing with a minimum of bends and restrictions. The same applies to the rest of the exhaust system. Large tubing and free-flowing mufflers are a must. You're dealing with a larger, hotter volume of exhaust gases and any restriction in the system is therefore amplified.

The nicest part about an exhaust system is that after you've installed it, it requires little periodic maintenance and absolutely no tuning or adjustment. It just hangs there, letting you devote your time to other areas that require attention. It is easy to forget the exhaust system, and that's OK, but when you have the wrong combination, you can spend a lot of money and waste a lot of time trying to figure out what isn't working right when the real culprit is poorly chosen exhaust system components. Do some research, follow the guidelines described here, get the highest quality parts you can afford, and you'll know that the exhaust system is doing its part to increase your engine's output.

Chapter 6

Electronics and Ignition

By far, the least understood (and most misunderstood) system on the third-generation Mustangs is the electronic computer control system which regulates all engine functions. The main reason for the increasingly complex computers and related systems is tougher emission standards. It is possible to design a brand-new, "cleaner" engine in terms of emission output, but it is much cheaper to use an existing engine along with electronic management controls to keep emissions down to acceptable levels. The small-block engine was originally designed to provide a broad range of power with good fuel mileage at a smooth idle. With the advent of emission controls in the 1970s, power output was compromised as was driveability, idle quality, and fuel mileage. Sophisticated electronic controls enable an engine to meet emission standards while restoring horsepower output, mileage, and idle quality.

Electronic Engine Control Systems

There have been four Electronic Engine Control (EEC) systems used on Ford engines. The current system, in use since 1984, is the EEC-IV and works in much the same way as its predecessors. EEC-I was first used on the Lincoln Versailles. It was designed to control ignition timing, EGR (Exhaust Gas Recirculation), and Thermactor (air pump) flow. It consists of the computer control unit, seven sensors, and the engine's ignition system—the distributor, coil, and the DuraSpark control box. The computer control unit is made up of two assemblies: the processor and the calibration assembly. The processor processes the information received from the various sensors, compares it to the values programmed in the calibration assembly, and then sends out signals to the ignition control box and actuator solenoids to adjust the system as needed.

The sensors measure intake manifold pressure, barometric pressure, water temperature, crankshaft position, carburetor throttle position, EGR valve position, and carburetor air inlet temperature. An interesting feature of the earlier EEC-I is the distributor. It is locked in place and cannot be rotated to adjust timing. There is also no mechanical advance mechanism as all these functions are controlled by the processor.

The EEC-II, introduced in 1979, worked in the same manner as EEC-I but with several refinements. First, the crankshaft sensor is mounted behind the engine's vibration damper and pulley. Second, and more significant is the use of an oxygen sensor located in the right exhaust manifold. The oxygen sensor measures the amount of oxygen in the spent exhaust gases and from this information, the computer processor adjusts the carburetor's air-fuel mixture, making sure that it is always within the calibrated parameters. Air-fuel adjustments are made through an electric stepper motor installed inside the carburetor.

In addition, EEC-II also controls fuel vapors that are stored in the evaporative control canister.

Similar to the previous control systems is the EEC-III, used on Ford engines from 1980-83. The major changes were made to the main processor assembly and the DuraSpark ignition control box. The EEC-III system uses a separate program module which plugs into a standardized main processor unit. Thus all EEC-III units have the same main processor but with varied program modules to suit the engine and car they are installed in. Also, many of the DuraSpark's functions have been incorporated into the main computer processor unit.

EEC-IV

The latest and most sophisticated Ford engine computer control system is the EEC-IV, in use since 1984. Through a series of sensors, EEC-IV controls fuel flow, ignition timing, and several other operations. EEC-IV performs in a way similar to its predecessors but with much greater speed, processing up to 1,250,000 commands per second. It uses a sixteen-bit microprocessor along with an 8K byte read-only memory chip. Most enthusiasts know this chip by its other name, PROM (Programmable Read Only Memory). PROMs tell the processor part of the computer what to do with the information that is received via the various engine sensors. We'll discuss PROMs a little later.

Let's look at the sensors that are used in the EEC-IV in current Mustangs:

MAS (Mass Airflow Sensor): measures airflow in terms of mass, which is independent of variables such as temperature, barometric pressure, and altitude.

ACT (Air Charge Temperature sensor): measures air temperature at the intake manifold.

BP (Barometric Pressure sensor): measures barometric pressure.

ECT (Engine Coolant Temperature sensor): measures coolant temperature and is used when the engine is cold. EEC-IV enriches the air-fuel mixture and advances timing 2deg to improve driveability when the engine is cold. This mode is in effect only at idle and at part-throttle. As the engine warms up, the settings gradually revert to their normal positions.

TPS (Throttle Position Sensor): measures throttle position and according to the information it sends to the computer, the computer adjusts fuel flow and timing accordingly. At wide-open throttle the computer turns off the air conditioner (if so equipped), the EGR valve, and maximizes fuel flow.

ISCV (Idle Speed Control Valve): It is through this valve that engine idle speed is regulated. Air is bypassed around the throttle plate which is then measured by the Mass Airflow Sensor.

HEGO (Heated Exhaust Gas Oxygen sensor): located in the exhaust headpipe, it measures air-fuel ratio. If it is too high or low (rich or lean), the signal sent to the computer will enable it to adjust fuel flow back to factory specs. Disconnecting the sensor will make the computer go into richer open loop mode. This may or may not (probably not) make the engine run any better. The oxygen sensor also compensates for a disconnected Air Charge Temperature (ACT) sensor or for increased fuel pressure—both "tricks" that are supposed to enrich the fuel mixture. Through the oxygen sensor, the computer merely compensates by reducing fuel to the injectors.

PIP (Profile Ignition Pickup): located in the Universal Ignition Distributor, it senses the position the distributor shaft is in relation to the crank and camshaft. From this information, the computer sets ignition timing and ignition advance. There are no centrifugal or vacuum advance mechanisms in the distributor. Maximum ignition advance with late-model 302ci engines is limited to 28deg.

There are other sensors that regulate emission-related functions, again all controlled by the EEC-IV unit. Turbocharged Mustangs also incorporate a knock sensor that detects engine knock which lets the computer retard timing to a safe setting.

The 1989 and earlier Mustangs also got a B/MAP (Barometric/Manifold Absolute Pressure) sensor. The information from this sensor and others was used by the computer to calculate a correction for airflow, which was based on a preset factory setting.

On V-8 engines it is located on the right inner fender, and on the left side on V-6 engines. The barometric sensors tell the computer of changes in atmospheric density and pressure while the MAP sensor picks up changes in intake manifold pressure.

Open Loop and Closed Loop Operation

The EEC-IV controls engine functions in two ways—through what is called an open loop system and a closed loop system. This is discussed in greater detail in the chapter on the induction system, but briefly, the engine is in open loop when it is first started, during quick throttle changes, and at wide-open throttle (WOT). In open loop mode, the engine is calibrated to produce maximum power. During closed loop operation, the computer is set to maximize fuel efficiency while meeting current emission standards.

As can be deduced, it is difficult to "fool" Ford's EEC systems into enriching the fuel mixture and allowing for more and quicker ignition advance. The only way to do this is to change the existing PROM chip. This can't be done with the EEC-IV, however; the PROM is soldered in and cannot be changed, unlike GM PROMs which are plugged in.

Aftermarket Chips

Currently, there are two chips on the market that modify the Mustang's computer existing parameters. One is from Hypertech, and the other is from Automotive Digital Systems, or ADS. (See Appendices for details.) Both achieve the same goal—enrich the

Here is a trick that is supposed to improve performance on fuel-injected Mustangs. The water temperature sensor has been disconnected to give the EEC-IV computer a false cold reading in order to send it into open loop mode. It doesn't work because the computer goes into open loop mode during wide-open throttle anyway, maximizing performance.

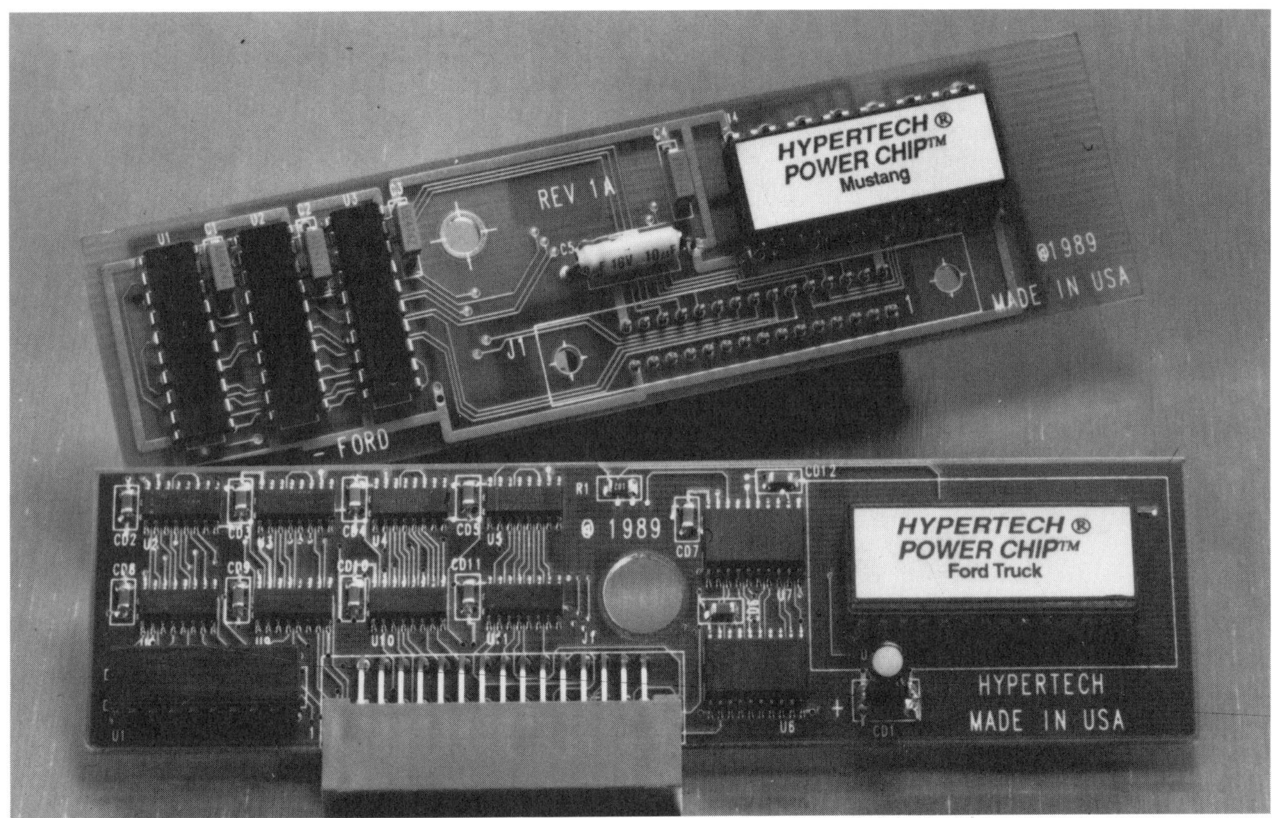

Hypertech's power chip for the Mustang. The chip substitutes its own values, replacing those that are initially set at the factory. For example, when the throttle is floored at a particular rpm, the computer looks at the factory-programmed values and then signals to the distributor the correct time to fire the plugs. With the Hypertech chip, the replaced values are more performance oriented. It is an effective way to get more performance from your EEC-IV computer. Hypertech

Autotronic Controls' MSD ignition increases spark duration by multiple firings, up to twenty per cycle. With multiple firings, there is more complete combustion. Dyno tests have shown that the MSD can improve horsepower output by 4 percent and prevent spark plug fouling. To connect the MSD unit on an EEC-IV equipped Mustang, you'll also need this special connector harness. Autotronic Controls Corp.

fuel mixture and ignition timing curves for better performance—but each does it in a different way. And both are very easy to install. The EEC-IV unit is located on the passenger-side footwell, behind the carpets. Once the carpet is removed, the unit can be brought out and the chip can be installed.

The ADS chip mounts in between the computer's wiring harness and the computer. It intercepts the signals that the computer receives, and modifies them so that the computer then issues commands for better performance. Two ADS chips are available, an A chip for Mustangs using the stock exhaust system and a B chip for those with a less restrictive exhaust system. Also part of the ADS system are a colder thermostat, an adapter plug for the computer, and an Octane Bar that fits in the distributor.

The Hypertech chip is made to fit in the computer's expansion port. It works by modifying the values that are preset at the factory. Thus, for example, when the throttle is floored, the computer receives data from the various engine sensors and then sets the timing and fuel curves according to the values that are preset in the PROM. The Hypertech chip substitutes its own values which produce better performance.

According to tests performed by *Hot Rod* and *Muscle Mustangs & Fast Fords* magazines, the results vary from about 1/4-1/2sec ET improvement on the drag strip with just the use of either chip.

There is very little you can do to the EEC-IV system to get better performance. One tip that most engine tuners recommend is to advance the initial timing to 14deg. It is worth several horsepower, but not much more than that because the EEC-IV is pretty well optimized already. For example, reducing initial timing to zero degrees results in only a 7hp loss. The EEC-IV is a very well thought out and flexible system.

For those interested in maximum power output using electronic fuel injection, the stock EEC-IV won't do the job. Using a camshaft that is several steps away from stock will get you driveability problems. You can use the stock EEC-IV computer, provided you can find someone to reprogram it, or you can purchase an aftermarket electronic system that you can program for specific fuel and ignition curves yourself. Digital Fuel Injection and Haltech Injection are two systems currently in use.

Ignition Modifications

As with all high-performance engines you should make sure that your distributor cap and rotor are of the highest quality and also use the best spark plug wires that you can afford. The stock spark plug wires have a carbon core which not only has high resistance, but eventually breaks down. Solid-core wires are the best in this respect, but unfortunately interfere with the car's radio and EEC-IV computer. Your best bet is to get one of the many spiral-core type wires available. These solid-core wires offer little resistance and suppress magnetic interference.

Ford engines would be best served with the addition of a multi-spark system, of which Autotronic Controls Corporation's MSD is the best known (see Appendices for address). During a firing cycle, rather than one spark, a series of sparks (usually up to twenty) is delivered to the spark plug and the results are obvious: much better combustion, noticeable improvement in idle quality, elimination of misfiring, the ability to fire fouled plugs, and more power. On engines with large, open combustion chamber designs (all current Ford engines) power can be improved as much as 4 percent. You can get the MSD ignition system through Motorsport.

Mounting an MSD unit is fairly easy. A good place to mount the control unit is on the left-front inner fender apron next to the shock tower. The rest of the installation involves plugging the unit's wire harness into the Mustang's wire harness. No cutting or splicing is required.

If you have a 1985 or earlier Mustang that did not come with the EEC-IV computer, there are several other things that you can do to maximize your ignition system's potential. The current EEC-IV equipped Mustangs have a Hall Effects distributor that sends a signal to the computer and the computer handles all ignition timing functions. Older engines with the DuraSpark system use a distributor that has a magnetic trigger with conventional vacuum and centrifugal advance systems which can be adjusted for better performance.

Depending on engine timing, the spark plugs are fired a certain number of degrees before the piston reaches the top of its stroke. This is to give the fuel mixture a chance to ignite (as it is not instantaneous) and expand, and thus drive the piston down on its power stroke. At higher rpm, the fuel mixture still needs the same amount of time to ignite, but because the engine is turning faster, the piston would be on its way down before the fuel mixture ignited. The spark

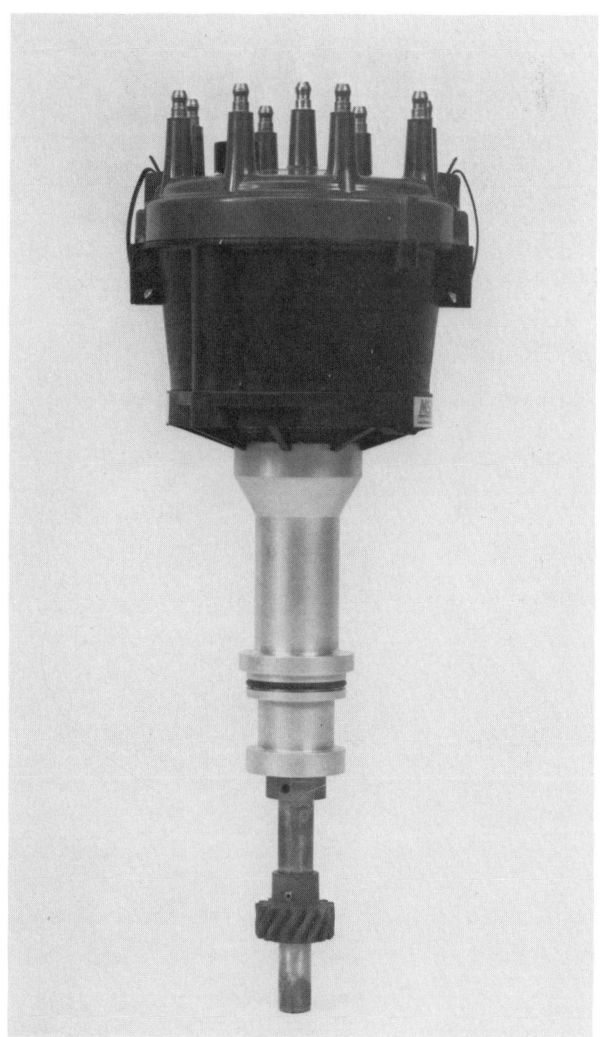

For racing you may want to consider using a higher quality distributor built to closer tolerances than the stock unit. This is a billet distributor from MSD. Autotronic Controls Corp.

Although the stock Ford coil has proven to be satisfactory for regular use, an aftermarket coil, such as MSD's Blaster, provides the extra reserve capacity needed in a high-performance engine. Autotronic Controls Corp.

advance mechanism in the distributor allows the spark timing to keep up the engine speed. This means that the spark has to be fired much earlier at higher rpm to compensate for engine speed. The centrifugal advance mechanism in the DuraSpark distributor advances the spark as engine speed increases, and retards it as speed decreases.

The rate of advance is controlled by two springs found underneath the distributor's breaker plate. By simply replacing the springs with lighter ones, the engine will accelerate quicker, resulting in better throttle response and more low-end power. Mr. Gasket and Motorsport both offer kits with different springs. A rule of thumb is to give the engine as much advance as it can tolerate without pinging. This simple and inexpensive modification is highly recommended.

There is also a vacuum advance mechanism on the distributor. This additional spark advance is controlled by the engine's vacuum. When engine vacuum is high, such as when the car is cruising, the engine can tolerate more advance than the centrifugal advance mechanism can provide, resulting in improved fuel mileage. It should never be disconnected as it is worth a 2-3mpg gain. Most Ford vacuum canisters can be adjusted to give more or less advance.

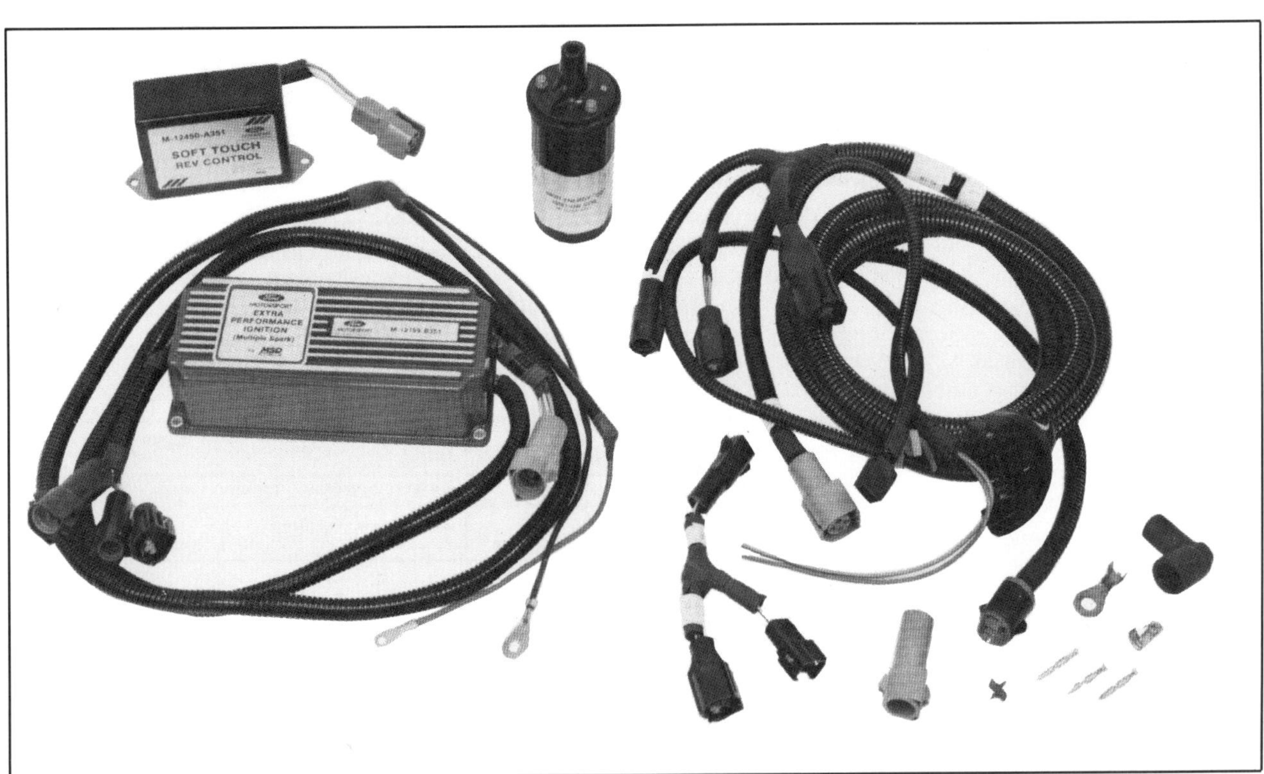

Motorsport offers this Ultra High Energy CD Ignition System which utilizes the MSD-AL control box, wiring harness, and coil. There is also an optional Soft-Touch rev controller which comes with three RPM Limiter Chips (6000, 7000, and 8000rpm). There is no point in equipping a street car with the Soft-Touch controller, though; the EEC-IV limits rpm to about 6200rpm anyway.

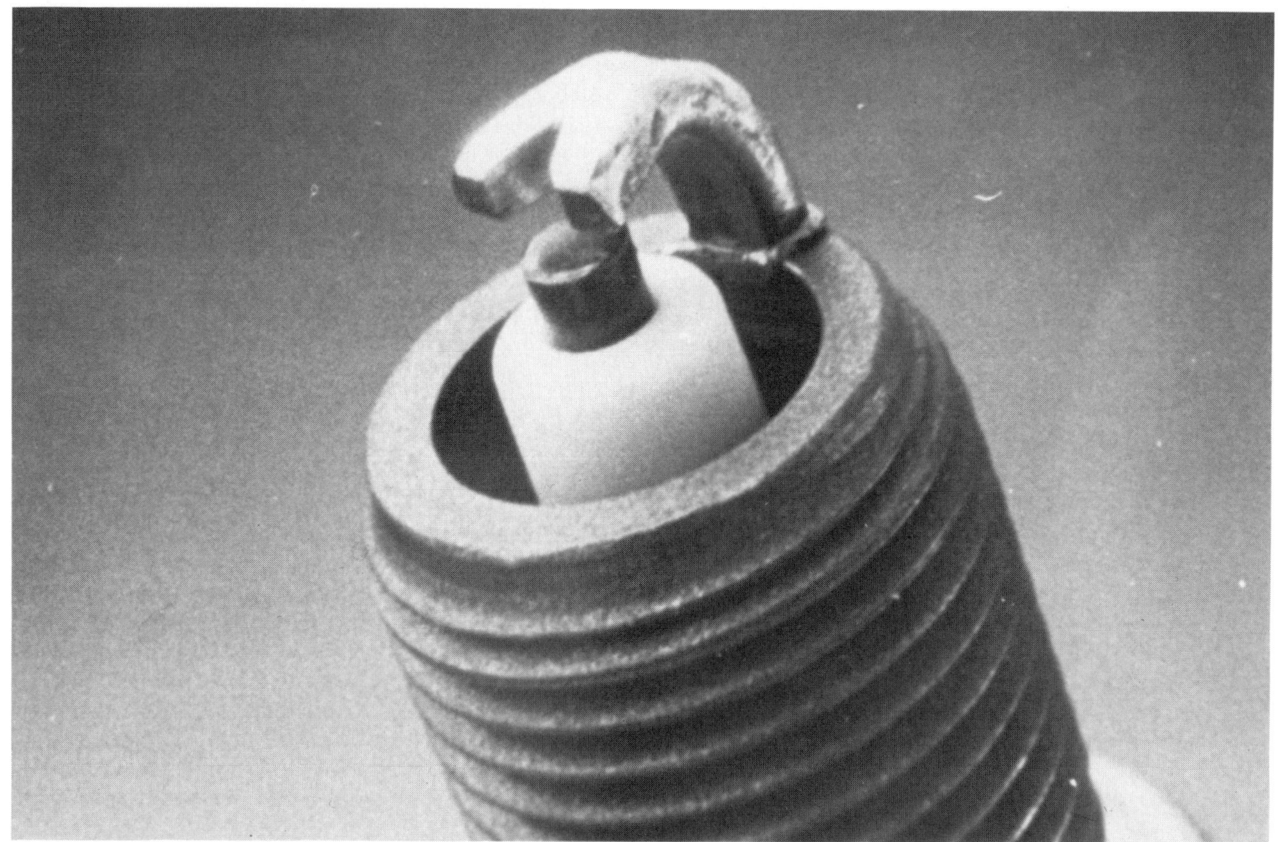

Ever heard of performance spark plugs? Splitfire, Incorporated's spark plug's V-electrode provides for better ignition for more complete combustion which results in lower emissions, better mileage, and more horsepower. They really work. Splitfire, Inc.

One final point concerns the distributor's drive gear. This is of importance if you are switching to a roller camshaft from a flat-tappet hydraulic cam. Roller camshafts require the use of steel gears while regular flat-tappet cam distributors come with a cast-iron gear. The cast-iron gear will quickly wear out with a roller cam. Bronze drive gears are usually recommended by aftermarket cam manufacturers and they will work either type of camshaft. However, since bronze is softer than cast iron or steel, it will wear at a faster rate.

Distributor Gear Selection Chart

Motorsport Part No.	Material	Color	Diameter Outside (in)	Diameter Inside (in)	Application
M-12390-A	Cast iron	Orange	1.249	0.467	289 and 302 w/hydraulic flat-tappet cam
M-12390-C	Bronze	Bronze	1.249	0.467	289 and 302 w/DuraSpark distributors
M-12390-D	Cast iron	Blue	1.249	0.531	302 flat-tappet cam w/EFI & all 351W models
M-12390-E	Bronze	Bronze w/ blue stripe	1.249	0.531	302 w/flat or roller cam w/EFI & all 351W models
M-12390-F	Steel	Yellow	1.249	0.531	302 w/roller cam & EFI models
M-12390-G	Cast iron	Green	1.421	0.531	351C, 351M, 400, 429, 460
M-12390-H	Bronze	Bronze w/ green stripe	1.421	0.531	351C, 351M, 400, 429, 460

Chapter 7

Supercharging, Turbocharging, and Nitrous Oxide Injection

There is no single engine modification that will yield more power than a supercharger. Without a doubt, supercharging is the most effective way of boosting power, bar none. Ford made several serious attempts with turbocharging on the four-cylinder Mustangs as well as the on the SVO Mustang with impressive results—the 2.3 liter four-cylinder which pumped out 88hp in stock form, put out 205hp in turbocharged form.

There are two methods of supercharging an engine: those using a belt-driven system, that is, driven by the engine's crankshaft by means of belts, called superchargers; and those that are exhaust driven, known as turbochargers.

If supercharging is so great, how come everyone isn't doing it? First, supercharging is still considered to be an exotic modification, meaning that the typical enthusiast doesn't know much about it. Second, supercharging is expensive. It often has been pointed out that when you add up the total cost of the usual modifications—new intake manifold, carburetor or fuel injectors, high-performance cylinder heads, hot-

Ford's second attempt at turbocharging was more successful in terms of reliability and power output. The 1984-86 SVO Mustangs were almost as quick as 302 powered GTs and handled better. The hood scoop channeled air into the intercooler. Ford Motor Co.

ter camshaft, and the like—the cost will be about the same as it would be to supercharge the engine from the beginning. This may be true, but the typical enthusiast usually modifies his or her engine piecemeal as the budget allows. On the other hand, supercharging an engine requires a fairly large initial expenditure, even for a mild application, say, a unit with a boost of 5-7psi. And if you really want to make a lot more power with higher boost pressures, you'll also have to get into the engine—which almost always requires new pistons and rods in addition to other modifications such as water injection and cooling system work. Supercharging your engine is an expensive proposition, but the results can be very satisfying.

Supercharging Defined

A supercharger is a device that forces more air-fuel mixture into the cylinders than the engine is able to draw in by itself. You may have heard of the concept of volumetric efficiency. For example, each cylinder of the 302 displaces 37.75ci of air when the piston is at bottom dead center. The force that fills the cylinder is atmospheric pressure, which is 14.7psi at sea level. If every time the piston went down the cylinder was completely filled, you could say that the engine was running at 100 percent volumetric efficiency. Unfortunately this rarely happens when the engine is running—atmospheric pressure isn't enough to fill the cylinders completely. The typical 302 HO engine as it leaves the factory is running at around 80 percent volumetric efficiency. The usual hot-rodding modifications—larger carburetors, highrise intake manifold, exhaust headers, and so on—will improve this figure but not to the 100 percent level.

Supercharging forces the air-fuel mixture in the cylinders to the point where 100 percent and even greater levels of volumetric efficiency can be attained. Restrictions that are inherent in normally aspirated engines such as small valves, less-than-ideal intake and exhaust ports, a low-lift camshaft, and poor exhaust manifolding are much less of a problem in a supercharged engine. The air-fuel mixture is anxious to get into the cylinder in a supercharged engine because the intake manifold acts like

The SVO turbocharged 2.3 liter was a very sophisticated engine. Besides using an intercooler to reduce intake temperature, the engine was strengthened to handle the additional horsepower. EFI was EEC-IV controlled and incorporated a knock sensor to control detonation. A nice system, but it lacked the 302's brute torque output which, after all, is what makes the 302 Mustangs accelerate as well as they do.

A variation on B&M's supercharger that uses two side-draft carburetors. Its lower profile allows it to fit under the standard Mustang hood. B&M Products

The Vortech is another centrifugal-type supercharger. In standard form it puts out 5psi boost, but it can be adjusted for 11psi. According to Vortech, air inlet temperature is 40deg less than the Paxton and the unit is lubricated by an engine-fed oiling system. Vortech Superchargers

a pressurized reservoir. The mixture is ready to rush into the cylinder as soon as the intake valve opens.

Supercharging also increases the effective compression ratio of the engine because a larger volume of air-fuel mixture is squeezed into the same space. Isn't that the same as using pop-up pistons? It is, but also remember that a supercharger forces the engine to operate at 100 percent volumetric efficiency. There is much more air-fuel mixture in the cylinder, which results in a bigger explosion. For this reason, it is not recommended that the static compression ratio in an engine be above 9.0:1, as the supercharger will blow the engine apart because of high cylinder pressures.

The major drawback of a supercharger is that it increases the temperature of the air-fuel mixture—air temperature rises as it is compressed. The higher the boost pressure, the higher the intake temperature. This can result in damaging detonation.

Belt-Driven Superchargers

There are many different types of superchargers. The most familiar one is the well-known GMC type used on dragsters, the Roots-type supercharger, most often referred to as a blower. This supercharger works much the same way as an engine's oil pump where two (or more) meshing rotors inside a housing compress the air-fuel mixture and force it on to the cylinders. It is a positive displacement supercharger, meaning that it moves the same volume of air during each lobe revolution. B&M Products of Chatsworth,

California (see Appendices), makes such a blower specifically for Ford 302 engines while Ford's 3.8 liter powered SC Thunderbird has a Roots-type blower as standard equipment. Roots-type blowers are driven by a belt-pulley system connected to the engine's crankshaft.

Positive displacement superchargers provide instantaneous response—there is no lag for boost to build up.

Another supercharger type that Ford enthusiasts are familiar with is the centrifugal type. Here an impeller, which looks like a fan, spins inside a housing. The air is accelerated by the spinning blades of the impeller. It is not a positive-displacement supercharger, however, as the amount of air flowing through it increases with the speed of the impeller. Thus, the impeller must spin at a very high speed in order to make boost, and boost drops off at low speed. Most common is the Paxton supercharger manufactured by Paxton Superchargers of Santa Monica, California, and like the Roots-type blowers, it is belt driven. (See Appendices for details.)

Exhaust-Driven Turbochargers

Another type of centrifugal-type supercharger is a turbocharger. Its main section is very much like the centrifugal supercharger, however, in a turbocharger, an additional impeller and housing is used, both sharing the same impeller shaft. Hot exhaust gas is used to spin this second impeller, thereby providing the motive power of the unit. The faster the engine turns, the more exhaust flow, and the more boost the turbocharger makes.

Turbochargers have some disadvantages when compared to belt-driven superchargers. Because

At a quick glance, it's hard to tell that this Mustang has Spearco's twin-turbo system. The system uses cast-iron replacement exhaust manifolds which tuck twin Garrett AiResearch turbochargers along each side of the engine, and they hook up to the stock exhaust system. The system is limited to 7psi boost and it is CARB certified. Spearco has higher capacity systems available as well. Spearco Performance Products, Inc.

both impellers share the same shaft, quite a lot of heat is transferred to the intake tract thereby reducing the turbo's efficiency. This can be alleviated by an intercooler—in effect, a radiator that is used to remove heat from the air entering the engine. Camshaft profile is also an important factor with a turbo: exhaust valve lift and duration have a direct bearing on how efficiently the turbocharger operates.

But probably the greatest drawback to a turbocharger is the problem of throttle lag. Because it takes time for exhaust flow to build up when the throttle is floored in a turbo application, it takes time for boost to build up as well. Although this problem can be minimized with careful design, it cannot be eliminated.

Draw-Through vs. Blow-Through Systems

There are only two ways a supercharger system can work. In a draw-through system, the supercharger is mounted in between the carburetor and intake manifold. The supercharger pulls or draws the air-fuel mixture through the carburetor (or fuel injectors), compresses it, and sends it on to the intake ports. The Roots-type blower is a draw-through system.

In a blow-through system, the carburetor or fuel injectors mount in between the supercharger and intake manifold. The supercharger pumps air (without any fuel) into the carburetor, or fuel-injection air tract, in the case of an EFI 302. The Paxton is a blow-through design.

Supercharger and Turbocharger Considerations

There is no point in installing a supercharger on a tired engine with loose rings and leaky valves. You're not going to realize much benefit, and you'll just hasten the engine's demise.

This is B&M's low-profile Roots-type blower for the small-block Ford which pumps out 410hp in this configuration. It uses J302 aluminum cylinder heads, a B&M camshaft, and a Holley four-barrel carburetor. A different hood or a hood scoop will probably be necessary. B&M Products

A question that often comes up with force feeding your engine is the amount of boost the typical engine can tolerate with no problems. A unit with a boost in the 5-7psi range is generally no problem for the stock 302 engine. The stock compression ratio is certainly low enough, and the engine can tolerate an occasional burst to 6000rpm without any problem. This is considered a mild application. Boost in the 8-10psi range is definitely borderline for a street engine, and above 10psi you are on very shaky ground. Remember that the 302 has lost about 70lb since the 1970s and a lot of that weight has come from the cylinder block. In order for the engine to tolerate a lot of boost, the block and associated parts must be strong enough to withstand all that extra pressure.

The more power an engine makes, the more heat it will produce. In a mild-boost situation, the stock radiator should be fine but anything beyond that will require a larger radiator. It is easy to overlook the cooling system. In addition, you should switch to a good synthetic motor oil if you go this route. Synthetic oils tolerate higher engine heat and also have the ability to draw heat away from hot engine parts much quicker than regular oils (see the section on synthetic oils in chapter 2).

High heat is also what causes detonation. There are three things you can do to eliminate detonation: use a higher octane gasoline, reduce the compression ratio, or retard engine timing. In a mild-boost applica-

The Paxton supercharger first came into use in 1952. It has been used on a variety of cars, including 1966-68 Shelby Mustangs when it was offered as an option. With its blow-through design, on EFI Mustangs all the Paxton does is force additional air through the intake tract. This particular installation includes nitrous oxide injection.

tion, you may not have to do much beyond using the best gasoline available, but you may also have to retard timing. It is also generally agreed that in a carbureted application, the carburetor must be enriched to the tune of 20-25 percent on the secondaries and about 10 percent on the primaries. Besides the fact that the engine will run better, the extra fuel acts as a coolant.

If you still encounter detonation, you should consider water injection. During a high-boost situation, a stream of water is injected into the air-fuel stream. The water vapor cools the cylinders enough to inhibit detonation. Water injection does not make more power, rather it permits the engine to run whereas before it would detonate—but only up to a certain point. Most manufacturers have water-injection kits available.

Turbocharged applications can also benefit through the use of a knock sensor. The knock sensor will retard timing to a safe level if detonation is sensed. The SVO four-cylinder engines came with a knock sensor.

Some turbo manufacturers use a system that retards ignition advance under hard acceleration to avoid acceleration. Again, it all depends on how much boost the system puts out.

The stock ignition system is sufficient to handle the spark requirements of a supercharged or turbocharged system. However, the addition of an MSD control unit along with high-quality spark plug wires,

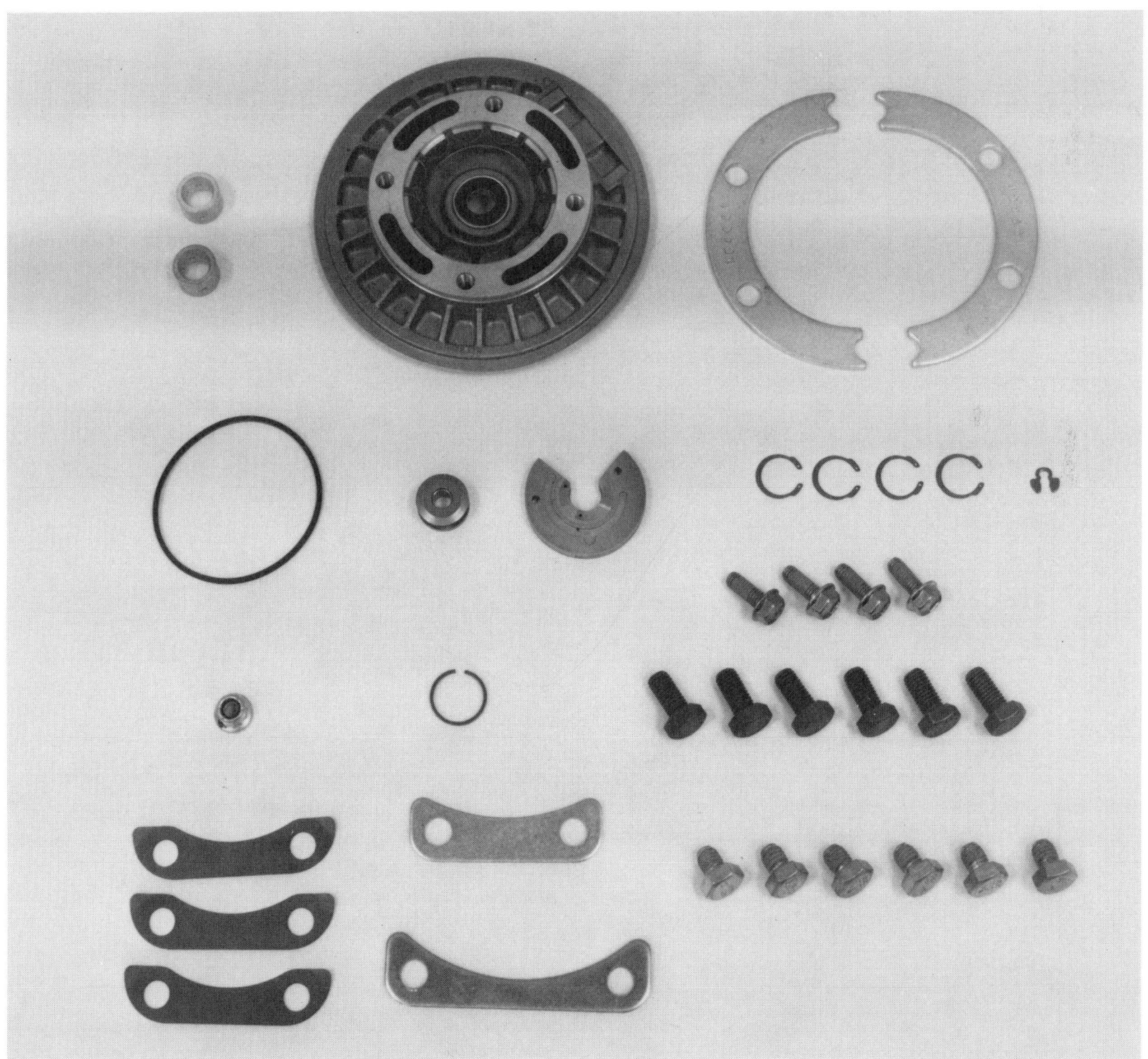

Turbochargers and superchargers do wear out; they can be sent out to specialized rebuilders or back to the manufac- *turer. Ford SVO owners can use this Turbocharger overhaul kit made by AiResearch. Ford Motor Co.*

distributor cap, and rotor is always recommended in a high-performance application.

It is logical to think that if the stock camshaft works fine in a supercharged or turbocharged application, then a high-performance camshaft with more duration and overlap is better yet because it would let in even more air-fuel mixture. This is not the case because what works in a normally aspirated engine doesn't work in such an application. In a normally aspirated engine, when both the intake and exhaust valves are open, overlap is actually helpful as the fast-moving exhaust helps to draw fresh mixture into the combustion chamber. In a supercharged or turbocharged situation, there is no need for lots of overlap because the intake mixture is always under pressure, rushing to fill the cylinder as soon as the intake valve opens. If both valves open, all that happens is that some of the pressurized mixture is pushed out the exhaust valve.

When it comes to camshaft recommendations, most cam manufacturers simply recommend their RV cams for such applications. In fact, the stock 302 cam is fine. The only other recommendation is to have the entire cam advanced 2-4deg. If you still feel that you need an aftermarket cam, have one ground with a dual-pattern profile, emphasizing exhaust duration. The supercharger or turbocharger gets more air-fuel mixture into the cylinders and consequently, it does take more time to get all the burned exhaust gases out.

It would also be a good idea to install heavier intake valve springs as boost can hold the intake valves off their seats. An intake valve that hangs up in a supercharged carbureted 302 is certain to spell disaster. The resulting backfire will most likely destroy the supercharger. This isn't a problem on an injected 302 since all that is pumped into the engine is more air.

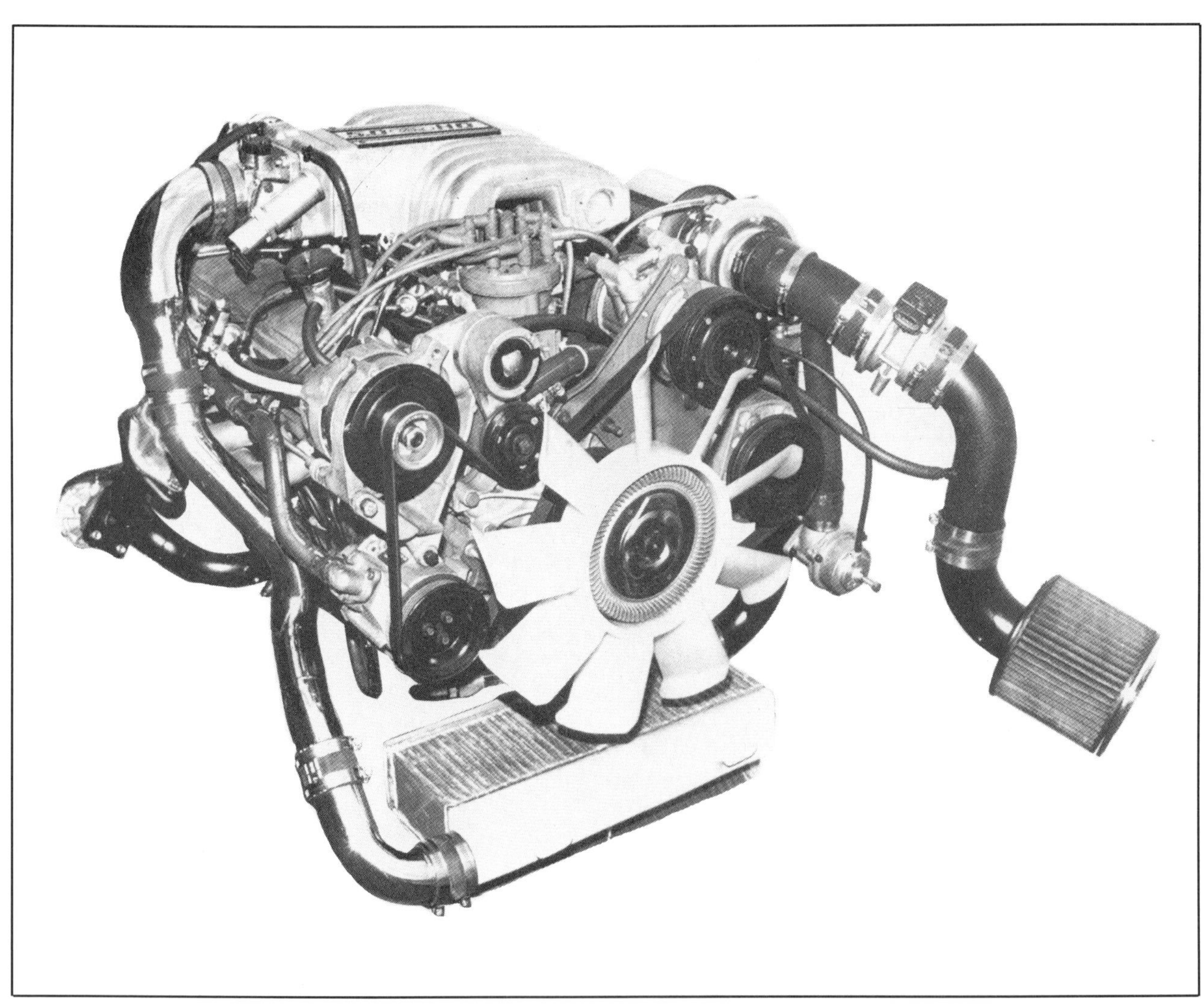

Turbo Technology's turbocharger for the 302 is more complex than a supercharger. This particular unit features a water-cooled turbocharger, and is said to increase horsepower to 450hp on an otherwise stock engine. Note the unique position of the unit's intercooler located in front of the car's antisway bar. Turbo Technology Inc.

It stands to reason that if the engine uses more air-fuel mixture, then you'll also need more fuel. It is best to follow the manufacturer's recommendations. Generally, you'll need more fuel volume and in some cases more pressure as well. On carbureted engines using a draw-through system, a high-capacity mechanical fuel pump such as the Carter shown in the Motorsport catalog should be sufficient. In blow-through systems you may also need more pressure, as fuel pressure should always exceed blower pressure by 3psi. On EFI systems, install the high-flow electric pump, Motorsport part number M-9A407-A50. It increases flow from 88 liters per hour to 110. An adjustable fuel pressure regulator, such as the one available from Kenne-Bell, is also recommended. You'll need about 100psi pressure on a system that has 10psi of boost.

If you are considering a high-boost system, you'll need to get into the engine as the stock pistons, rods, and block won't be able to handle the extra power. As stated earlier, the 302 engine has lost about 70lb since the 1970s and a lot of that weight has come from the cylinder block. The SVO four-bolt block is a must, as are heavy-duty rods with high-strength rod bolts and forged pistons. In addition, it is a good idea to have the block O-ringed, and use studs instead of head bolts. As with any high-performance engine, all specs should be blueprinted. Obviously, this is an expensive proposition, but if you want all the power that the 302 can produce, supercharging or turbocharging is the only way to go.

Recommendations

Kits are available in all supercharger configurations for the 302. Roots-type draw-through blowers are available from B&M, centrifugal blow-through superchargers are available from Paxton and Vortech Engineering, Incorporated, and turbocharger kits are

Ford's intercooler kit for the 2.3 liter. It can be adapted to fit other applications. Ford Motor Co.

available from Cartech Performance Systems, Texas Turbo Engineering, and Turbo Technology Incorporated (see Appendices for addresses).

Like any other engine modification, cost is an important factor when it comes to supercharging and turbocharging. A Roots-type blower, such as the B&M, is the least expensive and is particularly well suited for a carbureted application. Installation is not difficult either. On B&M's project Mustang, a dead-stock 302 pumped out 275hp with the B&M blower. With a camshaft change, output climbed to 336hp

This is the Cartech first generation turbo kit. From the air intake on the driver's side, the air is pushed through the intercooler mounted in front of the radiator and then to the intake manifold. With such long pipes, turbocharger sizing is critical in order to minimize throttle lag. Depending on any other modifications you've made, a single turbocharger system is good for 330-440hp. Cartech Performance Systems

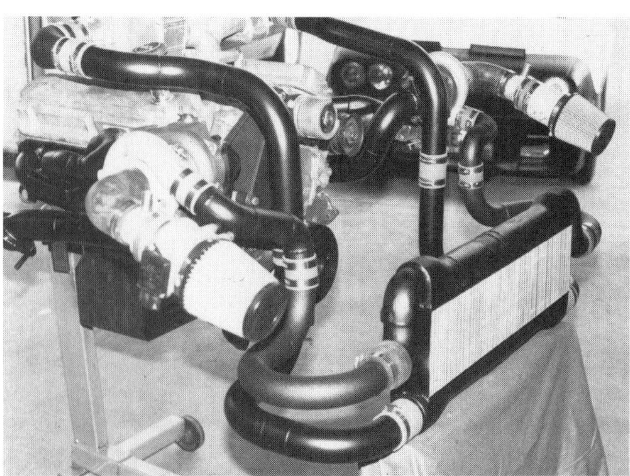

For serious, very high horsepower applications, Cartech has a twin-turbo kit. The system uses a twin throttle body plenum, special four-into-one headers, and an intercooler. Such a system requires major internal engine, cooling system, chassis, and driveline modifications. Using two smaller turbochargers rather than one large unit also tends to reduce throttle lag.

while the addition of J302 aluminum heads and a few other modifications brought output to 410hp. In all of B&M's tests, it was evident that the stock 302's ports and valves were a serious detriment to power output, especially on the exhaust side. It seems that with whatever type of supercharger or turbocharger you use, it would pay to have freer flowing heads.

For a fuel-injected engine a centrifugal-type supercharger, such as the Vortech and Paxton, has several advantages—cost and ease of installation are two. The Paxton also, at this writing, has a CARB (California Air Resources Board) exemption, making it legal for street use in all fifty states. You can expect about a 100-125hp increase with this type of supercharger and there are intercooler kits available to boost output even more, depending on the application. Once again, even minor porting will be extremely beneficial in terms of output.

The Roots and centrifugal type blowers, while meaning a major increase in the horsepower department, are still a mild-boost application. For someone who wants all-out performance, turbocharging is the way to go. The financial commitment for the kit alone can be over $3,000, and more for such things as timing controls, by-pass valves, and water injection. For serious applications running over 10psi boost, you'll also need to get into the engine with new pistons, head work, and so on as described earlier, so the 302 will live. It all depends on how fast you want to go and how much you want to spend.

The SVO Mustang came with a fairly sophisticated turbocharger system and it is possible to modify the stock system for more power. The 1986

The exhaust system on a supercharged or turbocharged engine should be as free-flowing as possible. As exhaust header scavenging principles don't apply on such systems, unequal tube length headers, such as these Cartech twin-turbo headers, do not limit output. Cartech Performance Systems

110

An intercooler should be used to maximize output from a turbo application—cooler air is denser, resulting in more power. The Vortech Intercooler kit fits behind the stock intake opening. Cartech Performance Systems

versions were putting out 205hp at 15.5psi boost. To get more power from the 2.3 liter you'd have to run a more radical camshaft, open up the cylinder heads with larger valves and ports, and resort to an aftermarket fuel-injection system, such as the Haltech. This would probably ruin its good driveability. One easy modification would be to install a freer flowing exhaust system with an efficient muffler, such as the Flowmaster. Any exhaust modification on a supercharged or turbocharged application is beneficial. One also has to consider the fact that the SVO's resale value is not the greatest. It may not make good sense to spend $3,000 on engine work on a car worth $4,500.

Although it hasn't been offered with the Mustang, the possibility exists that the supercharged 3.8 liter V-6, first offered on the 1989 Thunderbird, might find its way into a Mustang in the coming years. The 3.8 liter currently puts out 210hp, but those Mustang enthusiasts currently owning a 1983-86 3.8 liter equipped Mustang shouldn't get their hopes up thinking that this supercharger is easily adaptable to their engines. The supercharged V-6 has sequential multiport fuel injectors, a roller cam, a distributorless ignition system, a knock sensor, a stronger block and cylinder heads, special hypereutectic pistons, a stronger crankshaft, an intercooler, and a host of other features. In addition, the 3.8 liter uses a different EEC-IV computer.

Nitrous Oxide Injection

Considering the amount of power you can get from a nitrous oxide system, it has to be rated highly among the modifications that you can make. However, it is also dangerous because it is easy to lose an

The latest factory supercharging system is on the Ford Thunderbird SC and Mercury Cougar XR7. It is a sophisticated system using Eaton three-lobe rotors. The 3.8 liter uses a special block, heads, internal components, a distributorless ignition system, and a host of other unique features. Ford Motor Co.

111

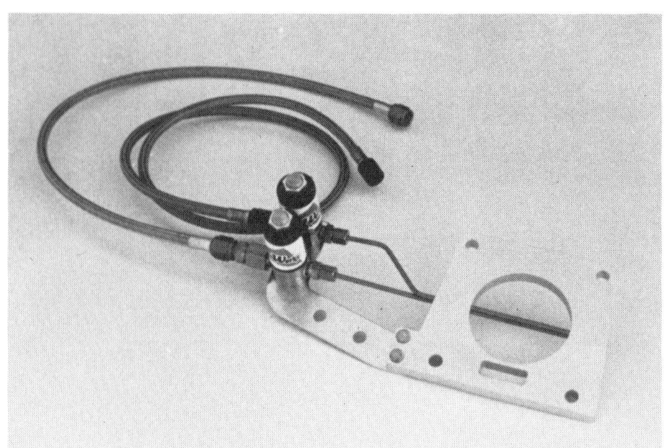

Easy installation and a large power jolt are some of the positive aspects of nitrous oxide injection. This system is made for Ford V-8 and V-6 fuel-injected engines and mounts in the system's intake tract. The Nitrous Works

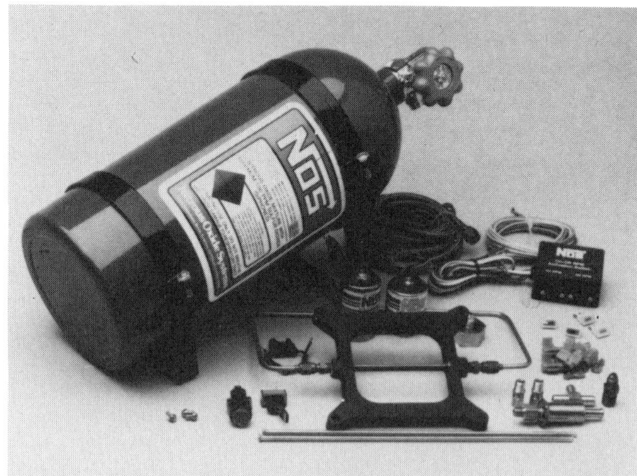

Nitrous Oxide Systems (NOS) of Cypress, California, is well known for its nitrous kits. This particular system is for a four-barrel carbureted engine. The tank is usually located in the trunk and will last between two to three minutes of continuous use—something you don't want to do since the engine will self-destruct. Nitrous use should be limited to short 10-15sec bursts. The most critical aspect of any nitrous installation is to make sure that the engine gets enough fuel when the system is engaged. An excess of fuel is required to keep the engine from detonating. Nitrous Oxide Systems

engine by keeping the gas pedal on the floor too long. Most nitrous oxide systems operate only when the gas pedal is floored.

If you remember, supercharging makes the intake mixture denser by compressing it so that more of it fills the combustion chamber. Nitrous oxide does the same thing, but by a different method. As the nitrous oxide gas decomposes, it releases the 36 percent or so of oxygen that it contains. By adding an additional quantity of fuel to this extra oxygen you have the makings of an instantaneous boost in horsepower. In addition, as the nitrous oxide changes from its liquid stored form to a gas, temperature drops, again creating a denser mixture. Still, there are problems. All that extra oxygen and fuel create a huge amount of heat in the combustion chamber and thus can cause detonation. For this reason, the amount of fuel that is injected along with the nitrous oxide gas is considerably more than is normally required in order to keep temperatures down. If there is a malfunction in the system, combustion chamber and piston temperatures will hit stratospheric levels, usually resulting in melted pistons. The same thing can also result if the nitrous is left on too long.

The typical nitrous oxide system will consist of a tank of nitrous oxide, which can be stored in a convenient place, such as the trunk. The pressure in the tank, 750psi, is enough to inject the gas into the intake manifold. An electric fuel pump is used to inject the additional fuel that is necessary. Both the nitrous gas and extra fuel are controlled by a pair of electrically operated solenoids which are normally connected to a switch that is activated only when the throttle is floored. How long a tank lasts depends on how efficient the system is, but two to three minutes is typical.

Used judiciously, a nitrous oxide system can provide a massive burst of power just when you need it.

Chapter 8

Transmission and Driveline

Modifying your engine for more power will invariably put more strain on the rest of your car's driveline. This consists of the transmission and rear axle. The first-generation Mustangs had plenty of built-in reserve capacity in this area, but the current third-generation Mustangs weren't originally designed for the amount of torque that the current 302 engine pumps out. Because the 302 was modified by the factory to put out more power, the Mustang's transmission and rear end have been a source of problems

The World Class T-5 five-speed manual transmission. When the transmission was originally designed, it wasn't intended for the 302's current torque output. With a 305lb-ft torque capacity, the T-5 is a marginal unit. Ford Motor Co.

Powershifting causes stress cracks (arrow) which eventually result in broken gear teeth and transmission failure.
Steve Collison

for the enthusiast, but there are a number of things you can do to correct them.

Manual Transmissions

A sore point in the Mustang's driveline is the Borg-Warner T-5 five-speed overdrive manual transmission. This transmission was introduced on 302

Gouging occurs when the gear teeth are overloaded as the mating gear tooth breaks through the oil's lubricating film. A synthetic fluid would stand up longer because it has higher film strength. Steve Collison

powered Mustangs in 1983 and even at that time when the 302 was putting out 175hp, the T-5 was considered to be a marginal transmission. Breakage was common, and even though the transmission has been strengthened and its torque-handling capability increased over the years, it is still no match for the 302. When the transmission was designed it was not envisioned that horsepower ratings would start rising again. It may be of some comfort to Mustang owners that Camaro and Firebird owners have exactly the same problems as they, too, use the T-5.

Of course the T-5 can last the life of the car, provided you don't beat on it or powershift it. You can say that any transmission has only so many powershifts in it before it fails, but in the T-5's case the number is minimal. One powershift won't generally break a gear, but the cumulative effect of many powershifts will. High-shock loads imparted during powershifting cause stress and fatigue cracks on the gear teeth until they eventually break off. This is especially so on the third gear.

Spalling can also occur on the pilot journal of the mainshaft (see photo). This occurs under severe use combined with poor lubrication under hard acceleration, when high g-forces push the transmission oil to the rear. Spalling will continually worsen, even under light loads, once it starts.

There are certain things you can do to help extend the life of your T-5. First, use a quality synthetic transmission fluid such as Red Line's MTL. Synthetics

114

<table>
<tr><td colspan="2">T-5 Transmission Usage</td></tr>
<tr><td>Part Number</td><td>Description</td></tr>
<tr><td>E3ZR-7003-A</td><td>Fitted on 1983 Mustangs, close-ratio box with 0.73 overdrive gear which interchanges only with 1984 T-5s. It uses a long throw shifter.</td></tr>
<tr><td>E4ZR-7003-DA</td><td>1984-85 Mustangs, close-ratio box with 0.63 overdrive gear, long throw shifter.</td></tr>
<tr><td>E5ZR-7003-FA</td><td>1985 Mustangs, wide-ratio box, short throw shifter. This and subsequent T-5s use fiberlined blocking rings.</td></tr>
<tr><td>E6ZR-7003-FA, FB</td><td>1986 Mustangs, wide-ratio box. Left side cover has electrical connection for neutral position sensor.</td></tr>
<tr><td>E6ZR-7003-FB</td><td>1987-89 Mustangs, wide-ratio box.</td></tr>
<tr><td>E9ZR-7003-A</td><td>Partial usage on 1989 Mustangs, wide-ratio box, seven-tooth speedometer drive gear, service replacement box.</td></tr>
<tr><td>F0ZR-7003-AA</td><td>1990-91 Mustangs, wide-ratio box, eight-tooth speedometer drive gear.</td></tr>
<tr><td>M-7003-CA</td><td>Motorsport World Class T-5, close-ratio box, no electrical connections on cover.</td></tr>
<tr><td>E4ZM-7003-A</td><td>Motorsport World Class T-5, close-ratio box with electrical connection on left cover for EFI cars requiring neutral position sensor.</td></tr>
</table>

have much higher film strength, can withstand heat better, reduce drag, and flow freely at very cold temperatures. Also change the fluid every 5,000 miles, if you decide to stay with conventional fluids. Don't use hypoid gear lubes in the T-5. They are too thick for the T-5's close tolerances and small oil passages.

Gear lube is also not compatible with the fiber-lined blocking rings on T-5s built since 1985.

It is also a good idea to install new shift fork pads whenever the transmission is opened up. They are inexpensive and tighten up sloppy shift forks. Speaking of shifting, the Hurst shifter for the T-5 feels great

Inadequate lubrication and overloading cause spalling (arrow) on the pilot journal at the front of the input shaft. *Once this starts, it will continue to worsen, even under light loads.* Steve Collison

Rounded teeth on this third gear are also evidence of hard usage. Steve Collison

and is recommended. It does transmit more noise, though, because it doesn't have the rubber insulation that the stock Ford unit has.

Still, the best life extender for the T-5 is to refrain from powershifting. And *never* powershift fifth gear, as most T-5s will fail.

Two T-5s have been available on the Mustang: a close-ratio box on 1983-84 models with ratios of 2.95, 1.94, 1.34, 1.00, and 0.63 (0.73 on 1983), and a wide-ratio box from 1985 on with ratios of 3.35, 1.94, 1.34, 1.00, and 0.63. Some 1985 cars got the close-ratio box, and some 1989 transmissions have 1.99/1.33 second/third gears. (See chart.)

Motorsport also offers a close-ratio, heavy-duty World Class T-5. It has a 305lb-ft torque capacity. Although it is a heavy-duty transmission, it too is not strong enough for the 302. Motorsport also offers the innards to convert a wide-ratio box to a close-ratio unit.

You can also fine tune the overdrive gear on your T-5. Custom overdrive ratios are available from Char-Trends of Maryland Heights, Missouri, which allow you to have a 0.59, 0.63, 0.73, or 0.80 overdrive ratio on the close-ratio T-5 and 0.68, 0.72, 0.83, or 0.92 ratios on the wide-ratio box. (See Appendices for address.)

Replacing the shift fork pads (arrows) is a good idea whenever your T-5 is apart. They'll tighten up the slack in the shift forks. Steve Collison

In very high horsepower applications, the T-5 won't work at all. In such cases you'll have to replace the T-5 with an aftermarket transmission such as the Richmond Gear five– and six–speed units, the B&W T-56 or the Tremac T-3550.

Clutch and Pressure Plate

If you're going to drive your Mustang hard you'll want to upgrade the clutch and pressure plate to withstand any additional power output from the engine. The first thing to consider is the flywheel. The stock flywheel is made from cast iron and is adequate for high-performance use, provided you don't rev over 5000rpm. In a high-performance situation, the stock flywheel won't do at high engine speeds; you're risking the possibility of a flywheel explosion. So even before you consider what kind of flywheel to get, you should invest in a steel bellhousing. The Lakewood steel bellhousing is available from Motorsport under part number M-6392A, and is designed for 302 Mustangs with the T-5 transmission.

Performance flywheels are made from either high-strength steel or aluminum. A lighter flywheel made from aluminum lets the engine rev faster once you get the car going, and is preferable in a road-racing situation. A heavier steel flywheel is recommended for street use as it holds more rotational inertia, allowing the car to accelerate faster from a standing start. These flywheels also have special frictional facings on the clutch side which complement a particular type of clutch.

A clutch disc consists of a splined hub that mates with the transmission's input shaft, an outer ring, and the lining material which can either be bonded or riveted. For street use, always use a clutch that has a cushioned hub. The cushioning effect is achieved by five small coil springs that are attached to the outer ring. The springs dampen the shock forces during engagement of the clutch. A race clutch disc will not have these springs, thereby transmitting the shock to the rest of the driveline, and the facing materials are often designed to wear away quickly.

A street clutch usually has an organic or non-organic type lining which allows for a smooth engagement while some high-performance units use a metallic lining. Like metallic brakes, these need to be heated up a bit to grab properly but they last considerably longer.

The biggest mistake that you can make is to install a heavy-duty pressure plate. This not only puts strain on your left leg, but it also puts a lot of strain on, and increases wear on the clutch linkage. The stock pressure plate is a diaphragm type, which is easier to disengage than Long or Borg & Beck type pressure plates. Early diaphragm clutches had a reputation of hanging up between shifts, but the

Powershifting and overloading will require the replacement of your T-5 or its internals. Shown is the countershaft cluster gear and third speed gear for the World Class T-5 which is available from Motorsport. Ford Motor Co.

The old standby for improving acceleration—changing the rear-axle gears. Changing rear-axle gears has a profound effect on the way your Mustang runs. Changing to a higher numerical ratio will improve acceleration but the engine will rev higher during cruising, thereby reducing mileage. Conversely, changing to a lower numerical ratio improves mileage at the expense of acceleration. You'll also have to change the speedometer gear in the transmission so that your speedometer will show correct miles per hour. Randy Ream

current units are reliable and dependable. Stick with a diaphragm clutch, but make sure to use quality parts.

The 1979-85 Mustangs came with a 10.0in clutch while 1986 and later cars came with a 10.5in unit. The SVO came with a 9.0in clutch. Highly modified Mustangs and those with nitrous or supercharging should use a heavy-duty clutch and pressure plate. The stock diaphragm pressure plate is made from cast iron while high-performance units can be made from nodular iron or steel.

If you are installing the 10.5in clutch assembly on a 1979-85 Mustang, you should also install Motorsport's clutch upgrade kit, part number M-7553-A302, which includes a beefed-up clutch release fork and a heavy-duty, self-adjusting, Teflon-lined clutch cable. The kit's components are standard equipment on 1986 and later Mustangs. You'll also need to replace the stock flywheel when you are replacing the 10.0in clutch with a 10.5in unit.

Automatic Transmission

Prior to 1984, the automatic used behind most Ford engines was the three-speed C-4 or C-5. The C-5 was basically a C-4 with a lock-up converter designed to give better mileage. Starting in 1984, they were replaced by the AOD (automatic overdrive) on the 3.8 liter and 302ci engines. The AOD is a four-speed

The 1986 and later 302 powered Mustangs got a larger 8.8in rear-axle assembly with twenty-eight-tooth spline axles. Heavy-duty applications would benefit from the use of thirty-one spline axles along with a thirty-one-spline differential. Ford Motor Co.

automatic, with the fourth gear having a 0.66 overdrive ratio.

The main advantage of the AOD is its overdrive gear, which produces good highway mileage. Another advantage is that the torque converter is completely by-passed in fourth gear, eliminating its inherent slippage. It is also by-passed to the tune of 60 percent in third gear as well.

Several modifications can be made to improve the AOD's performance. The first involves recalibrating the valve body's hydraulic pressure by installing a shift kit. The other involves tearing down the transmission and replacing weak stock components with stronger parts. These are fairly complex operations and aren't recommended for the typical enthusiast. If you have a 1987 or earlier AOD, you should plan on installing the AOD Rear Lube kit, Motorsport part number M-7060-A, which is incorporated in all 1988 and later units. It provides much better lubrication to the planetary gears. You'll have to take the transmission apart to install this kit, however. About the only other part that is available from Motorsport is a deep-sump transmission oil pan, which increases capacity by ½qt.

There are parts available from aftermarket suppliers, such as B&M Products, to enhance the AOD's performance and reliability. These include performance valve bodies, shift kits, and high-stall torque converters.

A high-stall speed torque converter may be OK on the drag strip, but *never* use one on a street car. A converter that has a higher stall speed allows more slippage before it engages—it is like revving up the engine without engaging the clutch in a manual transmission. By allowing for more slippage, the engine produces more off-the-line acceleration. The drawback to a high-stall converter is poor fuel mileage and a higher transmission fluid temperature. This can be quite detrimental to the transmission's

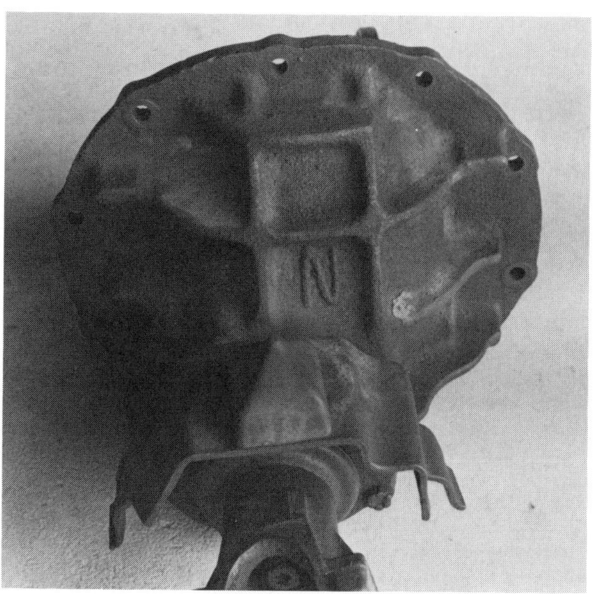

Although the 8.8in rear axle assembly is plenty strong, for all-out racing the old 9.0in rear is even stronger. The ones with the letter N on the case are made from stronger nodular iron. You might be able to find a used one at a salvage yard, but new assemblies are available from Motorsport. Randy Ream

life expectancy. Increasing transmission fluid temperature by just 10 percent can reduce the transmission's life by 50 percent.

Traction-Lok differential for the 9.0in rear. Ford has used the name Traction-Lok since 1969 to describe its limited-slip differential. The Traction-Lok's advantages are evident in bad, wet, icy weather conditions as it allows the transfer of torque to the opposite axle if there is slippage. It also works on the track. Randy Ream

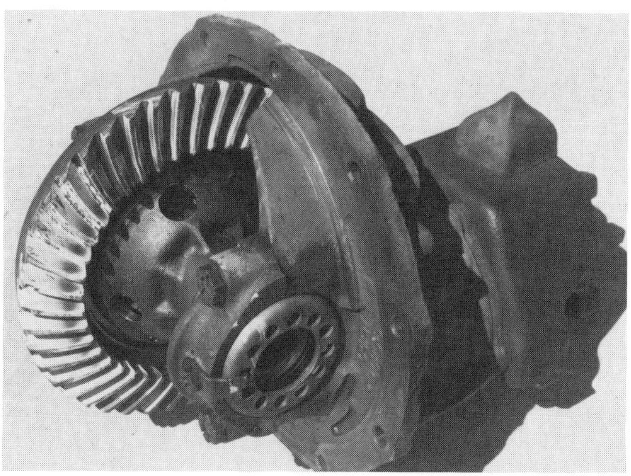

One advantage of the 9.0in rear is that the housing—the "pumpkin"—can easily be removed and replaced by another housing with a different gear ratio. Randy Ream

About the only other thing you can do for your automatic transmission is to install a transmission oil cooler. There are many available, including one from Motorsport, part number M-7A095-SR. It has a self-regulating feature which by-passes cold transmission fluid automatically until its viscosity decreases.

It is quite likely that anytime your engine overheats, your transmission fluid also will overheat as the stock fluid cooler is routed through the radiator. In such cases, it would be wise to change transmission fluid as well. If this isn't done, you will reduce the life of the transmission. You should also use a synthetic transmission fluid.

Rear Axle

The rear axle used to be a problem with 302 powered Mustangs because the standard axle came only with a 7.5in ring gear, which just wasn't strong enough to handle the 302's torque. Starting in 1986, an 8.8in rear replaced the 7.5in unit on 302 powered cars, thereby ending most rear axle problems. The 8.8in rear is strong but for very high power applications, it too should be replaced with the venerable 9.0in rear which is available from Motorsport along with a slew of performance axle shafts, differentials, carrier assemblies, and hardware. Nine-inch rears were commonly used on 1960s and 1970s full-size cars and most larger than 302ci equipped intermediates and Mustangs as well. You may be able to find one in a salvage yard, but it will have to be shortened to fit in the current Mustang.

If you have a pre-1986 Mustang with the 7.5in rear, the only thing that you can do is replace it; it can't be modified to withstand any extra torque. In fact, it can't handle the torque put out by the stock 1982-85 302.

Axle ratio selection depends on how you are planning to use your Mustang. With the advent of overdrive transmissions, choosing a high numerical axle ratio won't negatively affect mileage as badly as it used to with older performance Mustangs. Motorsport offers ratios from 3.08:1 to 4.10:1 for 7.5in and 8.8in rear axles.

If you have an open rear end, installing a Traction-Lok differential is recommended for improved acceleration. The Traction-Lok is a limited-slip type differential which divides torque between the two axles. If one wheel loses traction, the clutch assembly inside the unit disengages and the torque is transferred to the other axle. In an open rear, the car would just sit, with one wheel slipping. The Auburn cone-type differential is a limited-slip type unit available for both the 7.5 and 8.8in rears for severe use applications.

Over the years, there has been a lot of romance associated with the Detroit Locker differential. It

The Auburn locking differentials use cones instead of clutch plates and are available for Ford 7.5 and 8.8in rears. This is a limited-slip type unit but it is made for severe use, such as racing. Ford Motor Co.

The Detroit Locker differential is strictly a race-only item. With this type, both wheels are locked, whether going straight or around a corner. Ford Motor Co.

should never be used on the street, as both axle shafts are locked in place—there is no differential action when going around a corner—meaning that one tire is dragging. In addition, a Detroit Locker has to be preloaded every time you stop. You have to put your left foot on the brake while you rev the engine; when you hear a clunk, then you are ready to go.

As with any other mechanical part that requires lubrication, use a synthetic lubricant rather than conventional lubricants in your rear axle.

A quality clutch is necessary for any high-performance application—not only to make sure that the engine's power is transmitted to the rear wheels, but also for safety's sake. Stock cast-iron components aren't reliable under hard usage at engine speeds over 5000rpm. Shown are a billet flywheel (left), high-performance clutch disc (center), and a nodular case diaphragm pressure plate (right). Ford Motor Co.

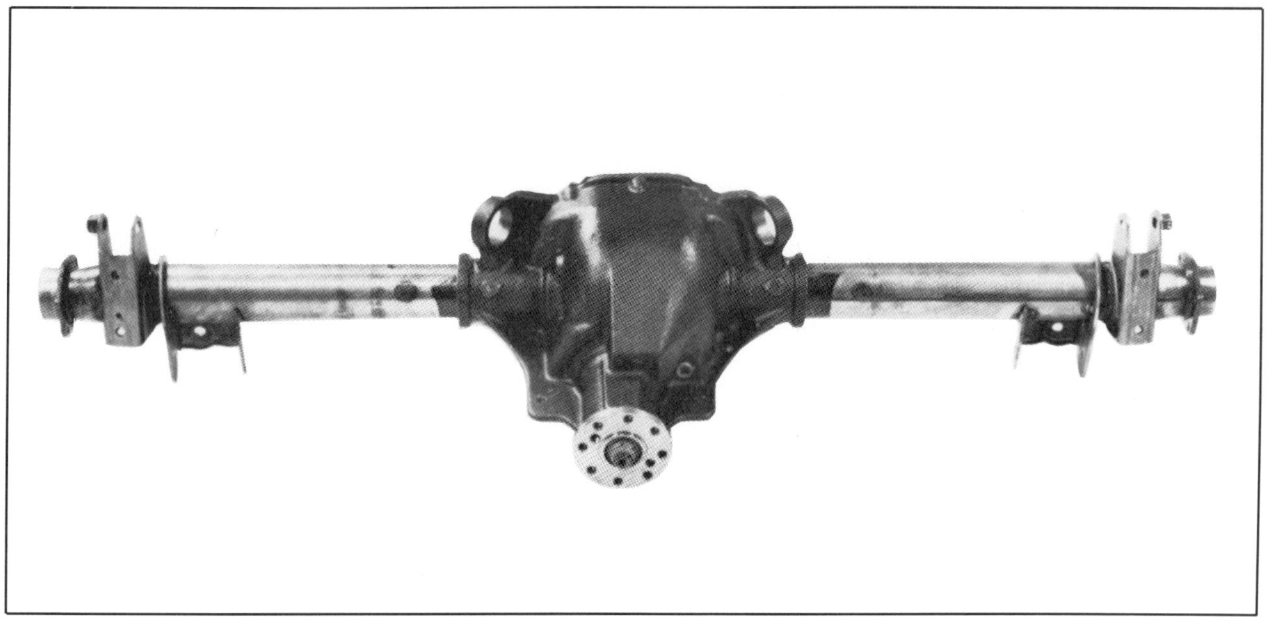

The 1985 and earlier Mustangs can benefit from the installation of a twenty-eight-spline 8.8in rear-axle assembly available from Motorsport. The 8.8in rear is about 35 percent stronger than the 7.5in stock unit and includes a Traction-Lok differential. It is a bolt-on installation. Ford Motor Co.

For all-out racing, this Tilton clutch assembly includes the very best components—flywheel, disc, pressure plate, and throw-out bearing. This one is for a four-cylinder Mustang. Racer Walsh Co.

B&M's Transpak kit is a must if your Mustang has the AOD automatic transmission. It improves shift quality while altering shift points. In addition, by reducing the overlap period when the transmission is in two gears during an upshift, the transmission's reliability is improved. B&M Products

122

T-5 Manual Transmission Speedometer Gear Usage Chart

The installation of speedometer drive and driven gears shown will provide approximately correct mile per hour readings with 7.5 and 8.8in axles on T-5 equipped Mustangs with Goodyear P225/60VR15 Gatorback tires.

Axle Ratio	Speedometer Part Number	Drive Gear Number of Teeth	Color	Speedometer Part Number	Drive Gear Number of Teeth	Color
3.27:1	E3ZZ-17285-A	7	Yellow	C0DZ-17271-B	19	Pink
3.45:1	E3ZZ-17285-A	7	Yellow	C1DZ-17271-A	20	Black
3.55:1	E3ZZ-17285-A	7	Yellow	C1DZ-17271-A	20	Black
3.73:1	E3ZZ-17285-A	7	Yellow	C4DZ-17271-A	21	Red
4.10:1	E3ZZ-17285-B	6	Black	C1DZ-17271-A	20	Black

Note: The 1990-92 Mustang GT and 5.0 liter LX models have an eight-tooth speedometer drive gear. Rear axle ratios numerically higher than 3.27:1 require a reduction gear unit in the speedometer cable.

The Centerforce clutch system from Midway Industries has a centrifugal assist feature which provides 30 percent more holding capacity than the stock clutch while maintaining stock pedal feel. Midway Industries, Inc.

Automatic Transmission Speedometer Gear Usage Chart

Axle Ratio	Gear Teeth	Tire Size	Part Number	Number of Teeth	Color
3.27:1	7	225/60VR15	C7VY-17271-A	19	Tan
3.27:1	7	225/60VR16	C7SZ-17271-B	18	Gray
3.27:1	8	225/60VR16	D0OZ-17271-B	21	Purple
3.45/3.55:1	7	225/60VR15	C8SZ-17271-B	20	Orange
3.45/3.55:1	7	225/60VR16	C7VY-17271-A	19	Tan
3.73:1	7	225/60VR15	D0OZ-17271-B	21	Purple
3.73:1	7	225/60VR16	C8SZ-17271-B	20	Orange

The speedometer drive gear is machined into the output shaft on rear wheel-drive automatic transmissions. Therefore, changing a drive gear requires a new output shaft—not a practical solution. To determine the number of drive gear teeth, remove the extension and count the teeth. Most have seven or eight teeth.

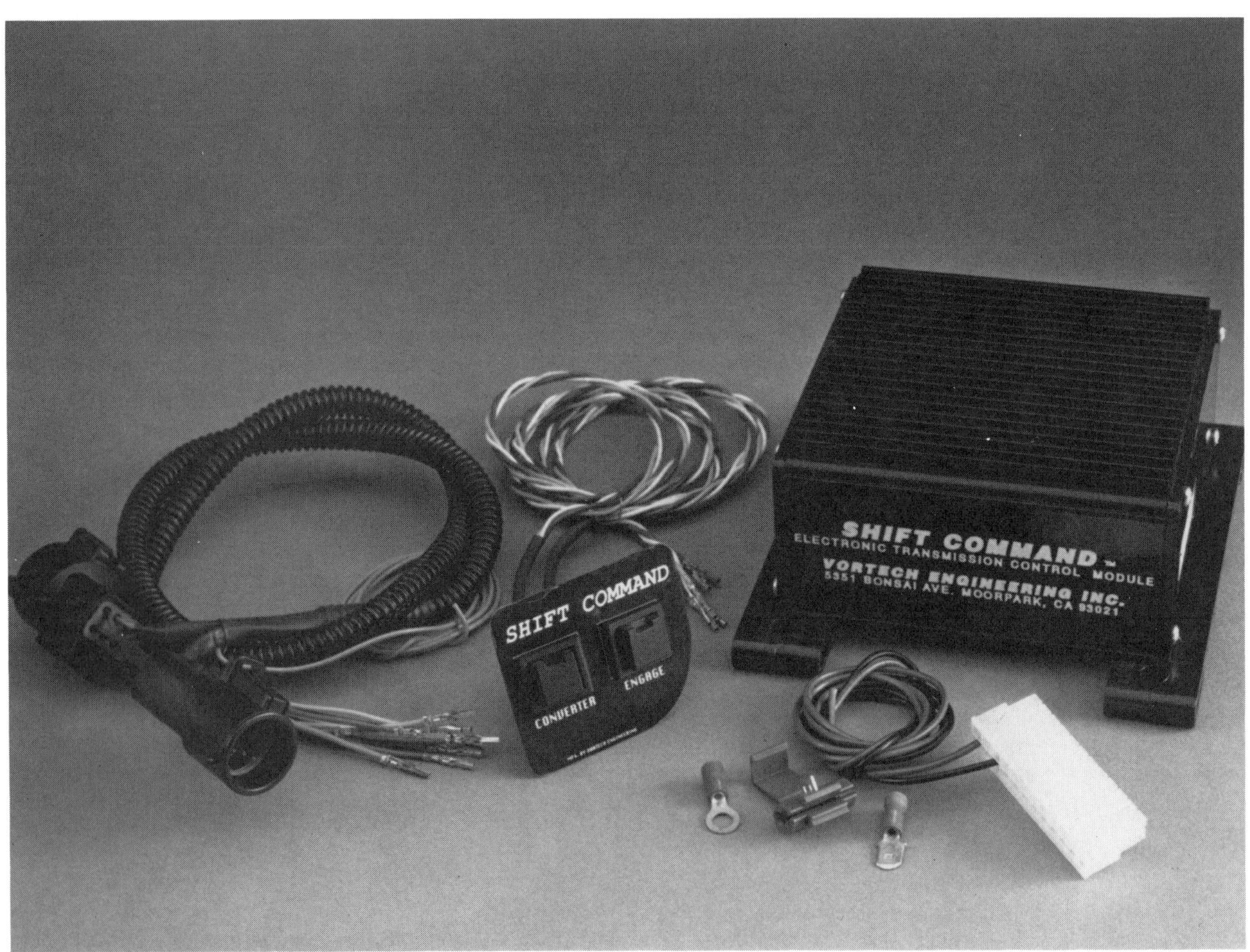

The Shift Command from Vortech allows you to defeat automatic transmission lock-up which results in more torque multiplication during acceleration. It also increases line pressure during shifting and raises shift points slightly during acceleration—in effect, it acts like a shift kit for pre-electronic transmissions. Vortech Superchargers

Chapter 9

The 2.3 Liter Four

The smallest engine to be found in Mustangs since 1979 is the 2.3 liter (140ci) inline overhead cam four. It has served as the base Mustang engine, with horsepower ratings hovering around the 90hp mark, and it generally hasn't been enthusiastically received by street racers and hot rodders. After all, how much can you get out of 140ci? Mustangs have always been V-8 territory, but the 2.3 liter that powered the SVO Mustang does produce a lot of power and has some very interesting features.

The 2.3 liter should not be confused with the 2.3 liter HSC engine which was introduced on 1984 Tempo/Topaz models. This 2.3 liter is a cam-in-block design with poor cylinder head combustion chamber design and porting, so it shouldn't be considered an engine with much performance potential. Its roots are from Ford's old inline six, on which the 2.3 liter HSC is based, but with two cylinders chopped off.

Although the 2.3 liter was originally built to replace the Pinto's 2.0 liter engine, it was designed to share many of the same parts to reduce production costs. For instance, both engines use a single overhead camshaft crossflow cylinder head for superior breathing. With a crossflow head, the intake manifold is located on one side of the engine and the exhaust manifold on the other side. The valves on the 2.3 liter are canted, like the 351 Cleveland V-8, which also promotes better engine breathing.

The 2.3 liter is a strong engine. It has a nodular iron crankshaft supported by five two-bolt main bearing caps. Rods are forged steel and the stock bottom end is considered safe to at least 7000rpm. There had been some breakage problems with the 2.0 liter's camshaft because it was supported by only three camshaft-bearing pedestals. For the 2.3 liter, Ford used four pedestals for greater support.

In addition, the camshaft is rifle drilled to provide oiling to the cam rocker arms and valvetrain. This was a problem on some 2.3 liters used prior to 1979; the rockers were made of a metal that turned out to be too soft. As the rockers wore, bits of metal plugged the oiling passages on the camshaft, resulting in camshaft failure due to lack of oil.

The 2.3 liter uses intake valves measuring 1.73in and exhausts at 1.50in. The valves are canted in opposite directions to improve combustion and produce more power. An unusual feature of the 2.3 liter's cylinder head design is the intake ports. The two outer ports are oval, while the inner two are round. In 1979, to increase flow velocity Ford made an additional change by altering the shape of all the ports to a D-port design. Although this head is considered to be superior to the earlier cylinder head, this was a running change, meaning that some 1979 engines have the older design while others have the D-port heads.

One anomaly of the 2.3 liter cylinder head is that all four intake ports are different, even though at first glance the two outer and the two inner ports look the same. This isn't important in a stock street engine, but if you ever decide to race your 2.3 liter, a porting job is necessary.

For all-out competition, Ford has available several other valves, 1.89 and 1.73in radius-flow underhead design intakes, and a 1.59in exhaust valve. There is also an aluminum head available, part number

The 2.3 liter four-cylinder engine has been the standard Mustang engine since 1979. Don't expect much from this engine in stock form, though, something which you probably already know if you own this version.

M-6059-A230, which weighs 25lb less than the iron head. It is designed to accept the 1.89/1.59in valves, and port configuration is different from the production head. The intakes are round and matched. The aluminum head should be used with the beefed-up heavy-duty block, part number M-6010-B230.

The Motorsport catalog also offers a good choice when it comes to camshafts, along with a stronger timing belt and a sprocket that can be used to advance or retard the camshaft.

Practically everything about the typical stock 2.3 liter is restrictive. The air cleaner is restrictive as are the intake and exhaust manifolds. The stock intake manifold, which looks fairly efficient, is actually very restrictive. It limits airflow to the engine to about 250cfm (cubic feet per minute). This means that if you install a larger than stock two-barrel carburetor, which flows only 225cfm, all that extra capacity would be wasted. Even a taller than stock air filter element results in a 25cfm increase over the stock air filter. A good replacement for the stock intake is Offenhauser's dual-port manifold and a small Holley 390cfm four-barrel carburetor. This is a popular combination as it provides decent mileage and 25hp more than stock.

Starting with 1989, the 2.3 liter came with a throttle-body injection system, but horsepower remained at 88. And in 1991 the 2.3 liter got a twin spark plug cylinder head and multi-port EFI for a 105hp output. The 1991 engine has also a distributorless ignition system.

A good set of headers and a turbo-type muffler are also worthwhile modifications and cost effective too, as the 2.3 liter needs only a single exhaust system.

These simple modifications will result in a 2.3 liter that produces about 145hp, not quite as much as a turbocharged engine, but for a lot less money. This will produce a livelier, more-fun-to-drive base Mustang. The reality, though, is that if you want enough power from a 2.3 liter to challenge a 302 V-8 you'll have to resort to supercharging or turbocharging.

That's what Ford did with the 2.3 liter. There were two attempts to turbocharge the 2.3 liter. The first was during the 1979-80 production year. In spite of some additional internal strengthening and the use of forged pistons, the engine had a high failure rate. Power output was 132hp in 1979, and 135hp in the 1980 version. By 1984, and with more development, Ford

For racing applications, the 2.3 liter heavy-duty block is available. It has a raised deck, with increased-thickness cylinder bore, main web, and bulkhead. These modifica-tions aren't necessary for a street application. Ford Motor Co.

All 1979 and later heads have revised D-shaped intake ports for better flow.

Exhaust ports are round on all 2.3 liter cylinder heads. They are fairly efficient.

You can get this head assembly, part number M-6049-A231, from Motorsport. It is basically a modified street head. The A231 head comes with 1.89/1.59in intake/exhaust valves and no intake valve shrouding. The larger valves help to make the engine come to life in the higher rpm range. Ford Motor Co.

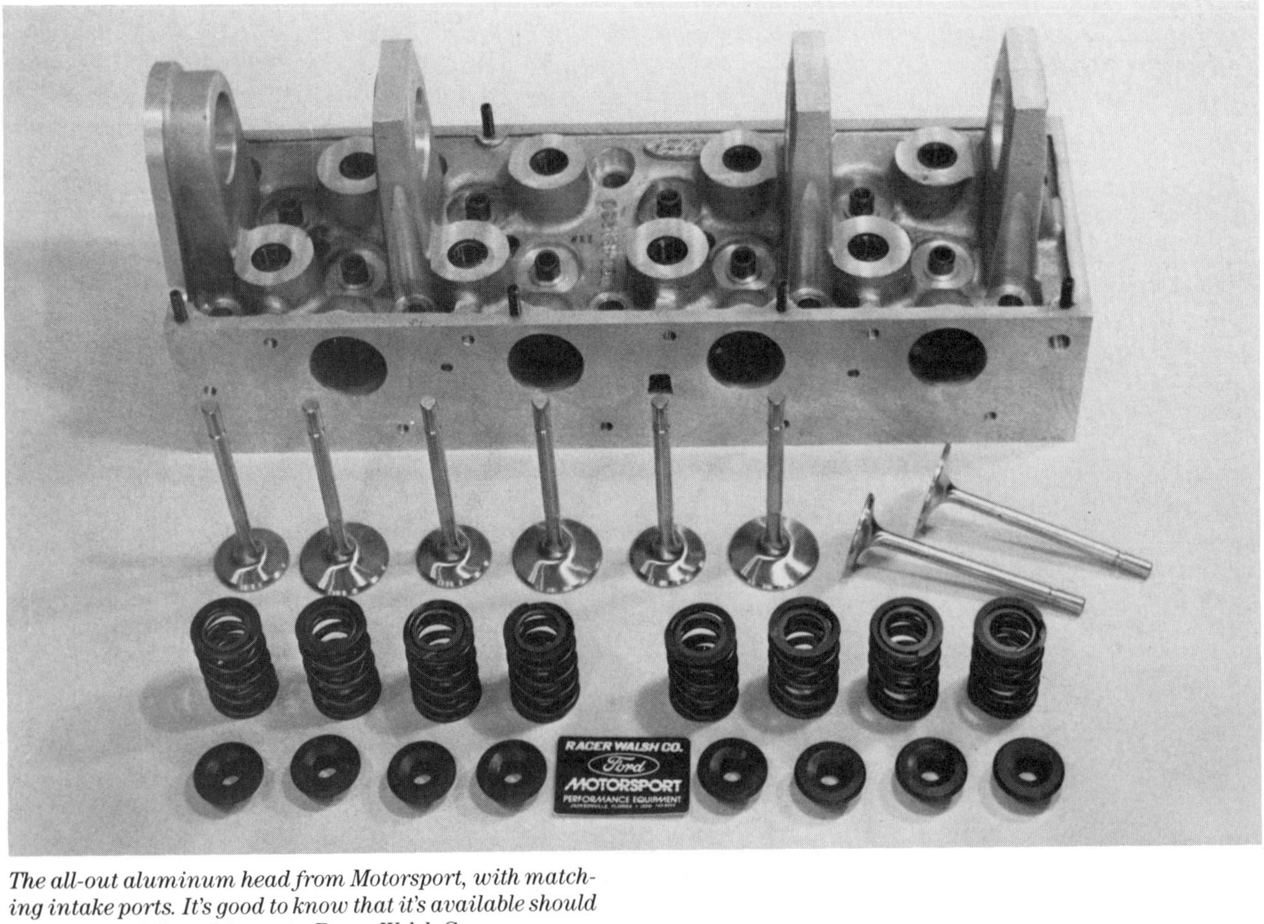

The all-out aluminum head from Motorsport, with matching intake ports. It's good to know that it's available should you want to follow this route. Racer Walsh Co.

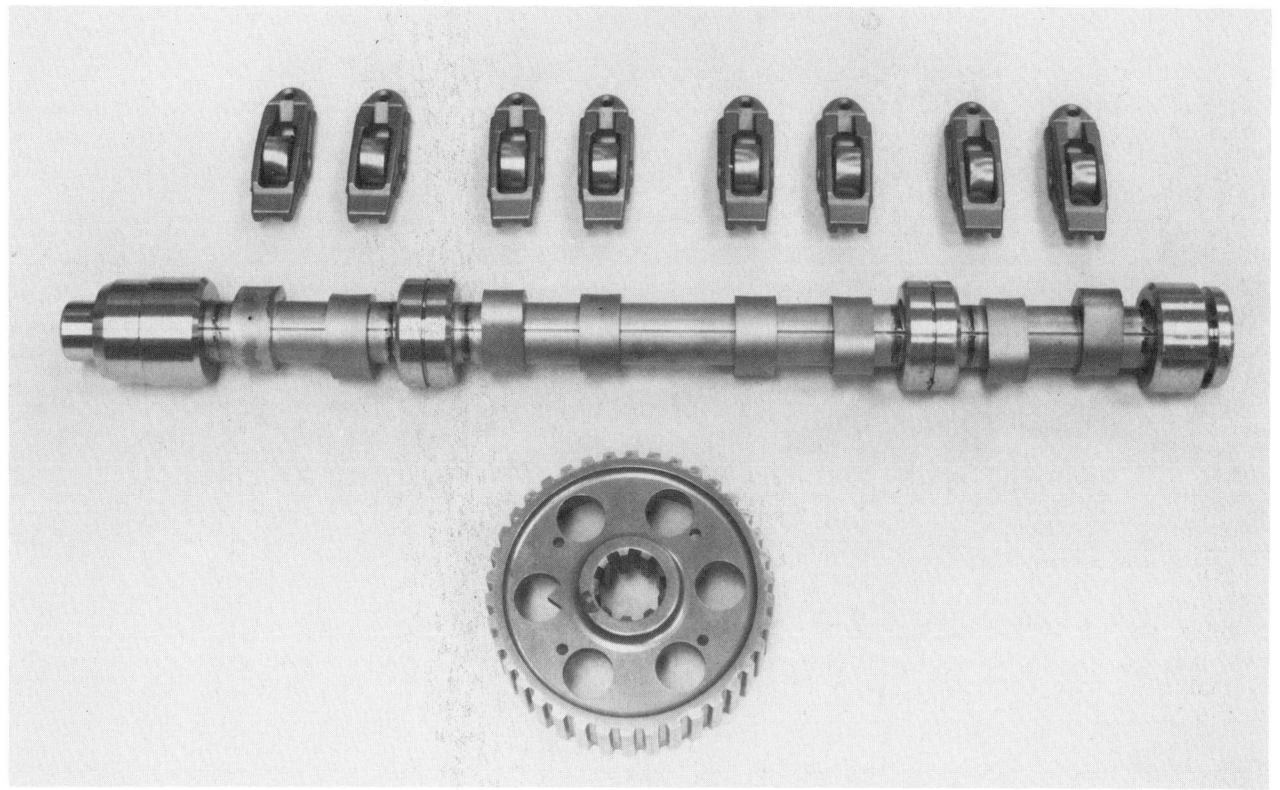

The Motorsport cam and kit, part number M-6252-A230, is described as an excellent mid-range cam for turbo and nonturbo applications. It comes with roller rockers and timing chain sprocket. Ford Motor Co.

reintroduced the turbocharged 2.3 liter, in two versions.

The Turbo GT Mustang came with a turbocharged fuel-injected 145hp version of the 2.3 liter, while the SVO Mustang got a more powerful 175hp version. The SVO's engine featured an intercooler to reduce intake temperature, and both engines used the EEC-IV computer to control all engine functions and turbo boost. The turbo 2.3 liter also used a knock sensor to control detonation. In 1985, the engine was revised through the use of larger fuel injectors, a revised intake manifold, a 1lb increase in boost (to 15lb), and a freer exhaust system for an impressive 205hp.

The turboed 2.3 liter was a great engine—it put out a lot of power, it was reliable, and turbo lag wasn't too bad. But the engine lacked the low-end torque of the 302 V-8 which the typical Mustang GT buyer wanted and appreciated. The 2.3 liter had to be wound out to produce any sort of power and the SVO Mustang was priced too high in relation to a 302 powered Mustang GT. Poor sales forced Ford to withdraw it after the 1986 model year.

There are several aftermarket turbo systems that provide reliable performance, but they are all expensive. Considering even the cost of the typical bolt-on modifications and the resultant horsepower increase, it is hard to justify spending so much on the 2.3 liter, considering how heavy the Mustang is. Even with turbocharging, a 2.3 liter powered Mustang can't keep up with a mildly modified 302.

Perhaps the best and most cost-effective way to improve the performance of a 2.3 liter Mustang is to swap a 302 V-8 for it.

One final point concerns cars that are governed by an EEC computer. You can't make most of the

Stock carburetor (left) and replacement Weber (right). The Weber has larger venturis and flows more than the stock unit. It is a good modification to make, but expect a small penalty in fuel economy. Racer Walsh Co.

There are plenty of aftermarket manifolds for the 2.3 liter.
These are from Offenhauser. Racer Walsh Co.

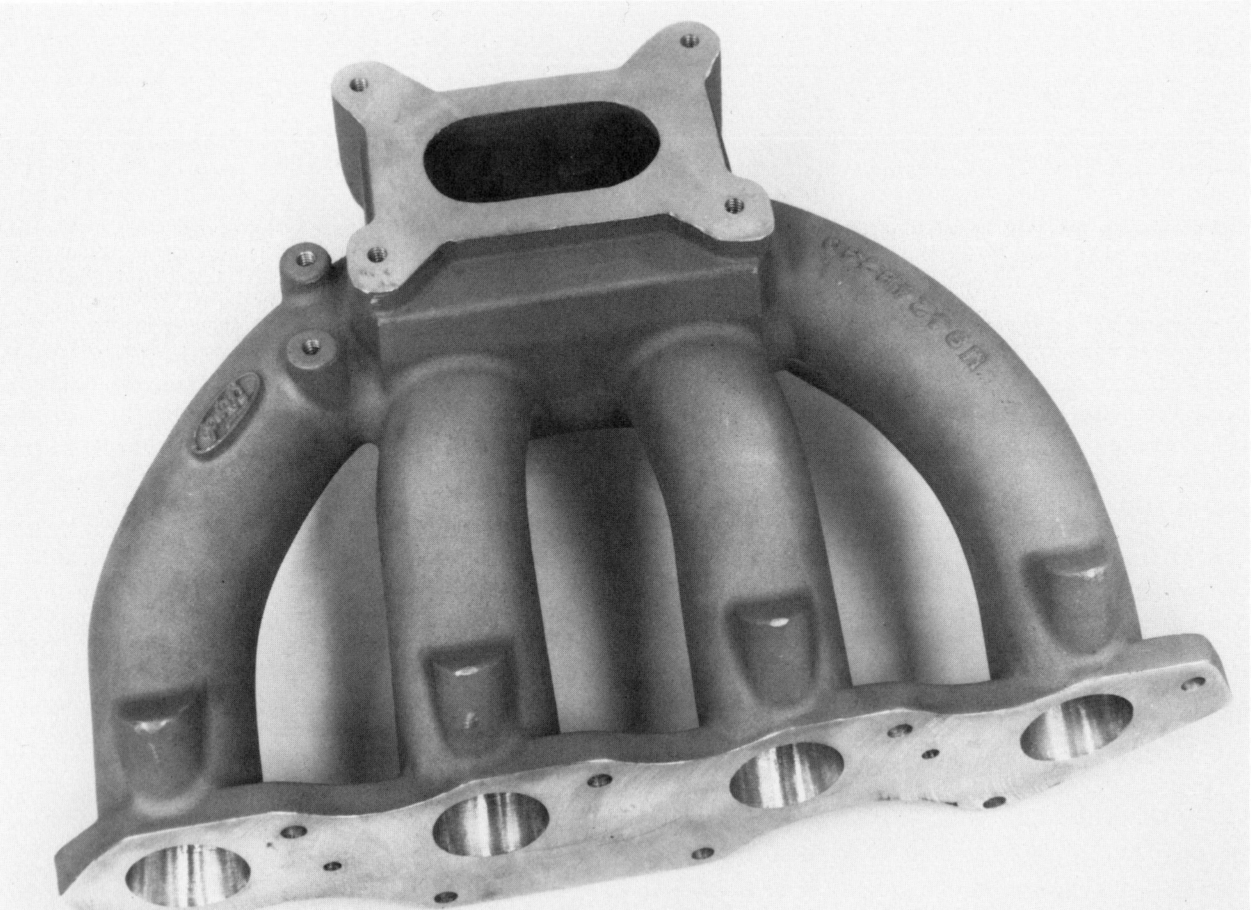

The Motorsport intake manifold is designed to work with
the Motorsport aluminum cylinder head. Note its round,
equal-sized ports. Ford Motor Co.

modifications suggested here (with the exception of the exhaust system) and expect the engine to run. Your only solution is to disconnect the computer and install a DuraSpark distributor and control box from an older engine. These should be quite plentiful in the salvage yard since Pintos from 1975 on came with this system.

The 2.3 liter is a good engine and its good points become evident in racing. For the street, the 2.3 liter will show itself well when Ford installs it in a lighter car.

For optimum street performance, Offenhauser's four-barrel intake with a Holley 390cfm carburetor is a good choice. Don't expect this setup to work with the EEC computer, though. Racer Walsh Co.

The Turbo GT engine of 1983-84. It was a much better engineered application as it included electronic fuel injection.

The SVO Mustang came with 175 and 205hp versions (in 1986) of the turbocharged 2.3 liter engine. Besides fuel injection and boost changes, the SVO engine has an intercooler to cool the intake air, something the Turbo GT engine doesn't have.

Chapter 10

The 3.8 Liter V-6

One of Ford's newest engines is the 3.8 liter (232ci) V-6 which powered Mustangs from 1983-86. It has a bore and stroke of 3.682x3.126in and weighs 298lb, considerably less than GM's 3.8 liter V-6. This low weight is due to aluminum cylinder heads which feature Cleveland-type ports and good-sized valves measuring 1.77in intake and 1.45in exhaust. The valves, however, are not canted like the Cleveland family engines and are arranged in a conventional straight line.

In 1983, the first year the engine was available, it was rated at only 112hp with the use of a two-barrel carburetor. For 1984-86 the engine came with throttle-body fuel injection and was rated at 120hp. Also from 1984, the only transmission available with the V-6 was the four-speed automatic overdrive.

There isn't much you can do to hop up the 3.8 liter since there hasn't been much in the way of aftermarket bolt-ons. But you can always improve upon the stock exhaust system by converting to a dual-exhaust system, and you could improve on the stock carburetor by installing an aftermarket Holley on the 1983 models.

Any other modifications will come at great expense. You can use the supercharger that is used on the Thunderbird Super Coupe, along with all other ancillary parts. However, be warned that the Thunderbird V-6 has been considerably modified and strengthened, as described in the chapter on supercharging. It is also possible to turbocharge or supercharge the V-6 as well with an aftermarket custom system.

The Motorsport catalog offers a number of options in terms of parts such as blocks, trick cylinder heads, valves, cams, manifolds, and so on, for the 4.5 liter V-6. At a quick glance, it would seem that the 3.8 and 4.5 are the same engines, but the 4.5 liter is designed strictly as a race engine, primarily for circle track racing, and has little interchangeability with the street 3.8.

The 4.5 liter is quite an engine. It can be bored and stroked to 315ci and the block has been designed

The 3.8 liter V-6 was optionally available on 1983-86 Mustangs. There isn't much one can do with this engine because there isn't much available in the aftermarket or from Ford.

The cylinder heads on this 3.8 liter are cast in aluminum. These heads have excellent flow, with the ports resembling those found on the 351 Cleveland V-8 heads. Valves are arranged in an inline configuration.

Exhaust ports are large and round, considerably larger than the 302 V-8. All in all, the 3.8's heads have been designed for possible use in race applications as the ports can be opened up even farther.

Combustion chamber configuration is of the open variety. There is plenty of room for larger valves. The 3.8 liter has shown itself to be a well-thought-out engine with no problem areas in everyday use.

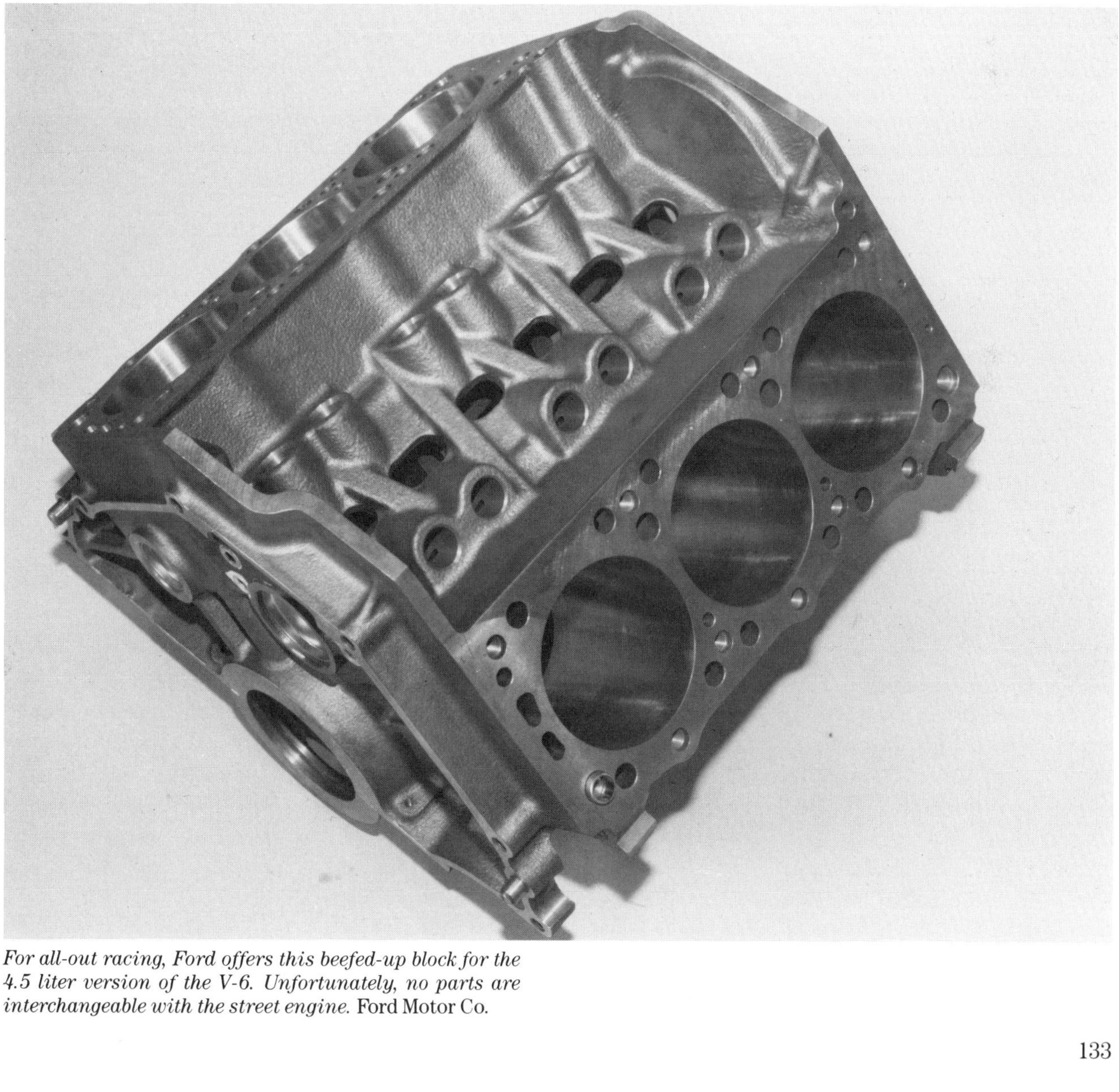

For all-out racing, Ford offers this beefed-up block for the 4.5 liter version of the V-6. Unfortunately, no parts are interchangeable with the street engine. Ford Motor Co.

to accept many small-block V-8 parts. There are two high-performance cylinder heads available for the racer with valves as large as 2.19in intake and 1.71in exhaust. The valvetrain has been designed to use most small-block V-8 parts such as the roller rockers and rocker arm studs and for improved gasket sealing, the 4.5 liter has an additional fifth head bolt.

It is possible that the 3.8 liter once again will be offered in future Mustangs but as of right now, it is difficult to take advantage of the V-6's potential.

A racing single four-barrel manifold for the 4.5 liter. Note its unusual runner configuration. Ford Motor Co.

There is no doubt that the 3.8 liter V-6 can make power. In the Thunderbird Super Coupe and Mercury Cougar XR7, the supercharged 3.8 liter pumps out 210hp at 4000rpm, and 315lb-ft of torque at 2600rpm—15lb-ft more than the Mustang GT's 5.0 liter HO V-8.

Chapter 11

Handling and Suspension

Back in the good-old 1960s, performance meant one thing: straight-line acceleration. Handling was more of an afterthought. There were the Boss Mustangs, of course, but they were a distinct minority. However, third-generation Mustangs are better-balanced automobiles because of the current emphasis on handling. During the 1980s, the message finally got through to Detroit that while handling meant a safer car, handling could *sell* more cars too. Not only do third-generation cars handle better than earlier models, but engine development has progressed to the point that current GT Mustangs are faster than most late 1960s hot-shot Mustangs. The result is a much more satisfying car.

Handling is a vast and sometimes complicated subject that can encompass many different things, but it all boils down to one thing: traction. I don't just mean traction during cornering; handling involves all facets of driving—during acceleration, braking, and cornering under all types of conditions and on different types of road surfaces. Good handling means control and predictability. A good-handling Mustang is a blast to drive while one that doesn't

Handling boils down to one thing—traction. In order to have good handling you must eliminate or at least minimize all the dynamic forces that try to keep the tires from doing their job. This stock Mustang exhibits some leaning which tends (in this case) to lift the passenger's side front wheel—thereby limiting the speed at which the corner can be taken. This particular Mustang LX convert- *ible isn't what you would consider to be best suited for autocrossing in a stock class: convertibles are heavier, the chassis is looser, and yet this particular car consistently beats all other competitors in its class, including other Mustangs and GM F-body cars. Knowing how to use what you've got is just as important as the equipment itself.*

Drag racing, on the other hand, calls for a different kind of handling. A looser, softer sprung front end will aid rear weight transfer and therefore traction as the car leaves the starting line. One thing you can do to help weight transfer is to disconnect the front antisway bar.

handle well will not only be difficult to drive, but also unsafe and dangerous.

Mustangs have always been designed with performance in mind. Third-generation Mustangs are engineered to handle better than previous Mustangs, but for most enthusiasts, there is always room for improvement. The guidelines given here are aimed at preserving a balance among the qualities that constitute good handling while maintaining a reasonable ride. The enthusiast who is concerned with performance is usually willing to give up some ride quality, but it is unwise to go overboard and sacrifice driveability and comfort.

There are some differences in suspension design on the third-generation Mustangs from the previous two. The front suspension, which previously used a double-wishbone system, was replaced by a MacPherson strut front suspension. A MacPherson strut system is simpler (meaning less expensive) because rather than using an upper control arm, a tube is attached to the top of the front hub, extending to the top of the spring tower. Inside this tube is a damper, and the tube also acts as the seat for the front springs.

All 1979-92 Mustangs have a MacPherson front suspension. The strut is attached to the hub and to the top of the shock tower, pivoting only on the lower control arm. Front suspension travel is not straight up and down but on an arc. The spring mounts in between the lower control arm and chassis.

Rear suspension uses coil springs and is located by four control arms—two on top of the axle housing and two underneath the axle, near the brakes.

136

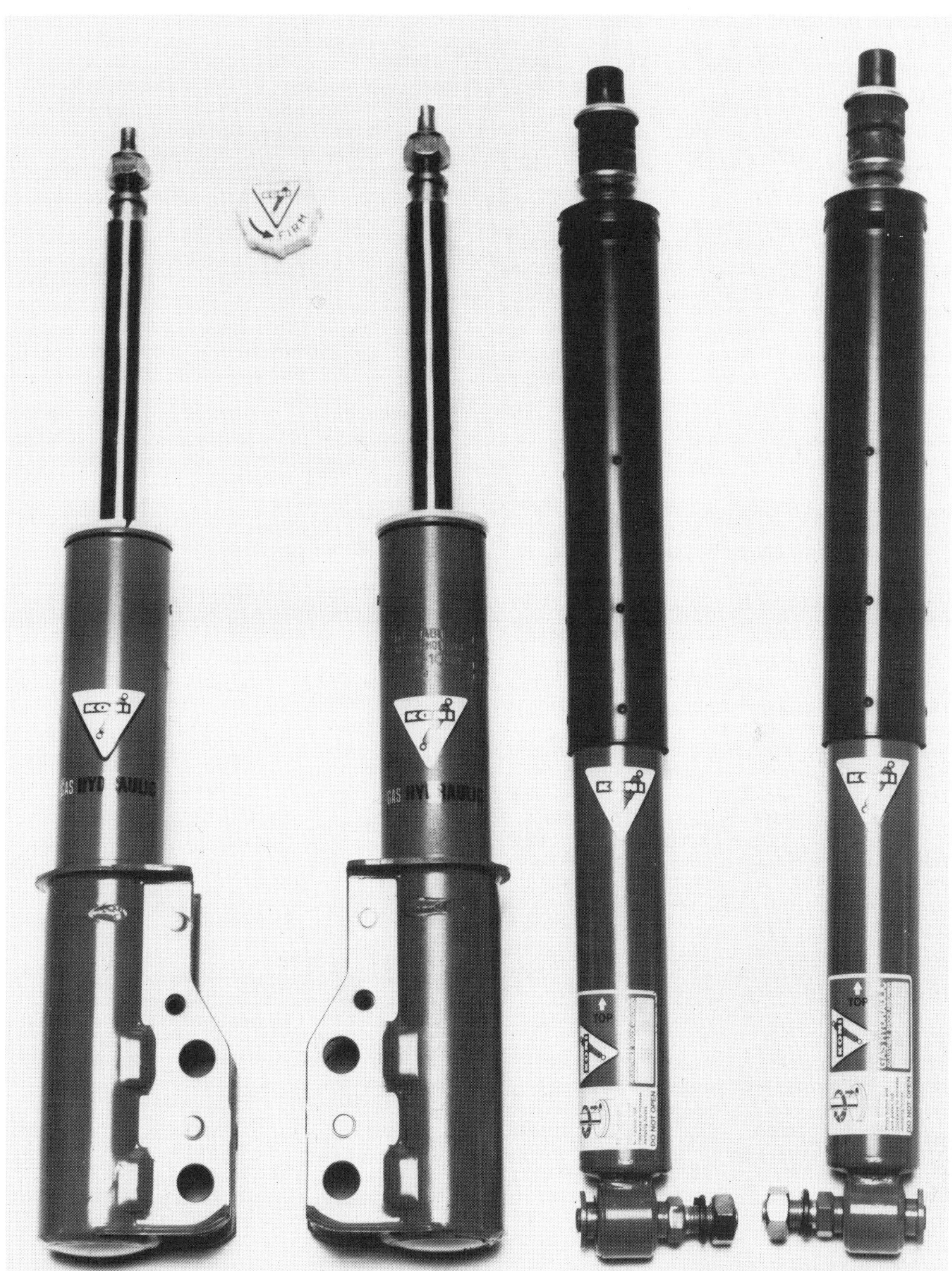

Low-pressure Koni gas shocks and struts were originally developed for use on the SVO Mustang. They are adjustable and will definitely improve the handling of any Mustang. Koni

Because the front hub assembly can only pivot on the lower attaching arm, front wheel up-and-down motion is on an arc. Weak front struts will invariably result in inner tire wear.

On the rear, coil springs replaced the leaf springs. Rear axle location was accomplished by four locating links, two on each side—one above the axle and one below it.

Understeer and Oversteer

Probably the most important terms to know and understand when it comes to handling are understeer and oversteer. All Mustangs are designed to understeer. This means that when your Mustang approaches and enters a turn it would rather continue in a straight line (because of centrifugal force). Enter a turn too fast and the car's front end will start to slide, and turning the steering wheel more will not do any good; the only thing you can do is to slow down and turn the wheel away from the turn. Most manufacturers consider understeering preferable because simply by following your natural driver's instinct you can still control the car and save yourself from spinning out.

In an oversteering situation, the opposite occurs. Because the rear tires slide out first, the car will continue turning tighter relative to steering input. Deliberate suspension design and rear weight bias cause this. If not corrected, the car continues making a tighter turn and at the limit of adhesion, the car will spin to the inside. Slight oversteer is preferred in racing because a skilled driver can control the car more easily and corner faster.

With most rear wheel drive cars you can also induce what is called power oversteer in a turn by stepping on the gas, assuming you have enough traction and horsepower.

Driving a Mustang that understeers excessively is no fun at all. A Mustang GT or any other Mustang with performance suspension components will still understeer, but at a lesser rate. You can reduce understeer by adding oversteer through these methods: increase front tire and wheel size; stiffen the rear springs; increase front tire pressure; or increase rear stabilizer bar diameter (or add one).

Springs

All third-generation Mustangs have coil springs at all four corners. Installing firmer springs is an easy way to improve handling, however, you should leave springs for last because you are better off if you can improve handling without resorting to firmer springs. Firm springs will make you aware of how many rattles your Mustang has and can take a lot of the fun out of driving. Suspension kits are available that provide everything you need to transform your Mustang's suspension, which usually include springs. But these springs normally will lower your Mustang as well. Although handling is no doubt improved, you are compromising your Mustang's ride, and losing ground clearance is not recommended in the real world. After all, it's no fun having your oil pan kiss the ground. See how your Mustang handles after you've installed better shocks, tires, and stabilizer bars and then determine if it's worth swapping springs.

If you have a non-GT Mustang, you can upgrade the stock springs to GT specs by using the Motorsport Sports Handling Kit, part number M-5300-B. The springs in this kit are variable rate, meaning that the first ¾in of spring travel is fairly soft, thereby making for decent regular driving. The springs will also reduce the height of a 1979-91 V-8 powered Mustang (and Mercury Capri) by about ¾–⅞in. The M-5300-C Super Sports Handling Kit has even firmer springs, with 650psi front springs as opposed to 425psi on the regular Sports Handling Kit. Both kits use 200psi rear springs.

Installation of the M-5300-B kit will improve handling while maintaining a decent ride. The M-5300-C kit will cause the car to ride considerably rougher.

Shocks

Shock absorbers control the up-and-down movement caused by the springs when a car hits a bump. Without shocks, your Mustang's ride would be an endless series of bounces. Shock absorbers absorb the energy generated when a wheel hits a bump and converts to heat. Previous to 1979, Mustangs used a shock absorber at each wheel. From 1979-on, Mustangs got MacPherson struts on the front.

How to Compute Spring Rates

To calculate the compression rate of a coil spring, use this formula:

$$\text{Spring Rate} = \frac{d^4 \times 11{,}500{,}000}{8 \times N \times D^3}$$

d = Coil wire diameter
D = Mean diameter (the inside diameter of the coil plus the diameter of the coil wire)
N = Number of effective coils. Because the top and bottom coils are compressed by the car's weight, the number of effective coils is the number of coils less 2
$11{,}500{,}000$ = Estimated Modulus of Rigidity of SAE 5160 steel springs
8 = A constant

Examples:
Stock 1988 Mustang front coil springs = 465psi
Stock 1988 Mustang rear coil springs = 253psi
Motorsport Super Sports Handling kit M-5300-C:
    Front rated at 650psi = 639psi
    Rear rated at 200-300psi = 258psi

The typical factory shock exerts its dampening force mainly on the rebound stroke. When a wheel hits a bump, the shock offers small resistance. The major portion of the shock's dampening force is exerted when the wheel is on the way back down to the road, and this results in a smoother ride. Most performance shock absorbers divide the dampening closer to a 50:50 ratio which improves handling at the expense of a harder ride. Most of the better shocks today use nitrogen gas to improve shock dampening and the gas does provide a mild booster-spring effect.

The best shocks, of course, are those that are adjustable. This way you can fine-tune them. Koni shocks have been a favorite with Mustang owners because of their high quality and adjustability, which includes adjustability on the front MacPherson struts. They are expensive, but Ford thought of them highly enough to make them standard equipment on the SVO Mustang. Other less expensive brands, such as Gabriel, also provide excellent performance. Screwdriver five-way adjustable struts and shocks are also available under the Illumina Five label from Tokico. These are also available in the Motorsport catalog under part number M-18000-B.

For 1987-92 Mustang GTs and LXs with the 302, you can install Motorsport's adjustable MacPherson strut and shock kit, made by Tokico. It consists of two struts and two shocks which can be controlled electrically from an interior-mounted switch. There are three ride settings, soft, normal, and firm.

Stabilizer Bars

If your Mustang doesn't have a rear stabilizer bar, adding one will improve its handling more than any other single modification you can make. Even if you've installed larger tires and better shocks, you need a rear bar. Stabilizer bars are designed to twist when a car leans during a turn. When both wheels are pushed up, there is no loading on the bar. Any resistance is exerted when one wheel hits a bump, or when the car is leaning in a turn. Thus a stabilizer bar will firm up ride, but nowhere near as much as stiffer springs. That's why it is recommended to retain stock springs, but use stabilizer bars to improve handling, thereby retaining a decent ride.

Generally speaking, you should not replace your Mustang's front bar (at least, initially) with a larger bar because you'll be adding understeer. You are better off installing a rear bar, if you don't already have one. Four- and six-cylinder Mustangs can use a $^{3}/_{4}$in rear bar while V-8 powered GTs can tolerate a $^{7}/_{8}$in bar.

The addition of a rear bar will do wonders. Dollar for dollar, a rear stabilizer bar is by far the most cost-effective suspension modification you can make.

You can also enhance the performance of any bars that are already on the car by substituting polyurethane bushings and end-link bushings for the stock rubber ones. Solid polyurethane bushings will make your bar act or have the same effect as a 20-25 percent larger bar. Also, bar response time will be

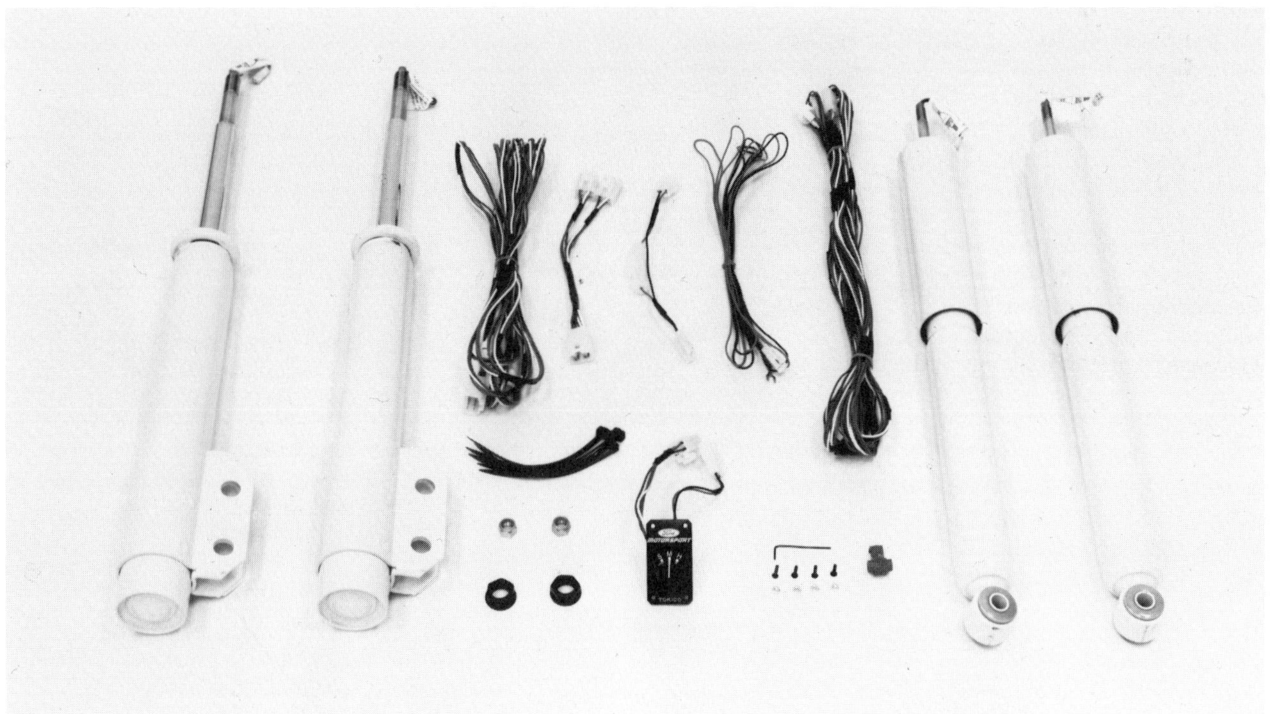

This is the Motorsport electrically adjustable suspension kit. There are three settings—soft, normal, and firm—and suspension is adjustable from the inside of the car. The kit is made by Tokico. Ford Motor Co.

Polyurethane antisway bar and end-link bushings are an inexpensive way to increase antisway bar performance. *They also decrease the bar's reaction time before they take effect.* Racer Walsh Co.

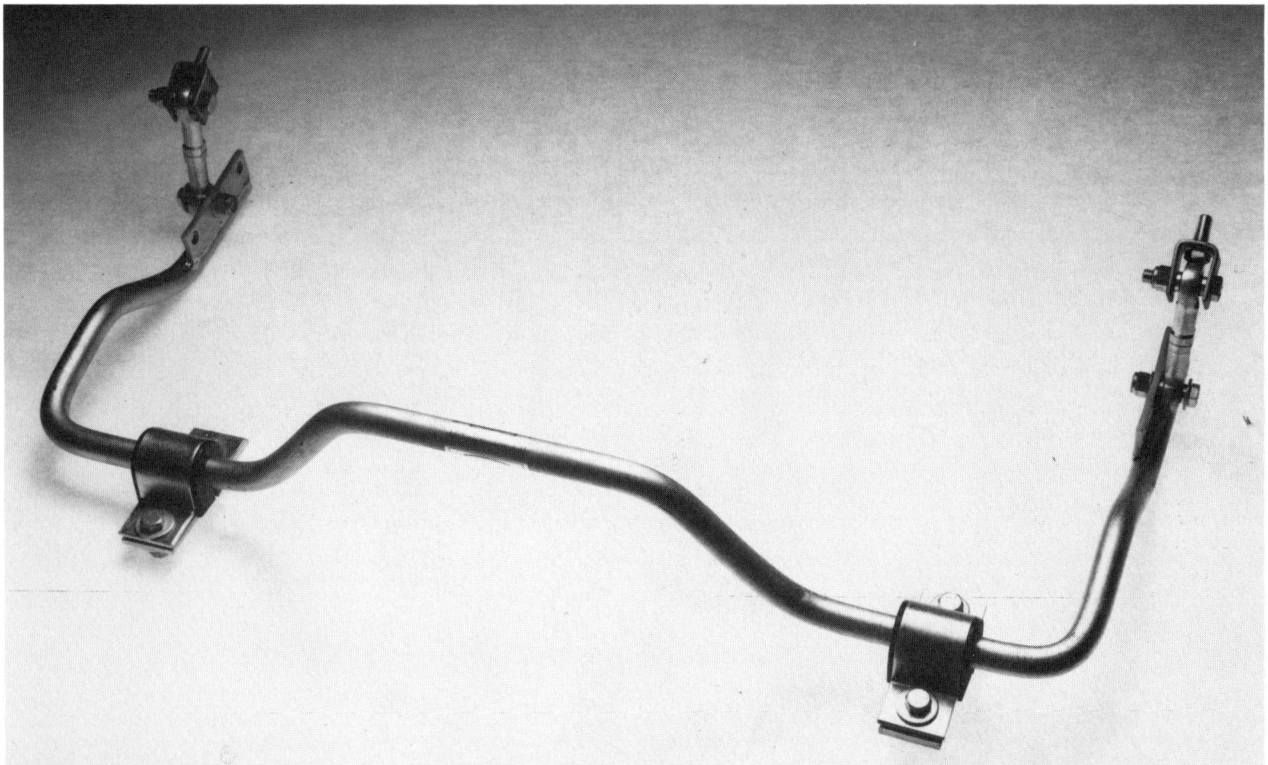

A competition antisway bar will usually have adjustable end links, enabling the bar to be tuned for a particular track or application.

quicker as there is no wait for the rubber bushings to compress before they take effect.

Another point worth considering when selecting a bar is the material it is made from. Stock Ford stabilizer bars are made from 4150H spring steel, a very good material. Some aftermarket suppliers use an even better 5150H or 6150H spring steel. Avoid bars made from 1018 cold-roll mild steel. This material is easier and cheaper to manufacture, but lacks the necessary spring qualities needed in a stabilizer bar. Also avoid bars with welded ends.

The following chart shows the difference or increase in torsional stiffness as bar size increases:

Front Bar		**Rear Bar**	
Size (in)	Stiffness Increase (%)	Size (in)	Stiffness Increase (%)
5/8	100	1/2	100
3/4	160	5/8	167
7/8	200	11/16	179
15/16	210	3/4	212
1	226	7/8	222
1 1/8	244	15/16	228

Current Mustang GTs come with a 1.31in front stabilizer bar and a 0.79in rear bar. These can be fitted on earlier Mustangs which came with smaller bars, or none at all when it comes to the rear. Again, they are available from Motorsport, kit number M-5627-A, and come with Teflon-lined bushings and urethane end-link bushings.

TRX-equipped Mustangs came with a 1.12in front bar and rear bars varying in size from 0-0.5-0.67in. If you own one of these, changing to the late-style bars along with 15 or 16in wheels and tires will go a long way in updating your Mustang.

Even with the larger Motorsport rear 0.79in stabilizer bar, the typical Mustang will still understeer. To reduce understeer you can use urethane instead of rubber on the rear bar mounting points but better yet, Steeda Autosports' supplemental rear bar

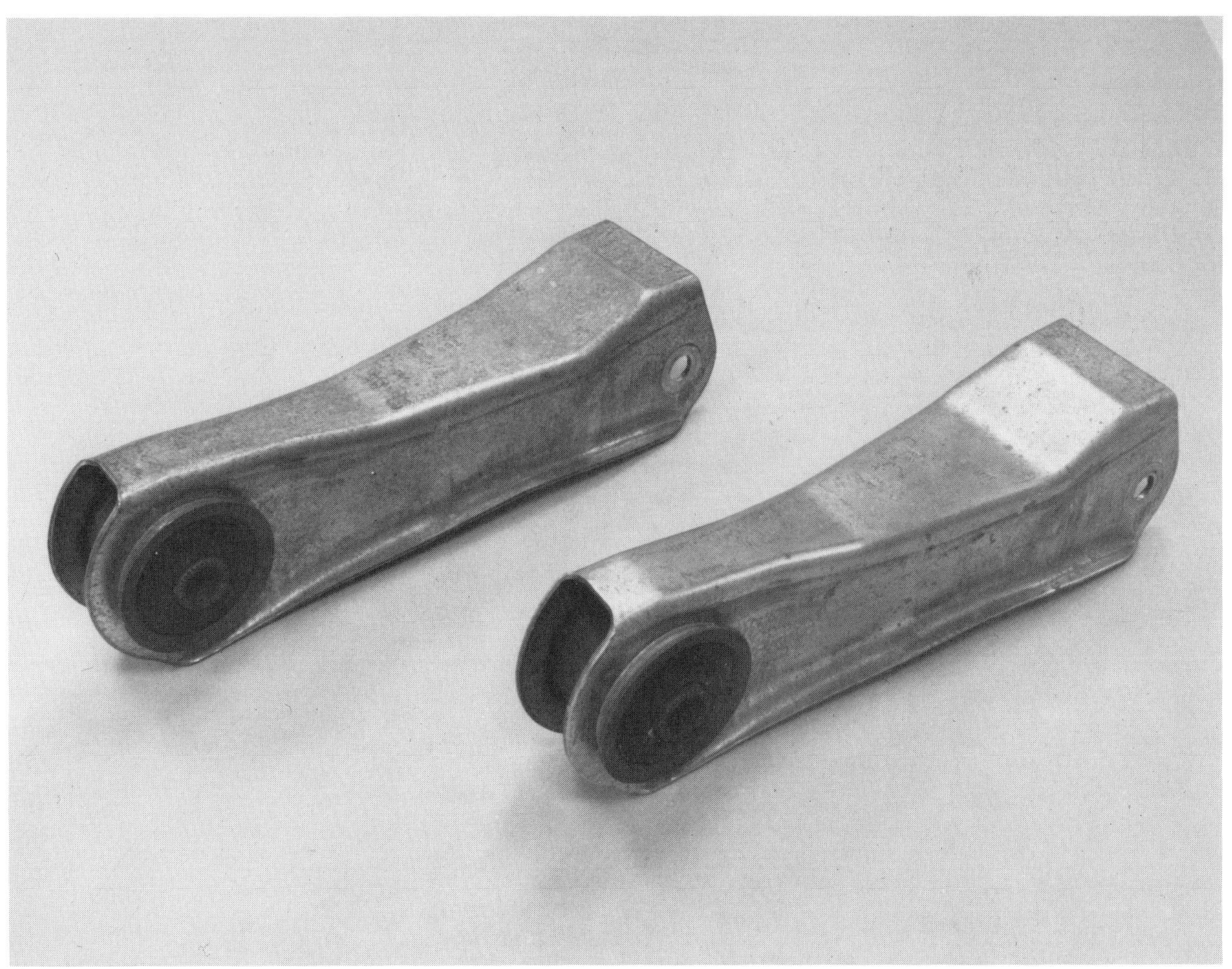

Motorsport offers this heavy-duty upper control arm kit for 1979-92 Mustangs. The bushings are twice as firm as the stock ones, *which translates to better traction and handling.* Ford Motor Co.

With this lower control arm kit, part number M-3075-A, owners of 1979-91 Mustangs can update their suspension to 1991 GT standards. The control arms come with low-friction ball joints and improved inner bushings. The 1983-91 GTs leave the factory with low-friction ball joints. Ford Motor Co.

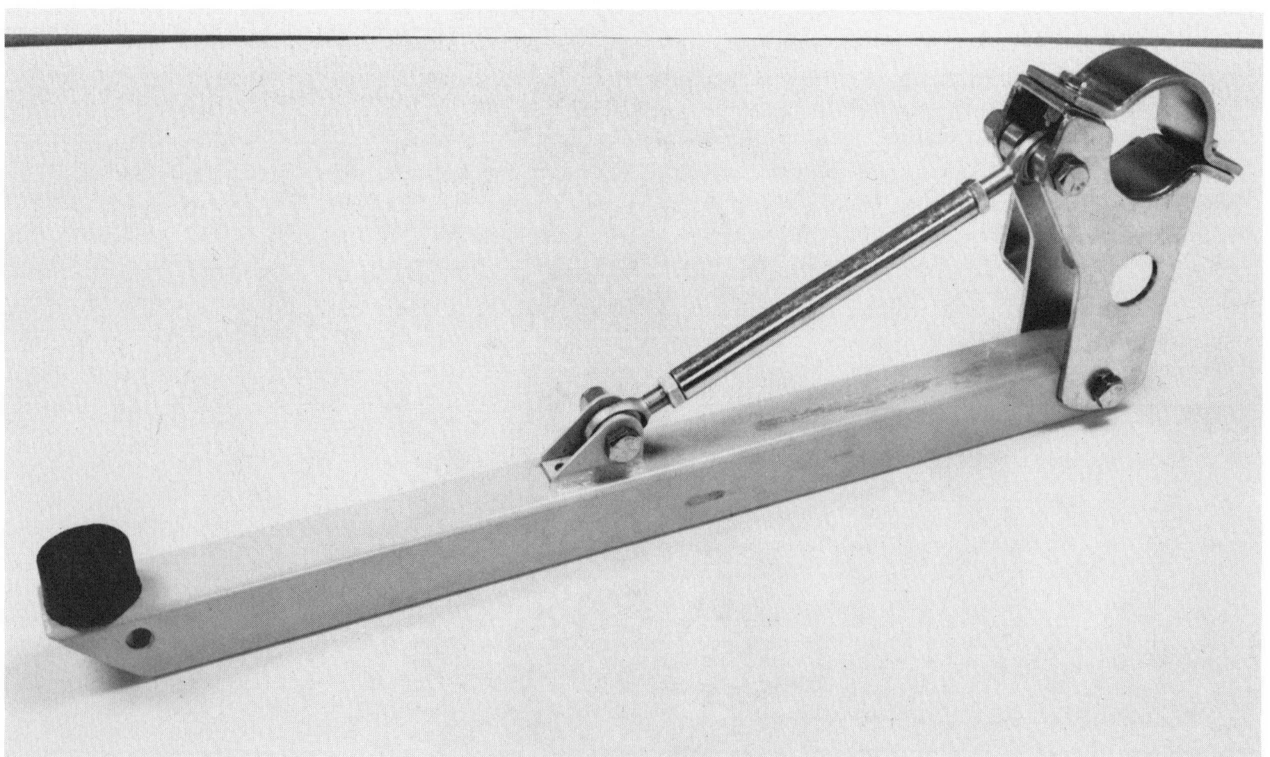

For drag racing use, the traditional Lakewood traction bars can do the job. They eliminate wheel hop and other traction problems, however, they also limit ground clearance. Ford Motor Co.

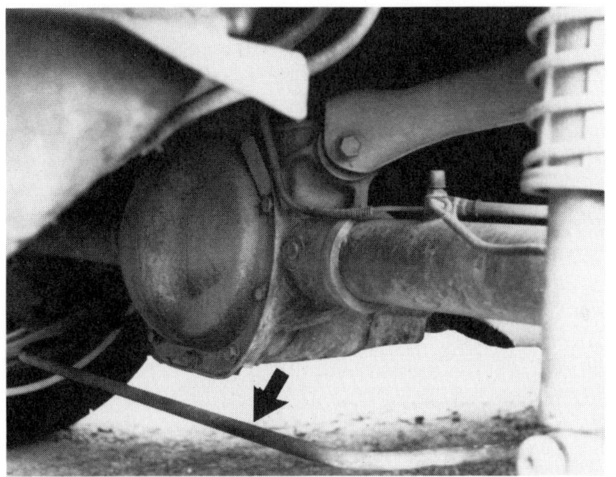

This TRX-equipped Mustang could benefit from a larger rear bar. The stock bar mounts on each lower control arm. A larger rear bar will make the most noticeable difference in the handling of your Mustang.

should be installed. This is an additional bar that mounts on the axle tubes and frame while the stock rear bar mounts only on the rear lower control arms. The bar measures 0.62in and has adjustable end links. The Steeda bar in conjunction with the stock bar works wonders.

Other Modifications

Other ways to improve handling include moving the battery to the trunk which improves weight distribution by about 1 percent. This is only practical on the two-door sedan models, however. Mustangs are front heavy, so any modification that reduces front end weight, such as a fiberglass hood, will improve handling. Aerodynamic aids such as wings, spoilers and side skirts will improve your Mustang's appearance, but their benefits are effective only at very high speeds.

Another useful modification is to install a rear Quadra-Shock kit. The Mustang GTs of 1982-84 vin-

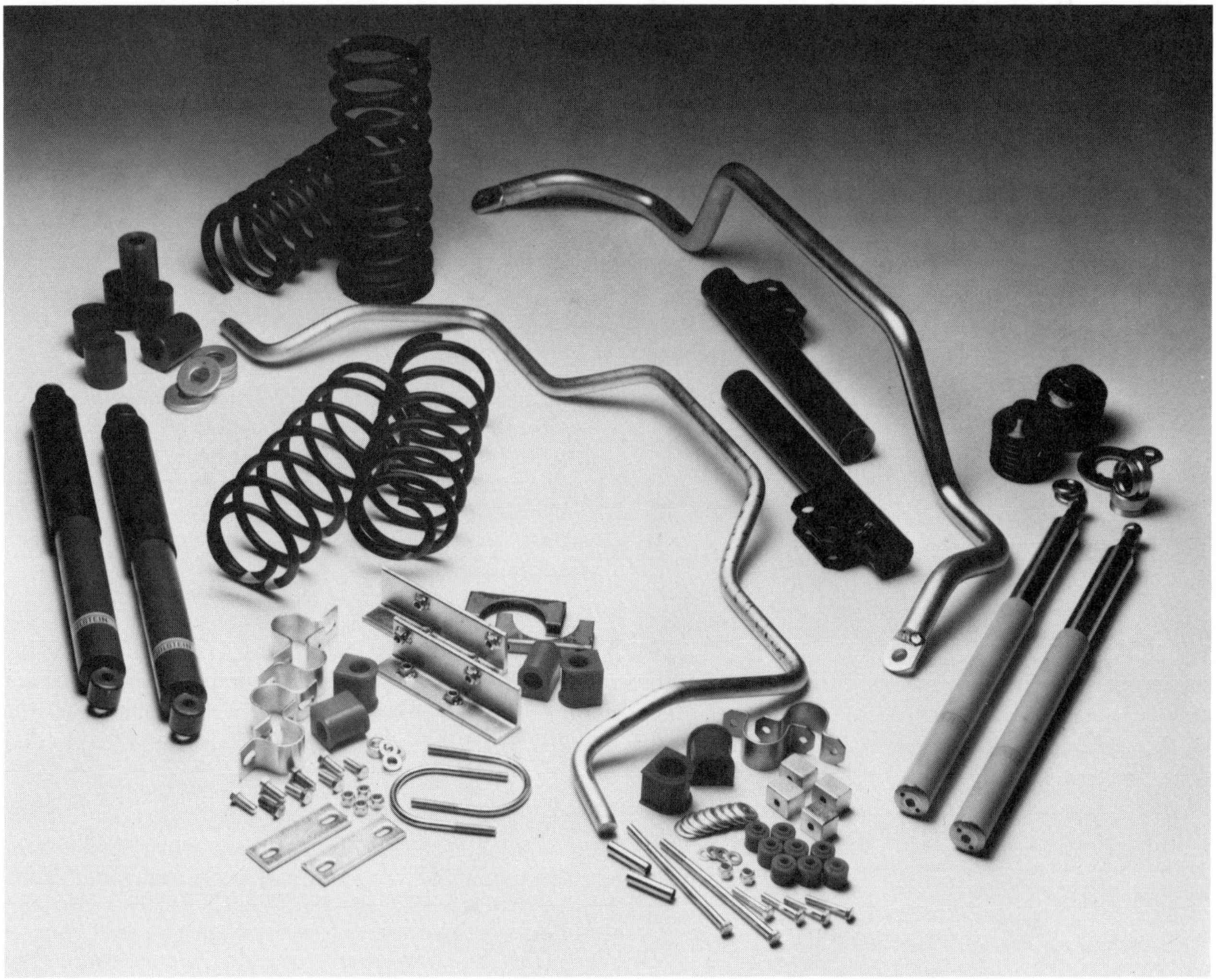

To completely transform a non-GT Mustang's suspension you'll need to use such a kit which includes shocks, struts, antisway bars and new springs, plus all the necessary hardware.

All 1982-84 GTs were plagued with rear-wheel traction problems due to the 302's excellent torque output. A big improvement came on 1984 SVO Mustangs and was later used on all 1985-92 302 powered cars in the form of a Quadra-Shock kit. An additional shock absorber is mounted horizontally behind the axle and controls rear-axle movement. The Quadra-Shock arrangement can be retrofitted on other 1979 and later Mustangs with the M-4263-A Quadra-Shock kit.

tage came with rear traction bars to control rear-wheel hop under hard acceleration. From 1985 on, all 302 powered Mustangs came with a Quadra-Shock arrangement which works much better. In addition,

When you subject your Mustang's chassis to higher cornering loads, the chassis will flex. This underhood brace will make a noticeable improvement. It is similar in concept to the old Export Brace and Monte Carlo bars used on 1960s Shelby Mustangs. A brace that bolts on is preferable to one that is welded on because it can easily be removed if necessary. Steeda Autosports

traction and handling were also improved from 1985 on as the rear lower control arms were relocated.

You can also reduce rear axle compliance by using the Motorsport heavy-duty upper control arm kit, part number M-5500-A. It comes with two new upper control arms with bushings that are twice as stiff as the stock ones.

Once you get beyond stabilizer bars, shocks, and springs you'll find that the Mustang platform is not as stiff as it could be. You can feel the body flex under hard cornering, especially the convertibles, which are already loose. As a car's cornering capability is improved, the loads transmitted to the chassis via the suspension attachment points are also correspondingly higher. If these attachment points aren't strengthened, the car's chassis will flex, which has a negative effect on handling. In time, cracks will develop at the suspension attachment points and on the suspension members as well. This can also be compounded by installing springs that are too firm for street use.

Subframe connectors, strut and shock tower braces, rocker stiffeners, and other chassis-stiffening components are available from various sources as well as in kit form in the Motorsport catalog under part number M-5024-A.

Other modifications, such as relocating suspension components, aren't recommended or needed for street use. They require a high degree of skill and knowledge and are designed to provide superior handling on the racetrack. It is best to leave the suspension in stock configuration.

One final point to consider is alignment. Alignment angles of the front suspension exert an influence on car's steering ease, steering stability, ride quality, and tire wear. This is a complex subject because these angles vary as the suspension does its job and the body moves up and down in relation to the wheels. The load in a car and its speed may also cause these angles to change. In addition, they are affected by changes in the car's attitude caused by acceleration, braking, and the type of road surface and cornering forces.

Camber is the amount (measured in degrees) that the front wheels tilt inward or outward at the top when viewed from the front of the car. When the top of the wheel leans inward, camber is negative. It is best to try for zero camber when aligning the front wheels. A little negative camber will help cornering, from $0-\frac{1}{2}$deg, but any more than this will cause uneven tire wear. With zero camber, the full width of the tire's tread makes contact with the road.

Caster refers to the angle made by a line between the upper and lower steering pivots (ball joints) and a vertical reference line. The angle is positive when this line tilts backward (when the upper ball joint is behind the lower ball joint). It is negative when this line tilts forward (when the upper ball joint is in front of the lower). Positive caster is beneficial as it keeps the wheels pointed straight ahead and reduces any tendency for the car to wander at high speeds. Caster also causes the steering wheel to return to the straight-ahead position as you exit a turn.

Toe is the difference (distance) between the front and rear inside edges of the front tires. Toe is usually set inward, or "in," and is measured in inches. Toe-in increases high-speed stability and takes the slack out of the suspension as the car moves from rest. Incorrect toe greatly affects tire wear.

Now that you know about caster, camber, and toe, there is not much you can do about it. Toe is

Not as readily visible are subframe connectors, necessary for increased chassis rigidity. These are a bolt-on design, making them easier to install than welded-on units. Saleen Performance Parts, Inc.

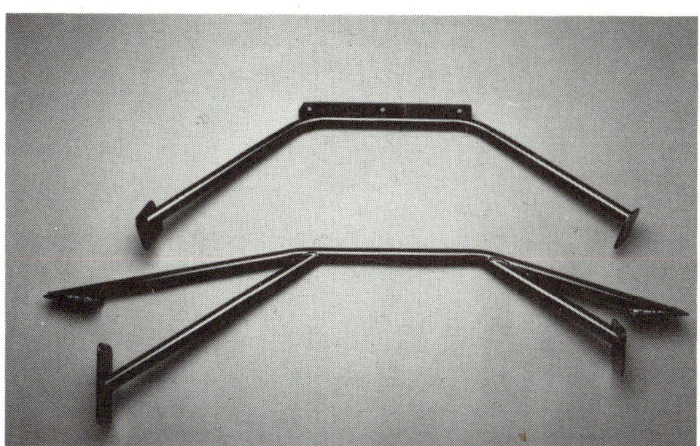

It is only when you push your Mustang hard through corners that you become aware of how flexible the front end is. A tower support brace will minimize this tendency but make sure you use a brace that has a large mounting pad. If the mounting pads are small, the chassis loads will be transferred to a small area, which will result in stress cracks. These two braces are from Global-West. The bottom brace is an SCCA legal unit which does not touch the fire-wall. Global-West Suspension Components

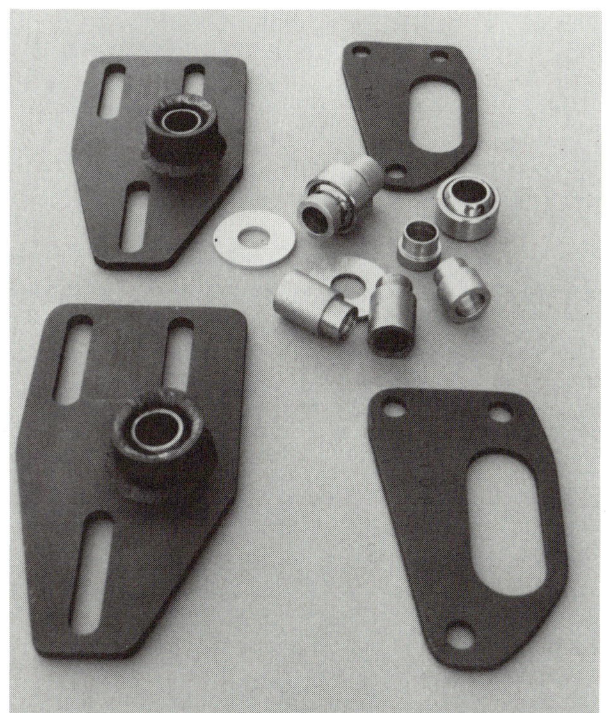

Global-West's McCastor Alignment Correction kit allows you to adjust for caster—something you can't do in a stock Mustang. This kit will work with lowered Mustangs. For

racing applications, Global has similar kits that already have negative camber built in. Global-West Suspension Components

adjustable, however. Of course, by using specially fabricated camber plates, camber also can be changed, but this is done only on race Mustangs. Caster can be adjusted, too, through the use of an aftermarket kit, such as Global-West's McCastor alignment correction kit.

If you own a Mustang GT, especially a 1985 and later model, consider yourself lucky. You already own one of the best-handling production cars built in the United States. You can fine tune the suspension to improve handling as discussed here, but your best bet is to improve your driving skills to take advantage of what you already have. You'd be amazed what the Mustang GT can do in the right hands!

Other less-endowed Mustangs will greatly benefit by these recommendations. You might not have the power to keep ahead of faster cars on the straights, but one thing is for sure, they won't be able to pass you on the curves!

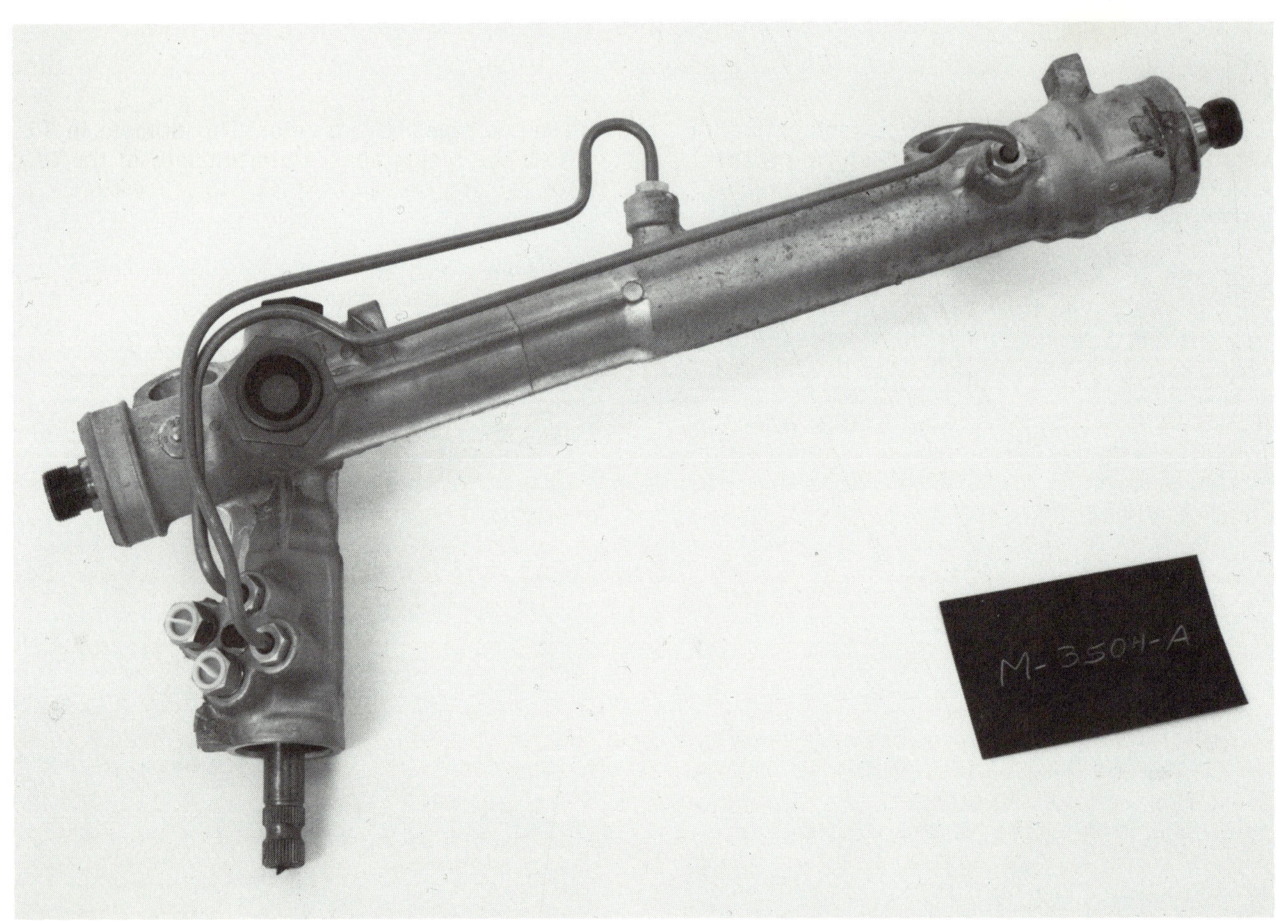

For quicker steering, you can install a high-effort 15:1 rack-and-pinion steering assembly on your Mustang. It provides quicker steering and better feel over the stock 20:1 ratio. Ford recommends that power steering pump number E6SZ-3A674-B be used. You can tell if your car already has a 15:1 rack if 15:1 is stamped on the housing. Ford Motor Co.

Chapter 12

Tires and Wheels

Once you find the right mechanical combination for your car and style of driving, you are still left with the greatest handling variable—tires. While over the past twenty years we've seen some progress with suspension components—larger antisway bars, new bushing materials, rear disc brake kits, and the like—it's tire engineering and technology that have changed by leaps and bounds. Aspect ratios, construction type, tread designs, in fact all facets of tire engineering are constantly evolving in the search for the ultimate tire—the tire that will perform well under every possible driving condition and last practically forever. Unfortunately, no one tire can do all that. One brand may provide superior dry performance but may not fare as well in the wet. Conversely, another tire may provide excellent braking response yet when compared to another, may not provide adequate acceleration traction. We're confronted with the old bugaboo—compromise. Everything automotive is a compromise, and it extends to tires as well.

If you've ever talked to anyone who autocrosses, you'll find that when the conversation shifts to what modifications they've made or what the trick setup is, the subject most talked about is tires. Tires are the key. For example, in SCCA's stock classes where no deviations from stock are allowed except for tires, a lousy driver piloting a car with great tires can beat a good driver with stock tires. Tires make all the difference, and whatever class you look at, the situation is the same. Of course, the tires used in a typical autocross event shouldn't be used on the street because they are made from very soft compounds (tread life is very poor). Two to three weeks of street use is all they're good for.

So, what is a performance tire? Simply put, a performance tire will respond to steering input with less lag than a non- or low-performance tire. It will be able to corner at higher speeds, in a predictably tight manner, and it will have a very noticeable on-center feel. Usually such a tire will have a wider tread and a smaller aspect ratio. One thing that *doesn't* make a performance tire, though, is raised white letters.

The advantage of a wider tread is obvious. Increase the tire's contact patch with the road and you should have better traction. The ultimate, in this case, is the racing slick. Unfortunately, in the real world, you may occasionally have to deal with rain. A

VEHICLE TOP SPEED MPH	INFLATION PRESSURE INCREASE[1] PSI	LOAD CAPACITY[2] (% of maximum branded load on tire)
100	0	100
106	1.5	100
112	3.0	100
118	4.5	100
124	6.0	100
130	7.5	100
137	7.5	90
143	7.5	85
149	7.5	80
155	7.5	75
161	7.5	70
168	7.5	65
174	7.5	60
180	7.5	55
186	7.5	50

1-Do not exceed the maximum pressure branded on tire sidewall.
2-Tire upsizing may be necessary to achieve these reduced loads.

The faster you go, the more air pressure your tires will require. This guideline is taken from the European Tyre and Rim Technical Organization Standards Manual. *According to the chart, for speeds up to 100mph, standard inflation pressure applies.*

tread pattern, necessary to remove water so that the tire won't hydroplane, also removes some of the tire's contact patch. Thus the tire designer has to compromise, making the tire safe in the wet, while minimizing dry traction loss. We'll look into aspect ratios a little later.

Construction Types

Original equipment Mustang tires in the 1960s were of the bias or the bias-belted types. In both of these types, the cords that make up the tire's plies run crisscross over the tread from bead to bead. This sort of construction, while very strong, causes the sidewalls to be stiff. Thus, for example, in a hard corner, there is a tendency for the tread to lift because the

The hot setup from 1979-84 was the Michelin TRX wheel and tire combination, which came with specific front and rear antisway bars, depending on the engine. It was a good system but the unusual rim size, 15.4in, limited tire availability.

sidewall is so stiff. Other disadvantages include tread squirm which causes wear, heat build-up, and expansion of bias-type tires with increased speed.

With the bias-belted tire, such as Goodyear's earlier Polyglas GT, two additional belt plies were added between the bias plies and tread. These served to strengthen the tread area, but at best, the bias-belted tires were a stopgap measure until the tire manufacturers tooled up for radials.

The main difference between the bias types and radial tires is that on radials the plies run directly across the tread. While strong, these radial plies are very flexible and require the use of belt plies under the tread to provide stiffness. You can visualize a radial tire by looking at an inner tube. By itself, it is wobbly and wouldn't be of much use as a tire. Wrapping a steel belt tightly around its circumference now provides a contact patch that will not distort, and because the sidewall is flexible, much more of the tire's tread remains on the ground during hard cornering. The radial's belts also restrict tire expansion as the tire rolls faster and faster. Ever see a fuel dragster burnout? The slicks, which are of a bias-type construction, expand tremendously under acceleration. This won't happen with a radial design.

Other radial tire advantages include less rolling resistance and better wear characteristics.

Aspect Ratio

Aspect ratio is a measure of the tire's height versus its width. Thus a 60 series tire has section height that is 60 percent of its width. A shorter sidewall (a lower aspect ratio) means that the tire will respond quicker to steering input. When you turn

On 1980-84 models, standard high-performance wheels measured 14in. A 14in rim diameter limited tire aspect size, however, since a very low profile tire would limit ground clearance.

your car's steering wheel, the tire doesn't immediately follow. First, the sidewalls bend and the force they exert will eventually overcome the tread's grip on the road and soon the car will turn. A shorter sidewall is stiffer, thus forcing the tread to react quicker.

The difference between the direction the tire is pointing and the direction it is steered is called the slip angle. Thus it can be seen that in any cornering situation, you have to steer farther into the direction you want to go than the tire will actually turn. However, a performance tire will generate a much smaller slip angle, thereby requiring less steering angle for a given corner.

You may ask, why have slip angles at all? Without slip angles, no matter how hard you turned the steering wheel your car would not turn because the tires would just slide. And as we have seen in the case with bias-ply tires, very stiff sidewalls have a tendency to lift the tread off the ground during hard cornering. The tire engineer has to balance a host of factors in order to maintain the correct amount of sidewall flexibility for a particular application.

Also, the slip angle and load exerted on a tire are related. When a tire is loaded it will generate cornering force at a lower slip angle. In a corner, weight distribution is shifted thereby loading one tire more than the other, even though they both may have the same slip angles. This means they are not generating the same amount of cornering power. The factory engineer's efforts to control weight transfer may be limited by corporate policy, but the enthusiast, through the correct use of springs, shocks, and antisway bars can further minimize it.

It is unlikely that you'll go to your local tire dealer and get into an involved discussion about slip angles with the salesperson. You have to rely on any test results you may have seen, the tire maker's advertising, your own experience, and any word-of-mouth information you have acquired to make a sensible choice. As a general rule, however, a tire with a smaller aspect ratio will make smaller slip angles. Installing a 50 or 60 series radial tire on your Mustang will provide better handling. You won't be at the cutting edge of tire technology since the current hot-shot street tires require 17in rims to compensate for a 35 series aspect ratio, but you'll be way ahead of anything that came as standard equipment on the base and six-cylinder models. Going beyond a 50 series tire with stock rims will drastically decrease ground clearance.

Tire Sizing

As a general rule, you should be able to go one size larger than stock. Typical Mustang wheelwells have plenty of space so you can go pretty wild, if you want to. It all depends on how you are using your car.

Tire size designations have changed several times in the last twenty years. Until 1968, US manufacturers used the Numeric System. For example, a tire with 7.00–14 designation meant that the tire had a cross-section width (not tread width) of about 7in when inflated. The two zeros stood for aspect ratio, generally an industry standard of 92, and the 14 stood for rim diameter. A tire with numbers other than double zero usually had a lower profile, which in most cases was around 80.

The 1984 SVO Mustangs were the first to come with 16in wheels and 50 series rubber—one of the reasons why the SVO handled so well. Its five-lug wheels mean that they are not interchangeable with regular Mustangs.

In 1985, 15x7in wheels replaced the TRXs, and Goodyear Eagles became the standard tires. The Eagles, known as Gatorbacks due to their tread design, have proved to be superior to the Michelin tires in terms of handling and also provide much better acceleration traction.

The Goodyear Eagle is a unidirectional tire, meaning it has to be installed with the tread pattern pointing toward the front of the car. Its only shortcoming is that it isn't great in the wet. For that reason, it was replaced by the Eagle GT4 tire in 1990—an all-weather design.

In 1968, the Alpha Numeric System was adopted. In this system, tires were designated by their load-carrying capability (letters A through N) and their aspect ratio. Thus with an F70x14 tire the F indicates its load capacity, the 70 its aspect ratio, and the 14 its rim width. If the tire was a radial, the letter R would be sandwiched between the F and 70 (FR70x14).

From 1976 on, the P Metric System came into use. It gave us more information. For example, a P205/70R-14 would break down as follows: The P stands for passenger tire, the 205 measures its section width in millimeters, 70 stands for aspect ratio, R is for a radial type (B for bias-belted, D for bias), and 14 is for rim width, still measured in inches. A speed-rated tire will include additional information. The speed rating, expressed by a letter indicating the tire's ability to withstand high speed, is placed before the letter showing what kind of tire it is. In our example, an H-rated tire would now read as P205/70HR-14. The following are the Speed Symbols currently in use:

Speed Symbol	Maximum Speed (mph)
Q	99
R	106
S	112
T	118
U	124
H	130
V (without Service Description)	130
V (with Service Description)	149
Z	149

Some high-performance speed-rated tires may also carry additional information known as the Service Description. This comprises the Load Index which ranges from 75 (851lb) to 100 (1,760lb), and the Speed Symbol. The Load Index is the same as the load capacity which is normally embossed on the tire's sidewall. Thus, in our example, a P205/70R14 93H tire has a 93 Load Index and is H-speed-rated. Today, all speed-rated tires up to and including H-rated use a Service Description. V-rated tires are marked in three different ways. For example, a P205/70VR-14 tire is certified for speeds above 130mph. A P205/70R14 93V has a Service Description designator and thus is rated for speeds up to 149mph. Finally, with a P205/70VR14 93V, note that the V-speed indicator appears in both size and Service Description, meaning that the tire is good to 149mph. Z-rated tires will continue to be identified with the Speed Symbol in the size designation. Pretty complicated, you say? It will probably get even more complicated.

For high-speed driving, additional inflation pressure and possibly reduced tire loading and upsizing is required. You can use the guidelines set forth in the *European Tyre and Rim Technical Organization Standards Manual* (see chart). What it means is that the faster you go, the more you have to increase inflation pressure without exceeding the maximum on the tire's sidewall. And the faster you go, the more the tire's load capacity is reduced so you may have to go to a higher load tire.

DOT Designations

Additional designations are required by the DOT (Department of Transportation) which include tread wear, traction, and temperature gradations. These designations were created to help the typical consumer compare one tire with another.

Tread wear is a comparative index that measures wear rate. A tire rated 200 will wear twice as long as one rated 100. This means that a tire with a low wear rating number will have tread made of a softer rubber and thus provide better traction. I feel that anything in the 300 range and above will give good wear but because the rubber compound is so hard, it may provide less than satisfactory traction, especially in the wet. For good handling, you should try to stay under the 200 range. If you are concerned about tread wear, try to modify your driving habits.

The greatest effect on tire wear is caused by braking. A tire will wear four times as fast in a typical moderate stop from 30mph under braking than from a rolling stop. A panic stop that doesn't lock the brakes will cause the tire to wear 2,000-3,000 times faster! Hard cornering will also accelerate wear. Doubling the cornering speed of any curve that you take will increase tire wear by sixteen times. Of course, burnout starts and panic stops greatly shorten tire life. In addition, the higher the temperature, the greater the wear. A tire will wear some 20

Firestone has recently entered the high-performance tire arena. This is their Firehawk SVX. Firestone

The Goodyear Eagle ZR50 S is a high-performance tire based on the original Eagle GT design. It is a Z-rated tire, good to speeds of 149mph and over.

percent faster if the outside temperature increases from 45 to about 70deg Fahrenheit. Conversely, tread wear is reduced when outside temperature drops from 90 to 50deg.

Traction, the second comparative index designed by DOT, is graded A, B, or C. This gradation measures the tire's ability to stop in the wet. There is no reason to get anything less than an A rating.

Temperature is also graded A, B, or C. This measures the tire's ability to withstand and dissipate heat. Again, an A rating is the only way to go, especially if you are going to drive fast, even for a short spurt.

What about rotation? Rotating your tires regularly is very important for long tire life. Regardless of what you may have heard, it is now OK to cross-rotate radial tires. For rear-wheel-drive cars, the right rear tire goes to the right front position, the right front tire moves to the left rear, the left rear to the left front, and the left front to the right rear. You should rotate your tires every 7,500 miles.

The hot factory setup from 1979-84 was the Michelin TRX wheel and tire combination which also came with specially matched springs, shocks, and stabilizer bars. From 1979-82, the Michelins measured 190/65R, and by 1983 tread width increased to 220mm while aspect ratio was reduced to 55. The TRX wheels and tires were highly rated at the time, but the TRX system had some limitations. Its unique wheel size, 15.4x5.9in, limited tire size and availability. The

TRX tires couldn't handle the resurrected Mustang GT's torque, which resulted in less than optimum acceleration traction.

Handling improved dramatically on Mustang GTs from 1985 on. The chassis was stiffened and the TRX wheels were discarded and replaced by conventional 15x7in aluminum wheels mounting Goodyear Eagle GTs. These provide superior traction, but like the TRXs they replaced, they fall short when it comes to rain and snow. You might as well park your Mustang GT at the first sign of moisture.

Since 1990, Mustang GTs have come with Goodyear Eagle GT+4 tires—an all-season performance tire which provides the usual excellent dry weather performance with dramatically improved wet and snow performance.

Another change occurred with all 1991 Mustang GT models, and LX models with the 302. They got larger 16x7in rims with P225/55ZR Eagle GT+4 tires.

Your best bet for improved handling is to get the largest wheel and tire combination that will fit your Mustang and budget. Stick to well-known tire brands. The factory setup between 1985 and 1990 is 15x7in wheels with P225/60VR15 tires. You can't go wrong with such a combination and you could probably fit a 235 size without any problem, as well as 15x8in rims. From there, it all depends on your budget. As long as you maintain a 24-25in overall tire diameter, you can go to a 16 or 17in wheel. The 1992 SAAC Mk 1 comes with 17x7.5in front and 17x8.0in rear wheels fitted with Goodyear 245ZR50x17 tires.

If it is time to replace your Goodyear Eagles, consider replacing your worn-out tires with the Eagle GT + 4s. Somewhat less expensive, yet still providing excellent all-weather performance are Firestone's Firehawk, B.F. Goodrich's Comp T/A HR, and General Tire's XP2000 AS.

Naturally, when you are replacing tires, get tires that are rated at least HR (good to 130mph) or VR (good to over 130mph).

Wheels

Standard Mustang wheels measured 13in for 1979-80; 14in rims were optional for that year and from 1981-on were made standard. From 1979-84, the optional wheels were the Michelin TRXs. From 1985-90, the optional wheels and those standard on the GT measured 15x7in and were of a conventional design. In 1991, the standard GT wheel measured 16x7in.

Most aftermarket replacement wheels are made of aluminum as are the optional Mustang wheels. Aluminum wheels are stronger than the stock stamped-steel wheels which can deflect under hard cornering, and they also contribute to reducing unsprung weight. Unsprung weight consists of weight that is not supported by the car's springs, such as wheels, tires, brakes, and hubs. A lighter wheel contributes to less overall weight and less unsprung weight which can be felt as less of a shock to the car's springs when going over bumps.

The majority of aftermarket wheels are made from aluminum or an aluminum alloy, and can either be cast or forged. Forged wheels are more expensive but they are stronger. There are also two- and three-piece modular wheels to choose from. By using different sections, wheel width and offset can be changed to accommodate different tires for different applications, thereby offering a distinct advantage to the racer.

The Plus System

The Plus System is an easy way to figure out what tire and wheel combination to use when going to a wider tire, yet still remaining within safe load-carrying capacities and maintaining the same overall diameter for speedometer accuracy.

For example, late-model base Mustangs come with 14x6in wheels fitted with P205/70R14 tires. The next size wider tire is a P215, but in order to maintain the same diameter (the P215/70R14 would be taller) you'd have to go to a lower profile tire on a taller rim, a P215/60R15. In this way you've lowered the tire's

You can upgrade your Mustang with better tires. This 1985 LX got a set of Firestone Firehawk FTXs measuring P225/60R14, putting down as much rubber as a Mustang GT. The Firestone Firehawk is also M&S (mud and snow) rated so it does provide good wet-weather traction while its 210 tread-wear rating means that it is a reasonably soft compound. The softer the compound, the stickier the tire is but at the expense of tread life.

aspect ratio while increasing the tire's contact patch. This is referred to as a Plus 1 because you've increased wheel diameter by one size and aspect ratio by one size. A Plus 2 would increase diameter and aspect ratio by two sizes. In our example, then, a Plus 2 would be a P225/50R16.

Naturally, when you are using the Plus System, you must refer to the manufacturer's tire availability and load-capacity charts in order to match the tires to the right wheels.

Of course, if you are on a tight budget (and who isn't?) and can't afford to get new wheels and tires, you may be better off getting the widest low-profile tires that will safely fit on your wheels and just changing the speedometer gear to compensate for the different height.

Figuring Out Effective Axle Ratio

The bigger the tire's diameter, the less acceleration you'll have while a smaller-than-stock tire will improve acceleration. The following formula will make it easy for you to determine what your effective axle ratio will be after changing from a stock (for example) P205/70R14 to a taller P255/60VR15.

$$\frac{\text{New tire revs per mile}}{\text{Original tire revs per mile}} \times \text{Original axle ratio} = \text{Effective axle ratio}$$

$$\frac{773}{825} \times 3.08 = 2.88$$

Tires, such as this Yokohama, that are used on cars that autocross should never be used on the street. The rubber compound, with a typical tread-wear rating of 50, is far too soft for street use. Tire pressure is upped to 42lb in front, while it is lowered to 24lb in the rear on this Mustang. More than anything else, it is the tire that makes all the difference in such an application, all things being equal.

Wheels do make the car. There is a variety of aftermarket wheels available. Of course, when the current Mustangs become collectibles, these wheels will probably be trashed—so save your original equipment wheels!

The 1992 Shelby Mustang comes with these distinctive 17in wheels which emulate the modular look. Tires are Goodyear 245/45/ZR17s. Whenever you are considering an aftermarket wheel for your Mustang, always choose an open design, such as these. The open design promotes brake cooling.

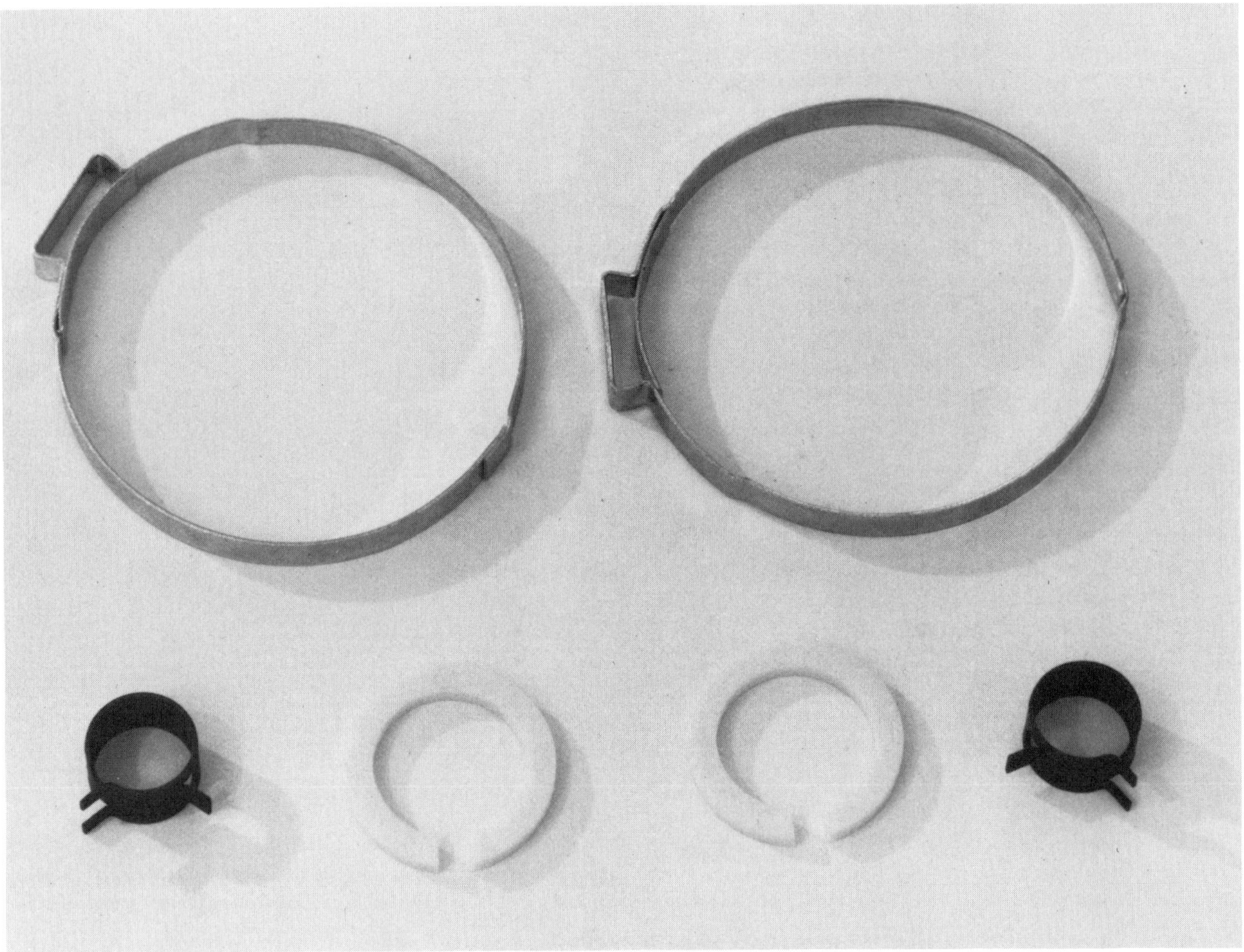

Mustangs equipped with 225/60 VR15 tires come with these stops which are designed to eliminate tire-to-body interference. If you install big wheels and tires on your car, this Motorsport kit, part number M-3500-A, is a must. Ford Motor Co.

You say you're experiencing tire wear problems on your lowered 1990-91 Mustang? You say you can't dial in enough caster? Well, these caster plates give increased suspension adjustment and end tire problems, too. Central Coast Mustangs

Thus in this example, installing taller tires will reduce your effective axle ratio from to 3.08:1 to 2.88:1. This will result in better mileage at the expense of acceleration. To regain equivalent acceleration, the rear axle must be changed. The following formula will tell you what axle ratio you will need.

$$\frac{\text{Original tire revs per mile} \times \text{Original axle ratio}}{\text{New tire revs per mile}} = \text{Equivalent axle ratio}$$

$$\frac{825 \times 3.08}{773} = 3.28$$

So in order to duplicate stock acceleration, a 3.28:1 axle ratio is needed. The closest one available in the Motorsport catalog is 3.27:1, which is close enough.

The ultimate wheels available are the two- and three-piece modulars. These are from Jongbloed and are shod with B.F. Goodrich Comp T/As. Their advantages are more readily apparent on a race car than on a street Mustang. Kamei USA Inc.

Chapter 13

Brakes

Most of the emphasis in this book is on making your Mustang go faster and handle better. In doing so, it's easy to forget about your brakes. The faster your Mustang goes, the more stopping power it needs. The

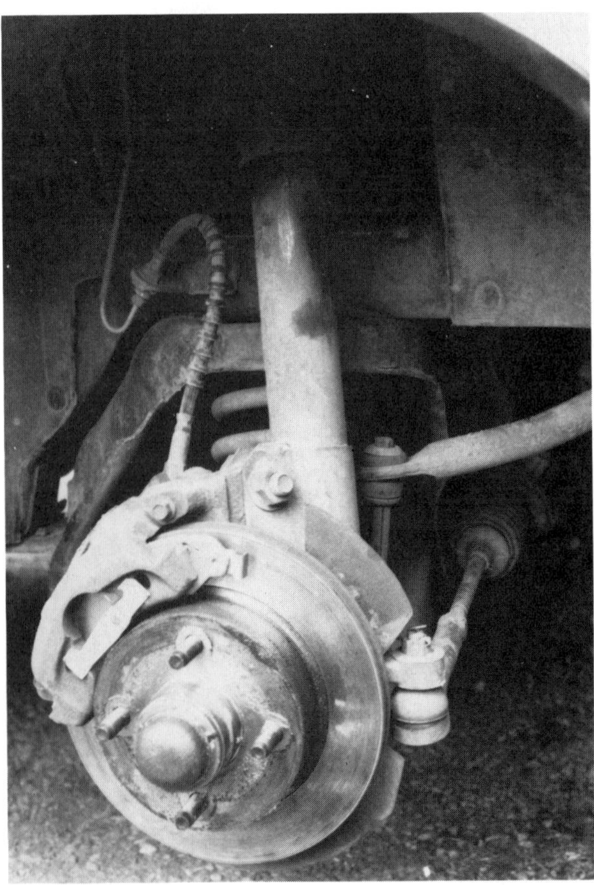

All 1979 and later Mustangs come with power front disc brakes and rear drum brakes. Rotor diameter measured 10in on all Mustangs built to 1986, except the SVOs which measured 11in. An advantage of disc brakes is greater swept (braking) area per given size and the rotor is always exposed to air and thus cools faster. Maintenance is also easier as pads can be quickly changed.

stock brakes are adequate for everyday use but the minute you start using your brakes harder than normal, you'll soon notice that the brakes will fade. What is happening is that your brakes take the forward motion (kinetic energy) of your car and convert it into another form of energy, in this case, heat. When brakes fade, it means that they cannot continue converting the car's forward motion into heat because they are too hot and need some time to cool and dissipate the heat. You can tell when your brakes are fading when it takes more and more brake pedal travel to stop or slow the car down, and sometimes even pushing the pedal to the floor won't stop the car. This is often accompanied by increased pedal effort—you have to press the brake pedal harder and harder. You can also smell what is happening as the brake pads and shoes heat up and start to smoke.

The problem with heat buildup is that it can damage your brakes beyond repair. The discs and drums may be scored or warped and under severe use, the disc pads and drum shoes can also disintegrate. If you are going to use your brakes hard, there are certain things you can do to reduce fade and improve your Mustang's braking performance.

All Mustangs built since 1979 come with power front disc brakes and rear drum brakes as standard equipment, which work fine under normal use. The front disc brakes do most of the work—usually two-thirds of the braking action is handled by the front brakes. The automobile industry gradually switched over to front disc brakes by the mid-1970s because disc brakes are more resistant to brake fade, provide greater braking power over a comparable drum brake, and are much easier to service and maintain. The main reason disc are better than drum brakes is that the braking surface is directly exposed to air so that cooling begins immediately. In a drum brake, the heat generated by braking action is inside the drum and it takes time for this heat energy to dissipate.

As the front brakes do most of the work anyway, Ford has stayed with rear drum brakes on the Mustang, with one exception—the SVO Mustang came with rear disc brakes in keeping with its road racing image.

From 1979-86, the front disc rotor diameter measured 10in while the rear drum diameter was 9in. Because of the Mustang's greater horsepower output, the rotor's diameter was increased to 11in in 1987. The effect of this was less brake fade under hard use. The SVO Mustang came with 11in front rotors.

The first step to better braking should be to change to larger front disc brakes. If you own a 1986 and earlier Mustang, you can install 1987 and later front 11in rotors and calipers for improved braking performance. You'll also have to change front spindles. The 1987 and later Mustangs will have to go to one of the 12in rotors available from JFZ Engineered Products, Incorporated, and Wilwood Engineering, as described in the next section. (See Appendices for details.)

Aftermarket Front and Rear Disc Brake Conversion Kits

One way to reduce brake fade is to replace the rear drum brakes with disc brakes. As mentioned, disc brakes provide better braking because they are

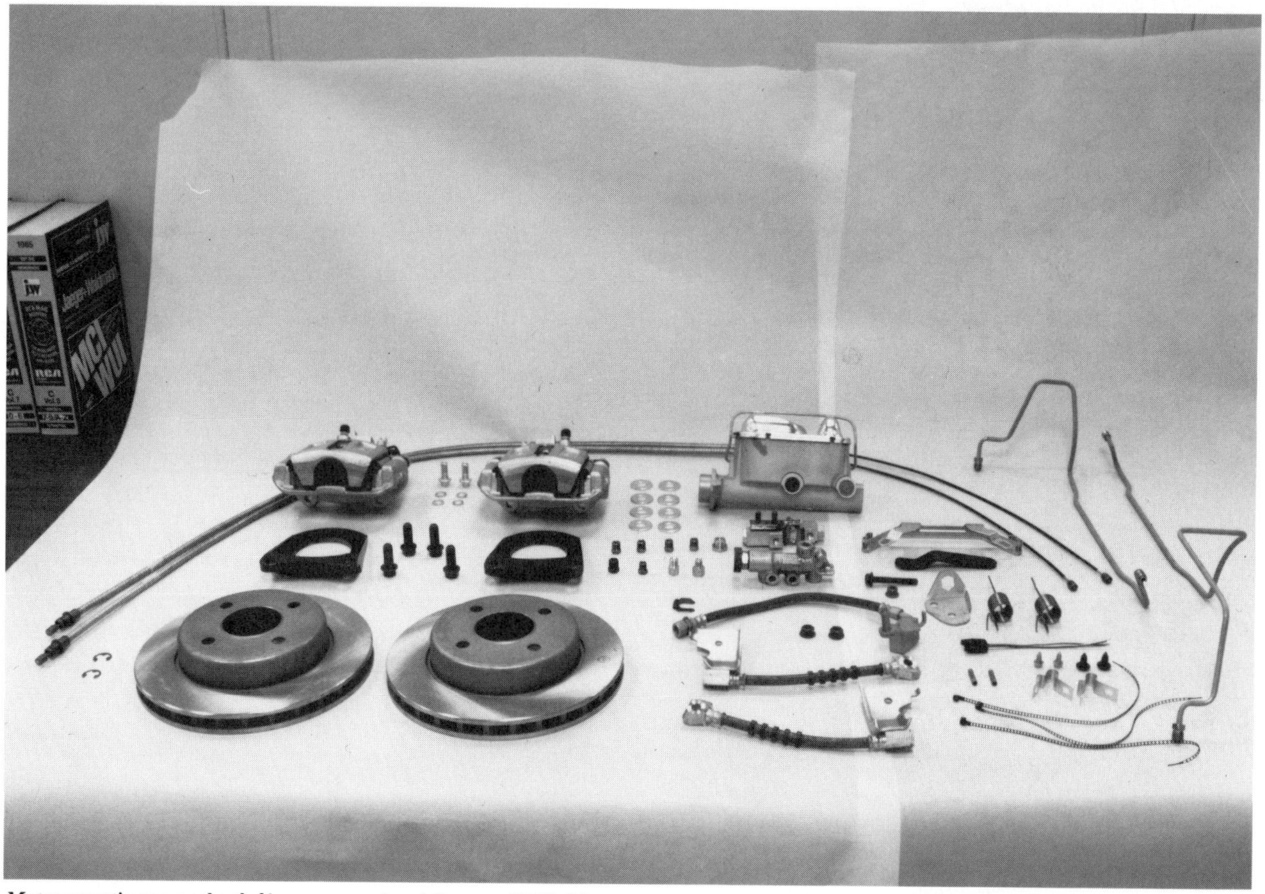

You can gain additional braking ability and fade resistance by switching earlier Mustangs to post-1986 11in rotors. You'll also have to change the front spindles and calipers.

Motorsport's rear wheel disc conversion kit uses 1987-88 T-Bird Turbo Coupe components. It is a bolt-on operation and includes all the parts necessary to complete the conversion including brake lines, master cylinder, proportioning valve, and parking brake cables. This kit is highly recommended for a hot street car. Ford Motor Co.

more resistant to fade. There are several ways to go about doing this and we'll look at what Motorsport has to offer.

The Motorsport M-2300-C Rear Wheel Disc Brake Conversion kit uses 1987-88 T-Bird Turbo Coupe rear disc brake components and can be installed on any 1979-92 Mustang. This is a bolt-on kit that requires no cutting or welding. Included in the kit is everything you need to complete the conversion (see photo).

One other kit that Motorsport offers, part number M-2300-E, is a four-wheel disc brake system that uses five-lug front and rear disc brakes. Included in the kit are two rear five-lug axle shafts. If you want four-wheel disc brakes with five-lug wheels (which you'll also have to purchase), this is the kit to buy.

Motorsport also offers 10 and 11in front five-lug disc rotors as well as rear five-lug axle shaft kits—the rear kits come with 9in drum brakes. One of the oldest suppliers of rear disc brake conversion kits for Mustangs is Stainless Steel Brakes Corporation. The Stainless Steel rear conversion kit uses 10in rotors and is similar to the Motorsport kit. Stainless Steel also offers an 11in five-lug rear rotor kit that comes with new axle shafts. This is identical to the 11in rear discs used on the SVO Mustang.

The systems described thus far are more than adequate for hard street and autocrossing use. For more serious applications there are disc brake kits available from JFZ and Wilwood. Both companies specialize in brake components for race car use.

For street use, JFZ offers their Series V Front Pro Street kit. It is a five-lug kit comprised of a 12.18in diameter vented rotor, billet aluminum hub, four-piston aluminum caliper, bearings, and necessary hardware. The rear kit also uses a 12.18in rotor, and once again, it is set up for five-lug wheels. The rotors are available in two thicknesses—0.810 and 1.25in.

Wilwood makes a Super Stopper front disc brake kit for 1987-92 Mustangs. These are available in four- or five-lug configuration and consist of 12.19in diameter vented 1.25in thick rotor, Superlite II aluminum

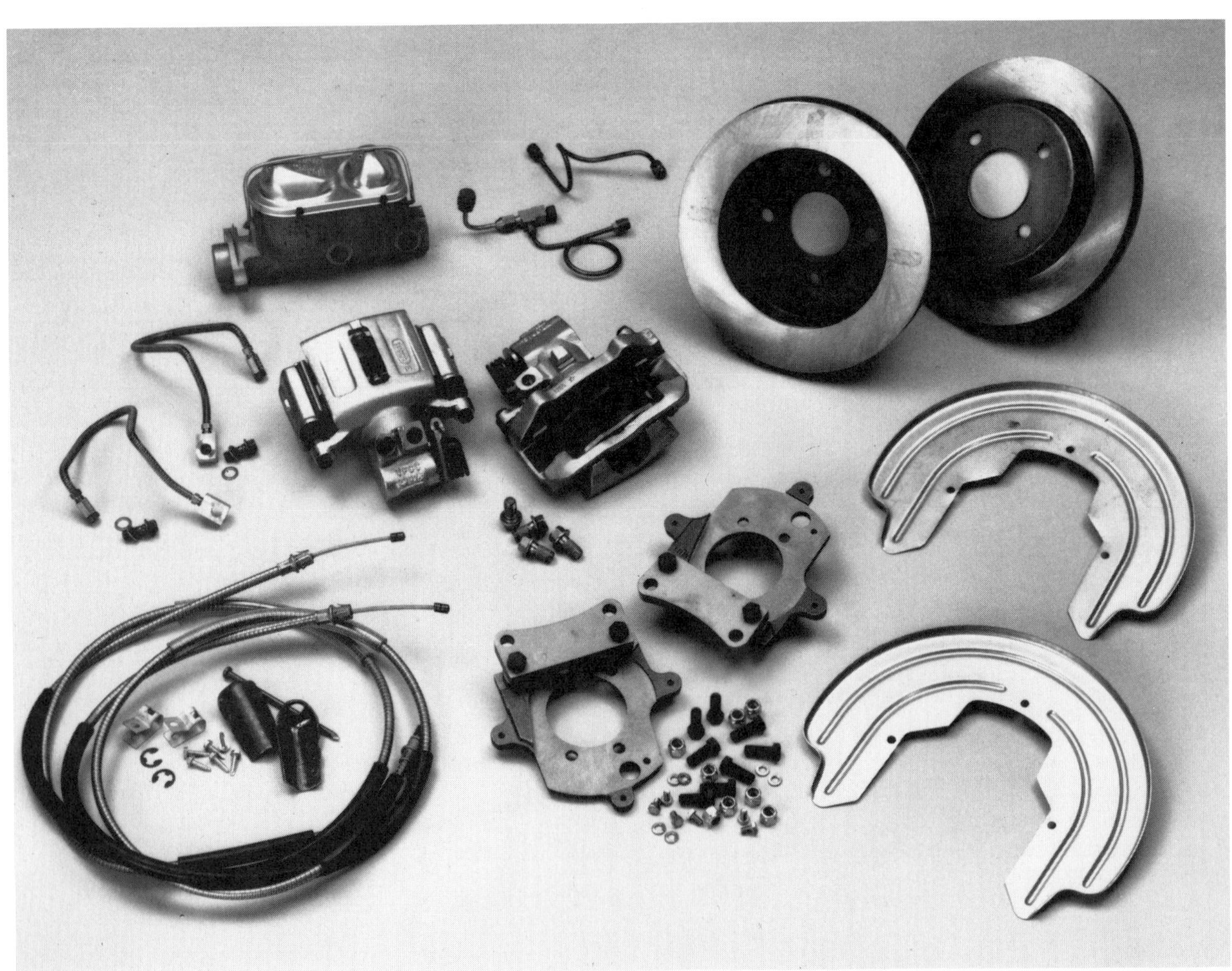

The rear disc brake conversion kit from Stainless Steel Brakes Corp. Similar to the Motorsport kit, it also retains the use of four-lug wheels. Stainless Steel Brakes Corp.

Wilwood's Super Stopper front disc brake kit features 12in vented rotor, billet aluminum hubs, and massive four-piston aluminum calipers. The kit comes complete with new front bearings and hardware and is designed for 1987 and later Mustangs that originally came with 11in rotors. Wilwood Engineering

four-piston caliper, and hardware. The whole setup weighs 7lb less than the stock components, thereby reducing unsprung weight.

Wilwood's rear disc brake kit features the same size rotor as the front, but also offers an optional mechanical caliper parking brake.

Brake Pads and Shoes

Some enthusiasts may think that they can improve brake performance by simply switching to pads and shoes using different types of friction materials. It would be great if there was a material that would last a long time, that could withstand high temperatures, that wouldn't damage the rotor or drum, and that would function quietly. Unfortunately there isn't. Instead there are several types of materials, each designed for specific purposes.

Organic

The most common material used for brake linings is made from organic sources. These include asbestos, cashew nut shell liquid, rubber chips,

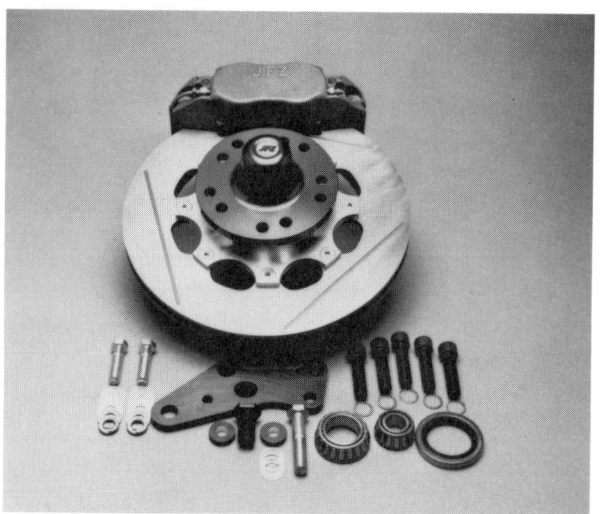

JFZ's front Series V kit also comes complete and uses grooved rotors for better fade resistance. It is designed to work on 1987 and later Mustangs. Rotor measures 12in. JFZ Engineered Products, Inc.

aluminum, brass, lead, curing agents, and phenolic resins used to bind them all together. Because of health questions, the use of asbestos has declined appreciably and is replaced by glass and synthetic fibers. These are molded to the shape required and either riveted or bonded (glued) onto a backing plate. For street use, either attachment method is acceptable, but bonded linings do not have high-temperature resistance so they should not be used in a performance application.

The advantages of organic linings are low cost, low rate of wear, and less noise. Their disadvantages become readily apparent under hard use, however: they fade and wear quickly as temperature exceeds 400deg Fahrenheit.

Metallic

Under hard usage, the organic materials in conventional linings quickly fall apart as they can't stand the temperature. Metallic linings, made from a metallic powder in a process called sintering where the powder is compressed and molded at high temperatures, can withstand the high temperatures encountered in a race application. However, there are some serious drawbacks to metallic linings. When metallic linings are cold, they don't work too well—they need to get hot to work properly. This is OK on the racetrack, but not on the street. Metallic linings also wear the rotor and drum surface more quickly, and they cost more. They should not be used on a street car.

Semi-Metallic

The semi-metallic lining is the best of both worlds. These linings are comprised of steel fibers bonded with organic resins to give excellent performance to about 1,000deg F. or so. However, they shouldn't be used in a competition application as the steel fibers will melt and fuse on the rotor or drum surface.

For everyday use, a semi-metallic lining works best. If you are going to do some serious autocrossing or road racing, switch to a metallic pad. This isn't hard to do on disc brake-equipped cars, and the aftermarket disc brakes are designed for even quicker pad removal and installation.

Finally, whenever you change to new pads, make sure that you break them in properly. This process, called "bedding," is done by driving your car and slowly warming up the brakes by doing several light to moderate stops followed by several hard stops. The brakes should then be allowed to cool.

The reason for this is to avoid glazing the pads or shoes. Glazing occurs when the lining material is first heated up. The organic components in the lining boil away and if the brakes are heated up too quickly, the material will resolidify on the pad or shoe. This hard surface can only be removed by refacing (or replacing) the pad or shoe.

Brake Fluids

Without hydraulic fluid, your braking system would not work. The fluid most commonly used today is a polyalkaline glycol ether mixture. Not all the brake fluids that you see in your typical auto parts store are formulated exactly the same, but they all must meet DOT standards. Brake fluid should have certain properties—for example, it should not compress, freeze, or boil, and it should be compatible with other glycol-based fluids.

The most important characteristic that a brake fluid must have is its resistance to boiling at high

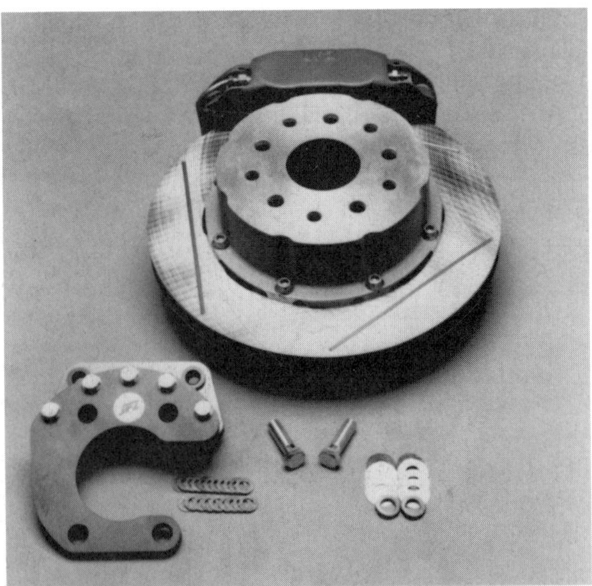

JFZ's rear kit for the Mustang. It is a high-quality piece, but it does require that the rear-axle shafts be changed to a five-lug configuration. The big four-piston caliper and 12in rotor provide massive stopping power. Whenever changing to rear discs or if you are road racing, a brake proportioning valve is a nice thing to have because you can alter front-to-rear brake balance. JFZ Engineered Products, Inc.

For severe use, Motorsport offers these 11in front rotors which also come with five lugs necessitating the use of five-lug wheels. To install matching five-lug wheels at the rear, you'll also have to get five-lug axle shafts which are available from Motorsport. Ford Motor Co.

temperatures. How does brake fluid boil? When the brakes are used hard, they get hot and that heat is transferred to the brake fluid. Like any other fluid that boils, tiny bubbles are formed in the brake lines and because gas bubbles compress, this results in a spongy pedal. Brake fluid boils at 550deg F. but depending on how much water the system is contaminated with, this boiling point drops. Brake fluid is very hydroscopic and readily absorbs water.

Brake fluid is rated by the DOT as follows:

	DOT 3	DOT 4	DOT 5
Dry boiling point	401deg F.	446deg F.	500deg F.
Wet boiling point	284deg F.	311deg F.	356deg F.

The dry boiling point refers to the boiling point that fresh, out-of-the-can brake fluid has. The wet boiling point refers to fluid that has been exposed to moisture under certain conditions that the DOT uses for testing purposes. DOT 3 and 4 standards apply to regular fluid; DOT 5 applies only to silicone-based fluid.

Tests have shown that the fluid's boiling point in the typical car will decrease by about 100deg after six months and by another 25-50deg in a year's time. If you plan to do any racing, you should change your fluid every week.

To avoid any future problems with corrosion in your brake system, change the fluid at least every year or 25,000 miles and stick to the same brand. If you change brands, make sure to flush all the old fluid out before replacing it with the new.

Although one may think that the fluid can be changed by simply opening up the bleed screws and pumping it out, this won't get all the fluid out because the bleeders are located at high spots—after all, they are designed to let air out, not fluid. You can refill and drain the system several times, each time diluting the fluid, but the only correct way is to disassemble the brake calipers, wheel cylinders, and master cylinder.

You may have heard about silicone-based brake fluids. Unlike the typical glycol-based fluid, silicone fluids do not absorb moisture so there is no problem with corrosion, and they have a higher boiling point as well. However, it is not recommended for race use because the fluid will compress slightly after exposure to high temperature—resulting in a spongy pedal. For race use, use a glycol-based fluid such as JFZ's Z-10 Racing Fluid, which has a dry boiling point of 570deg F.

If you do change to a silicone-based fluid, you must flush out all the existing brake fluid as outlined earlier to take advantage of its properties.

High-performance brake pads and shoes are a must. These are the Super Pro-Street Brakes from Kenny Brown. Note that both shoes and pads are grooved. For more brake fade resistance, you can add an additional groove on the drum shoes and a lengthwise groove on the disc pads. Project Industries

Other Modifications

A useful modification would be to install steel-braided hoses in place of the stock rubber brake hoses at the wheels. When the brakes are used hard, hydraulic pressure causes the stock rubber hoses to expand, which creates a softer pedal and requires more pumping. This is noticeable in a race application.

On race cars, you may have seen rotors that are grooved or drilled with holes. The grooves and holes can reduce fade by letting the gas and dust generated by the brakes go to the grooves or holes instead of forming a lubricating layer between the lining and rotor or drum surface. Grooves are preferable because stress cracks can form around the holes. This modification is not necessary on the street but if you insist on grooving, make grooves on your disc pads and rotors. Some disc pads and shoes already come with grooves—disc pads often come with a single groove and adding another one is acceptable. Brake shoes should have a groove every 2in or so. This no-cost modification will improve fade resistance. Don't overdo it, though, as too many grooves will increase wear, and always use a respirator mask (like the masks painters use) when cutting the grooves; asbestos is potentially dangerous. Don't get the dust on your hands or clothes, either.

Additional modifications and high-performance braking systems are described in Fred Puhn's *Brake Handbook*.

Chapter 14

Bodywork Modifications

Besides the usual mechanical modifications, the typical enthusiast will want his Mustang to stand out from a visual point of view as well. This has become quite common since the 1969 Boss 302, which popularized bodywork add-ons such as front spoilers, rear wings, and rear window louvers. The front and rear spoilers were designed to make the Mustang more aerodynamically stable while the rear window louvers are more of a styling add-on.

Spoilers and wings were touted as a way to improve mileage in the 1970s and early 1980s, besides making the car look more aggressive. The Cobra II and King Cobra both came with aerodynamic packages that included front and rear spoilers. When the third-generation Mustang was introduced in 1979, the pace car replica came with a front air dam and a rear spoiler which enhanced the car's image. The front air dam and spoiler were carried over to the 1982 GT. By 1984, the rear spoiler was replaced by a large rear wing on the GT models while the SVO Mustang got an even larger biplane rear wing. The SVO also came with rear wheel "spats" which are designed to direct air away from the rear wheels.

There is no doubt that the front air dam and rear wing do work. Racer Walsh ran a Mustang at Daytona with and without the air dam and wing and the car went 7-8mph faster with them on. Naturally, for a street car, the advantage of these aerodynamic aids can be seen as better fuel economy since it takes less power to push the car through the air.

In 1987, in an attempt to modernize the Mustang GT's appearance, Ford gave the GT a new aerodynamic look. The Mustang's nose was redesigned with flush fitting headlights while a ground effects package with scoops in front of each wheel opening extended around to the rear, giving the GT a much lower appearance. A large wing was used on the rear hatch. Since 1987, all GT Mustangs have come with this aero package.

While they might look good, you'll find that most, if not all, Mustangs that race on the Showroom Stock circuit do not use the GT's aero panels, especially the one on the rear. The side panels don't do much while the rear panel, because it extends below the bumper, actually slows the car down at high speeds because it catches air, like a parachute. You'll find that many of the aftermarket kits use a rear panel that has slots or is cut away to let the air pass. Substituting one of these on a GT Mustang is a worthwhile addition, or just using the stock LX rear panel will do the same job.

Most aftermarket kits are designed to give regular and older Mustangs the current GT's aero look, and most of them look similar to one another. One of the best kits available is from American Best Car Parts Incorporated/Xenon of North Hollywood, California. The parts are made from polyurethane and guaranteed for life. Polyurethane is stronger and considerably more resistant to cracks than fiberglass. (See Appendices for supplier's address.)

The 1982 Mustang GT used the same front air dam and rear spoiler that were first used on the 1979 Mustang pace car replica. The large hood scoop was nonfunctional. Tinting the side and rear windows and headlights, or adding headlight covers has also become popular. They may look good, but the loss of visibility at night is substantial.

The 1984 rear wing is a very effective piece, adding top-speed capability while improving mileage at current cruising speeds. Joy Jacobs

The GT's looks were substantially changed in 1987, giving the GT an aerodynamic look. While the front air dam and

rear wing are effective, the lower rear panel actually traps air underneath the car, like a parachute, slowing it down.

The Saleen Mustang came with a more efficient lower rear panel which let the air flowing underneath the car pass through. Rear window louvers are also a popular way of adding some individuality to the Mustang. They can be painted to match the car's exterior or left black.

You'll find that most racers competing in the Showroom Stock classes use the standard Mustang body panels and a rear wing. Steeda Autosports

You can update an older Mustang with Kamei's X1 kit. It includes spoilers, air dam, and side treatment. Kamei USA Inc.

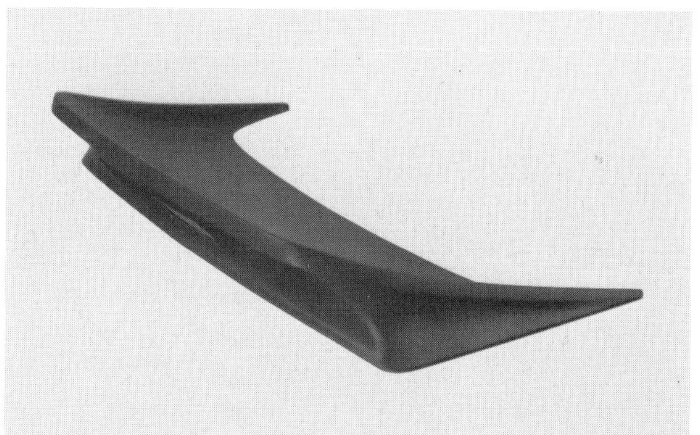

Steeda's latest rear hatchback wing. It has the advantage of weighing only 6lb. Its pronounced angle is designed to increase rear downforce at high speeds. Steeda Autosports

This is the Outlaw GT rear wing. It bolts on top of the existing rear Mustang wing, transforming it to a biplane design. Project Industries

The rear-facing hood on the Outlaw Mustang is a good design as its opening is in a low-pressure area. It comes on the Outlaw Mustang and is also available separately. Project Industries

Besides the kits, the use of a fiberglass hood is also popular. In addition to taking some weight off of the front wheels for better handling, the custom fiberglass hood gives any Mustang a high-performance look. A fiberglass hood is also usually necessary with some supercharged applications as well as some aftermarket fuel-injection setups.

And of course, if you don't like the stock rear wing, there are many aftermarket wings to choose from—and each seems to be bigger than the last one.

Other modifications include tinting the side and rear windows and the use of tinted headlight covers. These should be used with caution as they will decrease visibility at night. Although you don't see many Mustangs so equipped, front-end bras are available from many sources. They will protect the front end from bug splatter, but they can also remove your car's paint by the rubbing motion caused by wind if they aren't installed properly.

A large rear opening can be cut for an underhood air intake or to let hot underhood air escape.

Oversized scoops such as this are usually found on drag-racing cars. They are designed to be effective with intake systems using tunnel ram intake manifolds.

One of the most striking body kits for 1979-92 Mustangs is the GFX kit from Aeroform Motorsport. It goes beyond the usual bolt-on type kit as it requires extensive bodywork modifications, but the result is certainly unique and exciting. It comes in several variations that include optional hood designs and choice of headlights. Similar kits are available for coupe and convertible Mustangs. Aeroform Motorsport

Interior Modifications

As good as the Mustang's interior is, there is still room for improvement. For example, some prefer the feel of leather or wood instead of the vinyl that is used to cover the standard steering wheel. And although the Mustang's dash comes with the basic oil pressure, temperature, and amp gauges, it would be nice to get exact readings of temperature or oil pressure rather than just knowing it is in the "safe" zone. Another area, the Mustang's seats, have improved over the years but again they are a compromise designed to fit a number of differing physiques. Overall, a number of improvements can be made.

The stock Mustang interior was basically the same from 1979-86 (1984 model shown). It is well thought out and includes gauges that fill the minimum requirements for a performance car—tachometer, oil pressure, water temperature, ammeter, and fuel gauge. Glen Jacobs

In 1987, the Mustang's interior was redesigned but it still included the same standard gauge package. Seats featured adjustable thigh support. Note the cruise control switches that are built into the steering wheel. If you decide on an aftermarket steering wheel, you'll have to get one that has the same type of switches built into it.

Instruments

The Mustang is equipped with a speedometer, tachometer, oil pressure, water temperature, fuel, and ammeter gauges. With these gauges, all the basics are covered.

A speedometer measures how fast your car is going. Up until mid-1989, Mustangs came with an inadequate 85mph speedometer, which was well beneath what the typical 5.0 liter Mustang is capable of reaching. From mid-1989, a 140mph speedometer replaced the earlier unit. This was a welcome improvement, even though the typical 5.0 liter is capable of 150mph or close to it. For those wanting a speedometer that reads higher, Motorsport offers a 160mph unit, part number M-17255-J, that fits 1987-92 Mustangs. The bezel on 1990-92 Mustangs has to be modified slightly for a correct fit. With this speedometer, you'll be able to tell how fast you're going, which is especially important on highly modified cars. Motorsport also offers 140mph speedometers to fit 1979-86 Mustangs.

The stock Mustang tachometer works well enough but in a race application, you may want to install an aftermarket unit that is easier to see when you're driving hard. There are many available from

A car with the capabilities of the Mustang deserves a speedometer that reads at least 10mph higher than its top speed. This Motorsport 160mph speedometer is designed to fit 1987-92 Mustangs. The stock speedometer on 1987-89 Mustangs reads only to 85mph, but it was replaced with a 140mph unit during the 1989 model year. Ford Motor Co.

One of the oldest manufacturers of original equipment and aftermarket gauges is Stewart-Warner. Besides the one shown here, Stewart-Warner has a large variety of gauges available in different sizes to fit any need. Stewart-Warner Instrument Corp.

Auto Meter's three-gauge console designed for underdash applications. The mechanical gauges measure 2in. Auto Meter Products Inc.

Auto Meter's Sport-Comp Monster tach has a 5in face and an adjustable shift light. The best place to mount this tach is right on top of the dash. Auto Meter Products Inc.

A recent entry into the auto instruments market is Auto Avionics. These aircraft-quality gauges are offered in a variety of sizes and configurations. Auto Avionics Instrument Research, Inc.

manufacturers such as Stewart-Warner, Sun, and Auto Meter Products Inc. The most common place you'll find these installed is right on the dash pad. It may not be attractive or integral with the interior, but it gets the job done. Auto Meter's Shift-Lite Sport-Comp Monster tach has an interesting feature—an amber light that is activated when a predetermined rpm is reached so the driver doesn't have to look at the tach directly but can instead concentrate on driving. Another Auto Meter tach has a built-in memory function which recalls the highest rpm reached. (See Appendices for address.)

Three gauges are considered to be indispensable in a performance car: oil pressure, water temperature, and an ammeter gauge or volt meter to monitor the car's electrical system. Stock Mustang oil and temperature gauges don't indicate an exact reading but instead use a pointer that fluctuates between a low and high setting. The stock ammeter gauge shows either a charging or discharging condition in the engine's alternator. A volt meter may indicate the condition of an electrical system more accurately, as it indicates voltage.

If you aren't happy with the stock gauges, there is a slew of aftermarket gauges that you can use. They come in various sizes but the problem you may have is where to install them. In a race car, the gauges are mounted on a simple piece of sheet metal but on a street car, some kind of fabricated panel is required unless you install one of the available underdash panels. And some enthusiasts want to maintain the stock interior look, too. One panel that is currently made fits in place of the two center air conditioning

vents. The unit is called the Gauge Cage and it is designed to hold three gauges. Installation is simple and the loss of the center air conditioning vents is offset by the additional airflow directed to the remaining outer vents. The panel is available from most aftermarket Mustang performance parts vendors, or direct from the manufacturer, Greg E. Day of San Diego, California (see Appendices).

There is also the question of whether to install mechanical or electrical gauges. Both have their advantages and both are reliable, although you'll find that most racers use mechanical gauges. A mechanical gauge uses a mechanical method of measuring— for example, a mechanical oil pressure gauge has a small line carrying pressurized oil to it while an electrical gauge uses a sending unit to convert the mechanical movement into an electrical impulse which is then sent to the gauge via a wire. Electrical gauges have the advantage of easier installation.

Besides the three stock gauges mentioned, there are gauges for measuring practically any fluid pres-

If you want to maintain a stock appearance when installing additional gauges, you should use the Gauge Cage, available from Greg Day. It replaces the center two air conditioning vents for a factory look. Greg E. Day

Grant's Ultimate Wood Touring GT steering wheel uses a mahogany wood grip and center cover. It is a great way to add some individuality and class to your Mustang. Grant Products

sure and temperature found in a car: oil temperature, transmission and gearbox temperature, turbo boost, manifold pressure, exhaust temperature, brake line pressure, fuel pressure, blower boost, engine vacuum, cylinder head temperature, and air charge temperature. You just have to decide which functions you want to monitor.

Steering Wheels

When you look at the typical Mustang interior you'll be greeted with lots of vinyl- and plastic-covered surfaces—and that includes the steering wheel. The stock steering wheel is small enough and thick enough but if you want to dress up your interior, an easy way is to install an aftermarket steering wheel. Several manufacturers make custom steering wheels, including Grant Products of Glendale, California (see Appendices). Grant has a varied line of aftermarket wheels to suit any taste, from solid hardwood and leather to soft foam grips.

The traditional wood steering wheel is a good choice but there are leather-covered wheels as well. However, there are certain things to remember when it comes to Ford steering wheels. Some Mustangs equipped with cruise control have the cruise control switches located on the steering wheel. For such Mustangs, you'll need to find a steering wheel that accommodates these switches. Grant makes several wheels for cruise control Mustangs. You'll have to stick with the stock steering wheel on Mustangs built after 1990, though; these came with an airbag which is housed in the steering wheel.

Steering wheel installation is easy. All you'll need is a socket to remove the center wheel shaft nut and you'll probably have to purchase an inexpensive steering wheel puller, if you don't already have one. The whole process shouldn't take more than half an hour.

Custom Seats

No matter how good you think the stock Mustang bucket seats are, you haven't sat in a "good" seat until you've sat in a custom aftermarket seat such as a Recaro. They are designed with a lot more care and because they provide superior support, you'll have a much more comfortable ride and less fatigue over long trips. Custom seats are also designed to fit more snugly than the stock seats, which is especially important during "spirited" driving. Proper seating is one of the most overlooked aspects of driving and it is worth looking into what is available.

Besides providing a more comfortable ride, a racer will want to use the lightest possible seat in order to reduce vehicle weight. There are seats available for this purpose but for a street car, you'll probably want something that is more comfortable and adjustable. Many race seats are made to fit only one driver and they are bolted down in that driver's preferred position.

The typical stock seat is designed to fit what the car manufacturer considers to be the average driver in terms of height, weight, and driving style. Thus the typical seat may not fit all drivers comfortably and cause excessive strain. Recaro, with its L Modular System seats, can custom fit the same seat for people with differing physiques and heights. This is done by combining four different seat cushions and three different seatbacks. As you would expect, you can get these seats in a variety of fabrics and leathers as well as having the seat covered in your own fabric.

Recaro's ultimate seat is the CSE. It comes with electric seatback adjustment, electric air lumbar support, electric bilevel seat heating, power adjustable seatback side bolster supports, electrical height adjustment, an illuminated control panel located in the seat base, and an optional three-position memory system. Recaro seats are available from Keiper Recaro Seating, Inc. (see Appendices), among others.

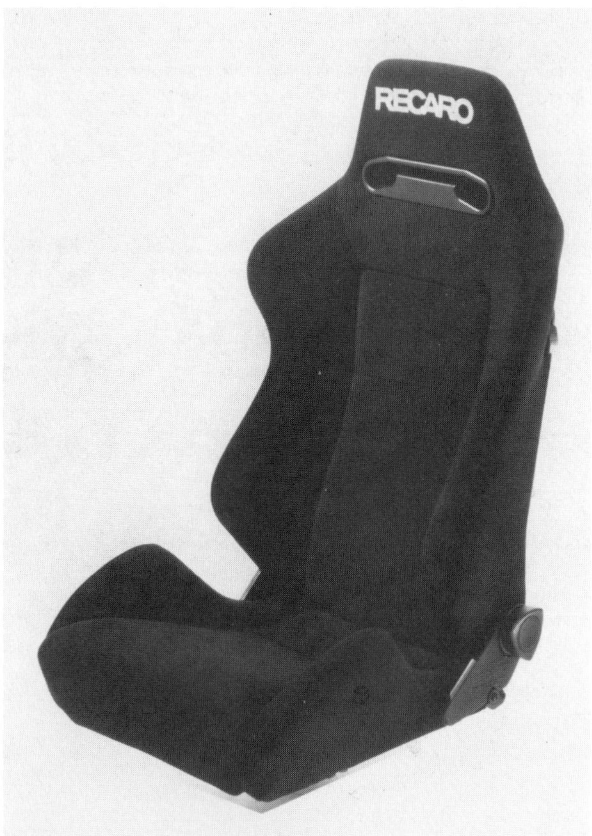

No wheel, no steal. Grant's Vehicle Security System is based on removing your car's steering wheel. You can remove or replace your steering wheel in less than five seconds with this system. Grant Products

The Recaro SRD seat, part of the L Modular System. This seat uses the SRD back which has a slot for a shoulder harness necessary for competition use. High sides are designed to keep the driver in place during serious driving. Keiper Recaro Seating, Inc.

George Klass' Mustang has seen some serious quarter-mile action. Lightweight competition seats are used along with a six-point roll bar. The dash-mounted tachometer is easier to see than the stock tachometer during a race. George Klass

A six-point roll bar is very intrusive in a regular street car, especially if you plan to use the back seats. Note how the shoulder harness fits through the slot in the driver's seat. George Klass

Hooker's chrome roll bar for street Mustangs is a four-point design. It looks great and the rear seats can still be used. Hooker Headers

A full roll cage and Flofit two-tone leather seats highlight the interior of this Saleen Mustang. Marshall Spiegel

Roll Bars

A roll bar is designed to protect the car's occupants in case the car rolls over, but they also have the benefit of reducing body and chassis flex. This is important in a road-race application. Roll bars are usually described as two-point, four-point, six-point, and so on. This refers to the number of places that it is bolted or welded on to the car's structure. The more points, the better as such a bar will form a protective cage around the driver and also provide more chassis rigidity. Although roll bars are important for a race car, they may be somewhat intrusive for normal use.

Roll bars are available from performance shops as kits or you can take your car to a shop versed in race car fabrication and have a custom-made bar fitted to your Mustang.

Chapter 16

Mustang Specials

Like the special Shelby Mustangs produced from 1965-70, today there are several high-performance aftermarket Mustangs available for the enthusiast. These cars have been modified and engineered for better acceleration and handling than the stock Mustang you can buy from your local dealer. The first of these was the ASC/McLaren which no longer is available—1990 was its last year of production. Better known are the Saleen Mustangs—again, they're no longer available new (1990 was the last year) but because they were built in relatively large numbers since 1985, you can find them on used car lots. Currently, there are three special Mustangs available—the Steeda GT, the SAAC Mk 1, and the Outlaw Mustangs from Project Industries. Because there are so many used Saleen Mustangs around, we'll take a look at them as well.

The Saleen Mustang certainly has made a name for itself during the past six years; it is the most recognizable Mustang Special. The Saleen name is synonymous with performance.

Saleen Mustang

Saleen Mustangs have been available since 1985 in either convertible or three-door form. Most of these were sold through selected Ford dealers. Following the pattern set by Carroll Shelby in the 1960s, Steve Saleen took regular Mustangs and modified them to his specifications. The most noticeable performance modifications were made in the suspension. Saleen Mustangs came with taller and wider wheels, usually of the five-lug variety, along with wider tires and a lowered suspension. Premium shock absorbers, a strut tower brace, four-wheel disc brakes, and special antisway bar bushings were also part of the package. In the interior, Saleen Mustangs were fitted with different seats, a special steering wheel, and unique upholstery. You'll find that most Saleen Mustangs also came with all the standard luxury Mustang options, including Saleen-installed high-power stereo systems.

Saleen Mustangs came with a distinctive rear wing, front air dam, and side skirt package. They also came with distinctive lower rocker panel stripes.

You could get a modified engine, but you'll find that most Saleen Mustangs have the stock 5.0 liter HO engine.

Steeda GT

The Steeda GT has been built since 1990 by Steeda Autosports, one of the major Mustang performance parts vendors. The Steeda is available through Ford dealers as well as directly from Steeda.

The first thing you'll notice about the Steeda is its aerodynamic treatment which is subtly different from the stock Mustang GT. The Steeda uses a rear valance panel designed to let air pass through in order to reduce drag. Also noticeable are the attractive Steeda Five Star wheels.

Not so noticeable, however, are the many suspension improvements made. The stock springs are discarded and replaced with higher rate springs that reduce roll and ride height. Polyurethane bushings are used wherever possible, and a strut tower brace helps to tighten up the Mustang's front structure.

Saleen convertibles are particularly attractive. Low-profile tires, shorter springs, and a modified aerodynamic package give the Saleen Mustang its understated look.

Improved braking can be provided by an optional four-wheel disc brake system. For the enthusiast wanting more, additional suspension modifications can be ordered, including subframe braces, Tokico cockpit adjustable struts and shocks, and larger antisway bars.

You can also outfit the Steeda with a variety of interior trim packages including leather and Flow Fit seats. And as you would expect, you can specify the kind of sound system you want as well.

Of course it's nice to drive a distinctive-looking Mustang, but the Steeda's engine has been modified to put out an EPA-approved 275hp. This has been accomplished by a modified fuel-injection system, high-ratio rocker arms, underdrive pulleys, an optimized EEC-IV computer, and a freer flowing exhaust system. The Steeda Mustang will accelerate 0-60mph in the mid-5sec range and hit the quarter mile in the mid-13sec range.

SAAC Mk 1

The latest Mustang Special is the SAAC Mk 1 produced by the SAAC Car Company, Incorporated—

The Steeda GT comes with a 275hp version of the 5.0 liter engine, along with a host of suspension and interior modifications. The car is EPA legal and is available from Ford dealers.

Except for the stripes and wheels, the SAAC Mk 1 looks stock. The engine and suspension have been extensively modified for a healthy boost in performance over the stock Mustang GT. It, too, is EPA legal and available through Ford dealers.

The Shelby's 295hp engine. It comes with GT-40 heads and intake, but excellent street manners are guaranteed as the engine uses the stock roller cam and EEC-IV computer. The triangular strut tower brace adds some chassis stiffening for better cornering.

affiliated with the Shelby American Automobile Club. Built with Carroll Shelby's blessing, the SAAC Mk 1 comes with a slew of performance features.

The engine, modified with technical assistance from SVO, pumps out 295hp and is EPA legal. It comes with GT-40 heads and intake manifold, and a special 2½in stainless-steel dual exhaust system with low-restriction mufflers. The engine uses the stock camshaft and EEC-IV computer.

Considerable work was done to the SAAC Mk 1 to improve handling. Koni shock absorbers and struts are used with firmer springs that also lower the car's ride height. For additional bracing, a three-point engine compartment brace is used in addition to an interior chassis-stiffening brace. And like the original Shelby Mustangs, the SAAC Mk 1 comes with a roll bar. Four-wheel five-lug disc brakes are used with semi-metallic linings.

The SAAC comes with distinctive 17x7.5in front and 17x8.5in rear wheels shod with Goodyear 245ZR50-17 Eagle GT tires.

In the interior, all regular Mustang luxury options are standard equipment, such as power windows, power door locks, air conditioning, and Premium Sound system. The standard interior is finished in leather only.

Like the early Shelby GT350, the car is finished in white only with two large blue stripes. A convertible is planned as well.

Performance figures given are similar to the Steeda GT with mid-13sec quarter-mile times, a top speed of over 150mph, and handling in the 0.9g range.

Project Industries Outlaw

The Outlaw XS built by Kenny Brown's Project Industries is available as an aftermarket conversion or as a complete car. It offers considerably more power than the other Mustang specials currently available because it comes with a Vortec V-1 supercharged 5.0 liter V-8 engine.

The base engine is rated at 385hp, but this can be optionally increased to 425hp with 435lb-ft of torque. Only the best components are used, including SVO four-bolt main block, SVO forged-steel crank, Crower rods, BRC pistons, the Pro-M 77mm Mass Air system, MSD ignition, the GT-40 intake, and Kenny Brown's Gold Heads. Interestingly, this powerhouse of an engine comes with the stock roller cam.

There is no way that the standard T-5 five-speed transmission can stand up to this kind of torque, so the Outlaw is fitted with either a six-speed manual transmission or a General Motors 200-4R four-speed automatic. Final drive ratio is 3.55:1, and the rear uses an Auburn differential.

The suspension benefits from the Kenny Brown MX-17 Advanced Geometry Suspension System include specific springs and a rear Panhard rod. The chassis is stiffened up with a three-point strut tower brace, a four-point lower chassis brace, and an eight-point double-cross subframe connector. SVO five-lug disc brakes are used on all four wheels. Wheels are 17x8.5in with Firestone Firehawk SXs measuring 275/40ZR17.

The interior is fitted with Recaro SR seats, the Kenny Brown Ultra Street Cage, and Schroth Harness Belts.

With all that power, the Outlaw XS is probably the fastest of the aftermarket Mustang Specials currently available.

As with the Steeda GT, all the parts that make the Outlaw what it is are available in kit form for the enthusiast who wants to upgrade his Mustang.

The Outlaw XS from Kenny Brown. With a stock 385hp and more available, the XS can obviously accelerate but with its advanced suspension system, it also handles like a racer. It comes with the Outlaw Power Hood and the Outlaw GT rear wing. Project Industries

Chapter 17

Additional Modifications

There are a few other things that you can do to improve the performance of your Mustang. Besides engine swaps, we'll take a look at some of the so-called free horsepower options that are available. Even if a certain modification yields only a small increase in power, the cumulative effect of several such modifications can make all the difference.

Underdrive Pulleys

One of the first modifications that anyone owning a 302 powered Mustang should make is to replace the stock pulleys with underdrive pulleys. This will reduce parasitic horsepower losses as the engine's accessories will be turning slower, resulting in about a 20hp increase. The pulleys that are usually replaced are those used on the alternator, crankshaft, and water pump. Owners who have installed mega-powered stereo systems are advised not to change the alternator pulley.

Steel pulleys will last longer than aluminum pulleys; Turbo Engineering also makes pulleys that reduce accessory speed by 57 percent, but these are recommended for race use only. If you drag race, you can also temporarily replace the stock belt with a shorter one (Gates part number K060705 for air conditioning equipped engines) which will by-pass the power steering pump and air pump. It should be replaced after you are through racing.

Engine Swaps

There is no substitute for cubic inches—that's an old hot rod saying and it is still true today. More cubic inches mean more power. You can put practically any engine in the Mustang if you have the mind to do so. Still, there are some swaps that are a lot more practical and easier than others. In all cases, though, you should note that a swap will make your Mustang illegal for street use under current EPA rules and regulations.

An obvious swap is the 351 Windsor engine. It will bolt right up on the block since the 351 block is practically identical to the 302's block, save for the increased deck height, making the 351 a taller engine. There are some problem areas, but nothing that can't be corrected. The Motorsport J351 headers will fit in a T-5 equipped Mustang, but they will require rerouting if a steel bellhousing is used. Because the engine is taller, a hood scoop will also be required to accommodate an air cleaner.

Kaufmann Products Incorporated of Downey, California (see Appendices), has a kit that will facilitate this swap, and another kit available for a 351 Cleveland engine. All things being equal, the Cleveland will outperform the Windsor.

Motorsport has put together a 351 HO engine for use in the Mustang and other Fox chassis cars, such as the Thunderbird. The very potent package consists of a marine 351 block used with high-silicon 10:1 flat-top pistons, aluminum J302 heads, DuraSpark distributor, police car oil pan, 7in steel crankshaft dampner, and an Edelbrock Victor Jr. intake manifold. A hydraulic cam is also used. The package is listed in the Motorsport catalog under part number M-06007-A351. For automatics, a dual-plane intake manifold will be used along with the GT-40 cast-iron heads.

By reducing parasitic losses, you can gain an easy 15-20hp by changing accessory pulleys. If you have a high-powered stereo system, leave the stock alternator pulley alone. Auto Specialties Inc.

With close to 400hp, this engine will make any Mustang really go.

Another swap that you see from time to time is Ford's 460ci engine. Kaufmann and Total Performance Incorporated of Mt. Clemens, Michigan, both offer kits for this swap. The engine fits surprisingly well in the Mustang's engine compartment, but its heavy weight exacts penalties when it comes to handling, front tire wear, and rear tire traction. (See Appendices for details.)

Weight Reduction and Ballast

If you aren't in a position to add cubic inches to your engine you can always reduce the weight that your engine has to push around—less weight means better acceleration. A word of caution is in order here, however. Some of the modifications suggested here will affect the safety and street legality of your Mustang. Lightening your car with fiberglass parts, for instance, can affect the crashworthiness of your car. Likewise, the removal of antisway bars and the use of skinny pro-stock type wheels and tires will negatively affect handling. And some of these suggestions are effective only on a drag racing car.

Kaufmann Products took one of their cars and put it on a diet to see how much weight could be removed. The test car was a 1987 LX hatchback with the 5.0 liter engine, five-speed transmission, and no air conditioning. With a full tank of gas, the car originally weighed 3,110lb. (Other Mustangs with a different option mix will show some variation from this figure.) Some modifications are truly "no-cost" mods (except for labor) while others will set you back a few dollars. The chart shows the various modifications made, along with the weight savings.

Modification	Weight Savings (lb)
Remove front antisway bar	21
Remove front energy-absorbing bumper assembly	24
Move battery to trunk	0
Replace hood with fiberglass replica	15
Remove trunk pad sound deadener mat	15
Remove tailpipes from the muffler on back	20
Remove rear fold-down seats	47

The 460ci V-8 looks amazingly at home in 1979 and later Mustangs whereas it is a very tight fit on first generation Mustangs. Kits are available from Kaufmann and Total Performance to facilitate this swap. Its heavy weight, though, is a detriment to handling and accentuates the Mustang's front-heavy weight distribution.

Modification	Weight Savings (lb)
Replace front seats with pro-stock type seats	24
Replace power steering rack with early 1981 manual rack and eliminate power steering pump	16
Remove rear antisway bar	14
Replace front wheels and tires with P165/15 tires and 15x3.5in aluminum wheels	32
Remove heater, stereo, speakers, under-carpet padding, center console, and miscellaneous interior items	63
Replace rear tires and wheels with drag slicks and 15x8.5in aluminum wheels	20
Remove spare tire, jack, and lug wrench	42
Remove exhaust system from header collector	51
Remove window crank mechanism, side window (replaced with plexiglass), and impact brace in doors	56
Replace cast-iron heads with aluminum heads	40
Replace radiator with aluminum two-core radiator	15

Also remember that gasoline weighs 6.2lb per gallon and if you are drag racing, there is no need to

The 460 needs a lot more radiator to keep it cool. This owner has wisely installed a larger unit. Engine swaps aren't just a matter of dropping in a bigger engine—you'll also have to make driveline and chassis alterations as the Mustang wasn't originally designed to cope with the torque produced by big engines.

run on a full tank. On the trimmed-down Kaufmann Mustang, the weight of the roll cage (80lb) and frame connectors (16lb) have to be added in so the Mustang, without driver, weighs in at 2,641lb. This is a substantial decrease from the stock Mustang and with the exception of the cylinder heads, the cost is minimal. The Mustang runs in the mid-11sec range at over 122mph. Removing weight does work!

Although there is no weight savings in moving the battery to the trunk, the resulting transfer improves weight distribution by 1 percent, assuming the battery weighs about 30lb.

Cooling System

The internal combustion engine makes a lot of heat; the reason for this is because it isn't that efficient. About 20 percent of the fuel energy is used to produce power and the rest of the heat energy produced must be dissipated elsewhere. Most of this heat originates in the combustion chamber. It must be dispersed to prevent thermal fatigue of the pistons, cylinder walls, and cylinder head. Depending on engine speed, up to 50 percent of the heat energy that is produced is dissipated through the radiator. At the same time, the combustion chamber must be kept cool enough to prevent preignition and detonation.

Higher combustion chamber temperatures, which result in higher horsepower output, also require the use of higher octane fuel. Because fuels today are lower in octane that they were in the 1960s, today's engines aren't producing all the power they are capable of. And anything that stops or slows down the transfer of the excess heat produced in the combustion chambers will reduce engine efficiency.

Most people use a mixture of antifreeze (glycol) and water in their cooling system. What is not well known is that antifreeze reduces or slows down the transfer of heat generated in the combustion chambers to the coolant medium. Plain water has almost 2.5 times greater thermal conductivity than glycol-based coolants. Another way of saying this is that plain water is capable of transferring twice as much heat out of the system as compared to a 50:50 glycol mix.

Water also has a very high surface tension. In the cylinder head, especially under load, the heat produced is not evenly distributed to the metal. Instead, there are localized hot spots and it is through these spots that most of the heat is transferred to the coolant medium. However, at these hot spots the heat is so great that the water or antifreeze mix actually boils, even though most of the cooling solution is below its boiling point. The culprit is the high surface tension of water which makes it difficult to release the water vapor from the hot metal surface. The vapor bubbles on the metal surface create an insulating area, which slows down heat transfer.

This is where Red Line's WaterWetter comes in. WaterWetter reduces the surface tension of water by a factor of two, resulting in much smaller water bubbles. This improves heat transfer on the localized hot spots by as much as 15 percent.

Red Line performed tests to measure how quickly heat was removed from a 304deg F. heated aluminum bar as it was quenched in different coolant combinations. All coolants were pressurized to 15psi and heated to 214deg. Water combined with WaterWetter required 3.2 seconds to reduce the temperature of the bar to 250deg; water alone took 3.7 seconds. A 50:50 mix combined with WaterWetter took 9 seconds; a 50:50 mix alone took 10.2 seconds, while pure antifreeze took 21 seconds.

Using antifreeze will raise cylinder head temperature by about 1deg F. for each percent of antifreeze mix used. Thus in the typical 50:50 mix you will see a cylinder head temperature increase of about 45deg. Not only will there be a power loss, but timing will have to be retarded or a higher octane fuel used to stop knocking.

Looking at it from another vantage point, using pure water with WaterWetter allows you to increase timing, which results in more power. Obviously this isn't a good idea in the northern areas of the United States, where temperatures drop below freezing during the winter.

But what about boiling over in the summer? Besides protecting the engine against freezing, a 50:50 mix of antifreeze solution and water raises the boiling point to 265deg F. at 15psi while water alone boils at 250deg at 15psi. That isn't much of a difference, but you can raise the boiling point of water to 265deg by using a 23lb pressure cap. However, you may not need to.

Racers use it and based on personal observation, water mixed with WaterWetter does work. For best results, flush out the existing coolant mixture and fill the radiator with fresh water, adding the specified amount of WaterWetter.

A natural engine swap into the Mustang engine compartment is the 351 HO SVO engine. It is rated at 388hp with 377lb-ft torque. It uses a 351 two-bolt marine block with a cast-iron crank, 10.0:1 hypereutectic pistons, heavy-duty marine/truck rods with ³/₈in bolts, aluminum SVO Windsor heads, hydraulic camshaft, aluminum roller rockers, and an Edelbrock Victor Jr. intake manifold which is designed to optimize high rpm horsepower. It does not come with air cleaner, carburetor, or exhaust headers. Ford Motor Co.

George Klass' 1987 LX Mustang has benefited from a substantial weight-reduction program, resulting in mid-11sec quarter-mile times. Some of the modifications can be used on a street car while others are suitable for track use only. Still, the less weight you lug around, the faster you'll go. George Klass

Performance Properties of Coolants

Result	Water Mixed with WaterWetter	50:50 Mix of Water and Antifreeze	70:30 Mix of Antifreeze and Water
Increase in cylinder head temperature	Baseline	+45deg F.	+65deg F.
Increase in octane (RON) requirement	Baseline	+3.5	+5.0
Change in spark timing to trace knock	Baseline	−5.2deg F.	−7.5deg F.
Change in torque	Baseline	−2.1%	−3.1%

Sources

Accel Performance Products
175 N. Branford Road
Branford, CT 06405
  Ignition components, starters, fuel
    pumps

Addco Industries, Inc.
Watertower Road
Lake Park, FL 33403
  Antisway bars, shocks, struts

American Best Car Parts Inc./Xenon
7400 Greenbush Avenue
North Hollywood, CA 91605
  Aerodynamic body styling kits

American Industries Inc.
443 W. Alameda Drive
Tempe, AZ 85282
  Manufacturers of Cyclone, Thrush,
    Blackjack, Eagle headers and
    exhaust systems

American Racing Equipment
19067 S. Reyes Avenue
Rancho Dominguez, CA 90221
  Wheels

Arao Engineering
21400 Lassen Street
Chatsworth, CA 91311
  302, 351, 429, 460 four-valve cylinder
    heads

ATO Racing Transmissions and
  Converters
2660 Mercantile Drive
Rancho Cordova, CA 95742
  Automatic transmissions

Auto Avionics Instrument Research,
  Inc.
P.O. Box 293
Monmouth Beach, NJ 07750
  Gauges

Auto Meter Products Inc.
413 W. Elm Street
Sycamore, IL 60178
  Gauges

Auto Specialties Inc.
13313 Redfish
Stafford, TX 77477
  Underdrive pulleys

Automotive Digital Systems
Highway 155 South
Tyler, TX 75703
  Computer chips

Autotronic Controls Corp.
1490 Henry Brennan Drive
El Paso, TX 79936
  MSD ignitions

B&A Ford Performance Inc.
Box 6553
Fort Smith, AR 72906
  351C heads to 302 conversion kits

B&M Products
9512 Independence Avenue
Chatsworth, CA 91311
  Automatic transmissions and
    superchargers

BBK Performance Specialists
3940-M Prospect Avenue
Yorba Linda, CA 92686
  Equal-length shorty headers and
    induction systems

Carroll Supercharging
14 Doty Road
Haskell, NJ 07420
  Superchargers

Cartech Performance Systems
11212 Goodnight Lane
Dallas, TX 75229
  Single and dual turbochargers

Char-Trends
2677 McKelvey Road
Maryland Heights, MO 63043
  T-5 transmission parts

Classic Motorbooks, Inc.
P.O. Box 1
Osceola, WI 54020
  Automotive literature

Competition Cams Inc.
3406 Democrat Road
Memphis, TN 38118
  Camshafts and valvetrain
    components

Compucar Nitrous Oxide Systems
509 Old Edgefield Road
North Augusta, SC 29841
  Nitrous oxide systems

Crane Cams Inc.
530 Fentress Boulevard
Daytona Beach, FL 32144
  Camshafts and valvetrain
    components

Digital Fuel Injection
37732 Hills Tech Drive
Farmington Hills, MI 48024
  Performance EFI systems and
    components

Dugan Racing Enterprises
1175-A Highway 23
Suwanee, GA 30174
  Mustang performance parts

Dyno Tunes, Inc.
4121 MacIver Avenue NE
St. Michael, MN 55376
  Mustang performance parts

Edelbrock Corp.
2700 California Street
Torrance, CA 90509
  Intake manifolds, carburetors,
    camshafts

Flowmaster Incorporated
2975 Dutton Avenue
Santa Rosa, CA 95407
  Mufflers

Ford Motor Company
Special Vehicle Operations and Ford
  Motorsport Performance
  Equipment
17000 Southfield Road
Allen Park, MI 48101
  Ford high-performance equipment

Gauge Cage/Greg E. Day
7350 Golfcrest Place
Unit 2007
San Diego, CA 92119
  Manufactures the Gauge Cage

Grant Products
700 Allen Avenue
Glendale, CA 91201
  Steering wheels

Headers by Ed, Inc.
2710-PS 16th Avenue
Minneapolis, MN 55407
  Custom-made equal-length headers

Holley Replacement Parts
11995 E. Nine Mile Road
Warren, MI 48089
  Carburetors and intake manifolds

Hooker Headers
1024 W. Brooks Street
Ontario, CA 91762
  Exhaust headers

Hypertech
1910 Thomas Road
Memphis, TN 38134
  Computer chips

Itac Automotive Technology
3121 Benton Street
Garland, TX 75042
  Haltech engine management
  systems

JBA (J. Bittle American)
9630 Aero Drive
San Diego, CA 92123
  Mustang performance parts

JFZ Engineered Products, Inc.
440 E. Easy Street, Unit 3
Simi Valley, CA 93063
  Disc brake components

K&N Engineering, Inc.
P.O. Box 1329
Riverside, CA 92502
  Air filters, oil filters

Kamei USA Inc.
4750 Eisenhower Avenue
Alexandria, VA 22304
  Mustang aerodynamic styling kits

Kaufmann Products Inc.
12400 Benedict Avenue
Downey, CA 90242
  Ford performance products

Keiper Recaro Seating, Inc.
905 W. Maple Road, Suite 100
Clawson, MI 48017
  Recaro seats

Kenne-Bell Performance Products
10743 Bell Court
Rancho Cucamonga, CA 91730
  Ram Air kits

Koni
8085 Production Avenue
Florence, KY 41024
  Shock absorbers and struts

M&H Tire Co.
77 Industrial Row
Gardner, MA 01440
  Tires

Midway Industries, Inc.
7171 Patterson Drive
Garden Grove, CA 92641
  Centerforce clutches

Milodon Inc.
20716 Plummer Street
Chatsworth, CA 91311
  Deep sump oil pans

Moroso Performance Products Inc.
80 Carter Drive
Guilford, CT 06437
  Oil pans, engine and driveline
  components

Nitrous Oxide Systems (NOS)
5930 Lakeshore Drive
Cypress, CA 90630
  Nitrous oxide systems

Offenhauser Sales Corp.
5300 Alhambra Avenue
Los Angeles, CA 90032
  Intake manifolds

Pacific Auto Accessories Inc.
5882 Machine Drive
Huntington Beach, CA 92649
  Aerodynamic styling kits

Paxton Superchargers
929 Olympic Boulevard
Santa Monica, CA 90404
  Paxton superchargers

Professional Flow Technologies
25740 John R. Road
Madison Heights, MI 48071
  Mass Air meter kits

Project Industries
Performance By Kenny Brown
8549 Lake Street
Omaha, NE 68134
  High-performance parts, Outlaw
  Mustangs

Racer Walsh Co.
5906 Macy Avenue
Jacksonville, FL 32211
  Ford performance parts

Red Line Synthetic Oil Corp.
3450 Pacheco Boulevard
Martinez, CA 94553
  Synthetic oils and WaterWetter

Saleen Performance Parts, Inc.
3210 Airport Way
Long Beach, CA 90806
  Mustang performance parts

Splitfire, Inc.
4065 Commercial Avenue
Northbrook, IL 60062
  Splitfire spark plugs

Stainless Steel Brakes Corp.
11470 Main Road
Clarence, NY 14031
  Four-wheel disc brake kits

Steeda Autosports
2241 Hammondville Road
Pompano, FL 33069
  Mustang performance parts, Steeda
  GT

Stewart-Warner Instrument Corp.
580 Slawin Court
Mt. Prospect, IL 60056
  Gauges

Sutton Engineering
3606 Killarney Court
Rolling Meadows, IL 60008
  EFI specialists

Texas Turbo Engineering, Inc.
9703 Plainfield
Houston, TX 77036
  Mustang performance parts

Total Performance Inc.
40631 Irwin
Mt. Clemens, MI 48045
  Ford performance parts

Turbo Engineering
5601 S. Proctor Avenue
Tacoma, WA 98409
   Turbochargers

Turbo Technology Inc.
6229 S. Adams Street
Tacoma, WA 98409
   Turbochargers

Vortech Superchargers
5351 Bonsai Avenue
Moorpark, CA 93021
   Superchargers

Watts Engineering
4115 S.E. 15th Street
Des Moines, IA 50320
   Rear-end specialists

Weiand Automotive
2316 San Fernando Road
Los Angeles, CA 90065
   Intake manifolds and blowers

Will-Burt Automotive
169 S. Main Street
Orville, OH 44667
   Trick Flow cylinder heads

Wilwood Engineering
461 Calle San Pablo
Amarillo, CA 93012
   Disc brake kits

World Products, Inc.
353 Oliver Street
Troy, MI 48084
   Dart Windsor cylinder heads

Race Sanctioning Bodies

International Hot Rod Association
   (IHRA)
Box 3029
Bristol, TN 37625
615-764-1164

International Motorsports Association
   (IMSA)
Box 10709
Tampa, FL 33679
813-877-4762

National Association for Stock Car
   Automobile Racing (NASCAR)
Box K
Daytona Beach, FL 32015
904-253-0611

National Hot Rod Association (NHRA)
Box 5555
2035 Financial Way
Glendora, CA 91740-4602
818-914-4761

Sports Car Club of America (SCCA)
9033 E. Easter Place
Englewood, CO 80112
303-694-7222

United States Automobile Club
   (USAC)
4910 W. 16th Street
Speedway, IN 46224
317-247-5151

Tuning and Rebuild Specifications

Capacities

Engine	Crankcase (qt) W/ Filter	Crankcase (qt) W/O Filter	Transmission (pt) 4-Spd	Transmission (pt) 5-Spd	Transmission (pt) Auto.	Axle (pt)	Cooling Sys. (qt)	Fuel Tank (gal)
1979-82 2.3 liter	5	4	2.8	4.75	16	3.25*	8.4	15.4
1983-87 2.3 liter	5	4	2.8	4.75	16	3.25*	9.4	15.4
1983-86 2.3 liter Turbo	5	4.5	2.8	4.75	16	3.25*	9.4	15.4
1988-92 2.3 liter	5	4	3.7	3.7	22	4.5	10.0	15.4
1983-86 3.8 liter	5	4	—	—	22	3.25*	13.4	15.4
1982-87 5.0 liter	5	4	4.5	4.5	22	3.25*	13.4	15.4
1988-92 5.0 liter	5	4	—	3.7	22	3.25*	14.1	15.4

*3.55 with Traction-Lok differential.

Crankshaft and Connecting Rod Specifications

1979-92 2.3 liter
Main bearing journal diameter	2.3990-2.3992in
Main bearing oil clearance	0.0008-0.0015in
Shaft end play	0.004-0.008in
Thrust on bearing	No. 3
Rod journal diameter	2.0464-2.0472in
Oil clearance	0.0008-0.0015in
Side clearance	0.0035-0.0105in

1983-86 3.8 liter V-6
Main bearing journal diameter	2.5190
Main bearing oil clearance	0.0001-0.001in
Shaft end play	0.004-0.008in
Thrust on bearing	No. 3
Rod journal diameter	2.3103-2.3111in
Oil clearance	0.0008-0.0026in
Side clearance	0.0047-0.0114in

1979-92 4.2, 5.0 liter
Main bearing journal diameter	2.2482-2.2490in
Main bearing oil clearance	0.0005-0.0015in (0.001–0.0015in No. 1 bearing)
Shaft end play	0.004-0.008in
Thrust on bearing	No. 3
Rod journal diameter	2.1228-2.1236in
Oil clearance	0.0008-0.0026in (0.0008-0.0015in through 1981)
Side clearance	0.010-0.020in

Valve Specifications

1979 2.3 liter
Seat angle	45deg
Face angle	45deg
Spring test pressure lbs. @ in.	159-175 @ 1.16
Spring installed height	1⁹/₁₆in
Stem-to-guide clearance Intake	0.0010-0.0027in
Stem-to-guide clearance Exhaust	0.0015-0.0032in
Stem diameter Intake	0.3420in
Stem diameter Exhaust	0.3415in

1980-92 2.3 liter
Seat angle	45deg
Face angle	44deg
Spring test pressure lbs. @ in.	159-175 @ 1.16*
Spring installed height	1⁹/₁₆in
Stem-to-guide clearance Intake	0.0010-0.0027in
Stem-to-guide clearance Exhaust	0.0015-0.0032in

Valve Specifications

Stem diameter
    Intake   0.3420in
    Exhaust   0.3415in
*1979-81 intake 71-79 @ 1.56.

1983-86 3.8 liter V-6
Seat angle   44.5deg
Face angle   45.8deg
Spring test pressure lbs. @ in.   215 @ 1.79
Spring installed height   1³⁄₄in
Stem-to-guide clearance
    Intake   0.0010-0.0027in
    Exhaust   0.0015-0.0032in
Stem diameter
    Intake   0.3420in
    Exhaust   0.3415in

1979-92 4.2, 5.0 liter V-8
Seat angle   45deg
Face angle   45deg
                               (1979, 44deg)
Spring test pressure lbs. @ in.   205 @ 1.36
Spring installed height   1³⁄₄in
Stem-to-guide clearance
    Intake   0.0010-0.0027in
    Exhaust   0.0015-0.0032in
Stem diameter
    Intake   0.3420in
    Exhaust   0.3420in

Piston and Ring Specifications

2.3 liter
Piston clearance   0.0014-0.0022in*
Ring gap
    Top compression   .010-0.020
    Bottom compression   .010-0.020
    Oil control   0.015-0.055in
Ring side clearance
    Top compression   0.002-0.004in
    Bottom compression   0.002-0.004in
    Oil control   Snug
    Wear limit   0.006in
*1979-81 Turbo 0.0034-0.0042in, 1983-86 Turbo
0.0030-0.0038in.

3.8 liter
Piston clearance   0.0014-0.0028in
Ring gap
    Top compression   .010-0.020in
    Bottom compression   .010-0.020in
    Oil control   0.015-0.055in
Ring side clearance
    Top compression   0.002-0.004in
    Bottom compression   0.002-0.004in
    Oil control   Snug
    Wear limit   0.006in

Piston and Ring Specifications

4.2 liter, 5.0 liter
Piston clearance   0.0018-0.0026in
Ring gap
    Top compression   .010-0.020
    Bottom compression   .010-0.020
    Oil control   0.015-0.055in
Ring side clearance
    Top compression   0.002-0.004in
    Bottom compression   0.002-0.004in
    Oil control   Snug
    Wear limit   0.006in

Bolt Torque Specifications (in lb-ft)

Engine	Cylinder Head	Rod Bearing	Main Bearing	Crankshaft Pulley	Flywheel to Crankshaft
2.3 liter	80-90*	30-36	80-90	100-120	54-64
3.8 liter	**	31-36	65-81	85-100	75-85
4.2, 5.0 liter	65-72***	19-24	60-70	70-90	75-85

*Torque in two steps: first 50-60, then 80-90lb-ft.
**Torque in four steps: (1) 37lb-ft, (2) 45lb-ft, (3) 52lb-ft, and (4) 59lb-ft. Then back off two or three turns on all bolts and repeat sequence.
***Torque in two steps: first 55-62, then 65-72lb-ft.

Tune-Up Specifications

2.3 liter 1979-82
Spark plugs   AWSF-42
    Gap   0.034in
Ignition timing   Manual 6B, automatic 20B
Fuel pump   5.5-6.5psi
Idle speed   850rpm, manual and automatic

2.3 liter 1983-85
Spark plugs   AWSF-44
    Gap   0.044in
Ignition timing   See emissions sticker
Fuel pump   5.5-6.5psi (1984 5-7psi, 1985 6-8psi)
Idle speed, rpm   Manual 850rpm, automatic 800rpm
                               (1984-85 750rpm)

2.3 liter Turbo 1983-86
Spark plugs   AWSF-32
    Gap   0.044in
Ignition timing   See emissions sticker
Fuel pump   39psi
Idle speed   See emissions sticker

3.8 liter V-6 1983-86
Spark plugs   AWSF-52 (1984 AWSF-54, 1985
                               AGSP-52, 1986 AWSF-54)
    Gap   0.044in
Ignition timing   See emissions sticker
Fuel pump   6-8psi (1984-86 39psi)
Idle speed   1983-84, 550rpm; 1985, 600rpm;
                               1986, 550rpm

Tune-Up Specifications

5.0 liter V-8 1979

Spark plugs	ASF-52, ASF-52-6 Calif.
Gap	0.044in, 0.060 Calif.
Ignition timing	Manual 12B, automatic 6B
Fuel pump	5.5-6.5psi
Idle speed	Manual 800rpm, automatic 600rpm

4.2 liter V-8 1980-82

Spark plugs	ASF-42
Gap	0.044in
Ignition timing	Automatic 10B
Fuel pump	5.5-6.5psi
Idle speed	Automatic 550rpm

5.0 liter V-8 1982

Spark plugs	ASF-42
Gap	0.044in
Ignition timing	Manual 12B
Fuel pump	5.5-6.5psi
Idle speed	Manual 800rpm

5.0 liter V-8 1983-85

Spark plugs	ASF-42
Gap	0.044in
Ignition timing	See emissions sticker
Fuel pump	6-8psi
Idle speed	Manual 700rpm (550 w/TBI)

5.0 liter V-8 1986-92

Spark plugs	ASF-42
Gap	0.044in
Ignition timing	See emissions sticker
Fuel pump	39psi
Idle speed	See emissions sticker

Wheel Alignment Specifications

Caster	
Range	½-2deg positive
Preferred setting	1¼deg positive
Camber	
Range	¾deg negative–¾deg positive
Preferred setting	0deg
Toe-In	1/16-5/16in

Index